Revolution beyond the Event

Revolution beyond the Event

The afterlives of radical politics

Edited by
Charlotte Al-Khalili, Narges Ansari,
Myriam Lamrani and Kaya Uzel

First published in 2023 by
UCL Press
University College London
Gower Street
London WC1E 6BT

Available to download free: www.uclpress.co.uk

Text © Authors, 2023
Collection © Editors, 2023
Images © Copyright holders named in captions, 2023

The authors have asserted their rights under the Copyright, Designs and Patents Act 1988 to be identified as the authors of this work.

A CIP catalogue record for this book is available from The British Library.

Any third-party material in this book is not covered by the book's Creative Commons licence. Details of the copyright ownership and permitted use of third-party material is given in the image (or extract) credit lines. If you would like to reuse any third-party material not covered by the book's Creative Commons licence, you will need to obtain permission directly from the copyright owner.

This book is published under a Creative Commons Attribution-Non-Commercial 4.0 International licence (CC BY-NC 4.0), https://creativecommons.org/licenses/by-nc/4.0/. This licence allows you to share and adapt the work for non-commercial use providing attribution is made to the author and publisher (but not in any way that suggests that they endorse you or your use of the work) and any changes are indicated. Attribution should include the following information:

Al-Khalili, C., Ansari, N., Lamrani, M. and Uzel, K. (eds.) 2023. *Revolution beyond the Event: The afterlives of radical politics*. London: UCL Press. https://doi.org/10.14324/111.9781800081185

Further details about Creative Commons licences are available at
https://creativecommons.org/licenses/

ISBN: 978-1-80008-120-8 (Hbk)
ISBN: 978-1-80008-119-2 (Pbk)
ISBN: 978-1-80008-118-5 (PDF)
ISBN: 978-1-80008-121-5 (ePub)
DOI: https://doi.org/10.14324/111.9781800081185

Contents

List of figures	vii
Notes on contributors	viii
Acknowledgements	xi

Introduction   1
Charlotte Al-Khalili, Narges Ansari, Myriam Lamrani and Kaya Uzel

Part One: The shifting grounds of revolutionary temporality

1 The remains of revolution: disagreements about revolutionary failure in Nicaragua   21
David Cooper

2 Picturing absence in post-revolutionary Yemen   43
Gabriele vom Bruck

3 Smoking, praying, killing: the politics of boredom in post-revolutionary Libya   73
Igor Cherstich

4 Religious transformations after the 1979 Iranian Revolution: from Imam Husein as exemplar back to intercessor   102
Mary Elaine Hegland

Part Two: Rethinking revolutionary afterlives: anthropology and beyond

5 The 'revolution before the revolution': radical organising across the *longue durée* in twentieth-century Peru   131
David Nugent

6 Cosmogony and second nature in revolutionary Cuba   154
   Martin Holbraad

7 On the question of optimism in troubled times: revolution,
   tragedy and possibility in Caribbean history   175
   Brian Meeks

   Afterword   197
   Behrooz Ghamari-Tabrizi

Index   202

List of figures

2.1 'Ali b. Muhammad's father, 1950s. — 47
2.2 The young 'Ali (centre), his father (left) and grandfather (right), 1950s. — 48
2.3 'Ali b. Muhammad wearing an Egyptian-style uniform a few years before the Egyptian army entered Yemen in 1962. — 48
2.4 Students at the military academy of Sana'a, 1950s. — 49
2.5 Sayyid Hamud al-Wushali, early 1950s. — 52
2.6 Ahmad Qa'id. — 53
2.7 Yemeni boy visiting his uncle abroad shortly before the revolution. — 57
2.8 Graduate of the Police Academy, 1963. — 59
2.9 Colonel 'Abdullah al-Sallal, leader of the Yemeni revolution. — 61
6.1 'To fight against the impossible and win'. State-sponsored political billboard, photographed in Cuba in 2008 (Source: Wikimedia Commons, https://upload.wikimedia.org/wikipedia/commons/2/23/Castro_sign.jpg). — 165
6.2 Change and endurance in revolutionary transformations as related to Roy Wagner's distinction between the innate and the artificial (Wagner, 1981). — 171

Notes on contributors

Charlotte Al-Khalili is a social anthropologist trained in philosophy. She is a Leverhulme fellow in Sussex University and an associated member of CéSor (École des hautes études en sciences sociales/École pratique des hautes études. Her research explores the nexus between revolution and displacement, looking at the effects of the 2011 revolution and its aftermaths on displaced Syrians' lifeworlds. Mapping out Syrians' evolving understandings, imagination and conceptualisations of revolution and displacement, her PhD (UCL, 2019) analysed the emergence of alternative definitions of these phenomena. Her postdoctoral research has traced the religious genealogy of revolutionary groups from the 1980s and currently focuses on Syrian conceptions of predestination and martyrdom in the revolutionary and migratory contexts. She is the author of the forthcoming book *Waiting for the Revolution to End: Syrian displacement, time and subjectivity* (UCL, 2023).

Narges Ansari is a social anthropologist. Her doctoral thesis, funded by a European Research Council studentship, considers conceptions of agency and subjectivity within Shiʻa rituals of mediation in the revolutionary and post-revolutionary context of Iran (UCL Anthropology, 2023). She was the 2022 recipient of the British Society of Middle Eastern Studies Early Career Development Prize.

Myriam Lamrani is a Marie Skłodowska-Curie Research Fellow at Harvard and Panteion universities. She studies the ways in which images of migration shape national identities in Greece and Mexico and has conducted field research in both countries. She received her doctoral degree from UCL in 2018 for her work on devotion to death and Mexican politics, funded by the European Research Council. In 2020, she was awarded the J. B. Donne Essay Prize on the Anthropology of Art from the Royal Anthropological Institute and has written in leading academic journals. Her work on intimacy with violence and the representation of death in Mexico was published in *American Ethnologist* (2022).

Kaya Uzel is a PhD candidate in anthropology at UCL. His research into the aftermath of Burkina Faso's 1983 revolution under Thomas Sankara has been supported by an interdisciplinary studentship funded jointly by the Economic and Social Research Council and the Arts and Humanities Research Council. He has taught in the Anthropology departments at UCL and Goldsmiths College, University of London, since 2018.

Igor Cherstich is a social anthropologist and a lecturer at the Thomas Coram Research Unit, University College London. He has carried out extensive research in Libya both before and after the revolution of 2011, focusing on Sufi miracles, esoteric knowledge, revolutionary politics, state surveillance and tribal dynamics. He is the co-author of *Anthropologies of Revolution* (2020) and the co-editor of a special issue of *Middle East Critique* on 'The multiple narratives of the Libyan Revolution'. He has published on Libya in both academic journals and national newspapers, and has commented on Libyan affairs on television and radio.

David Cooper teaches anthropology at the University of Bristol. His research is based on fieldwork in rural Nicaragua, and has examined revolutionary and populist politics, land rights and popular religion.

Behrooz Ghamari-Tabrizi is professor of Near Eastern Studies and director of the Sharmin and Bijan Mossavar-Rahmani Center for Iran and Persian Gulf Studies at Princeton University. He holds a PhD in sociology from the University of California, Santa Cruz. He is the author of three books on the historical context and different aspects of the Iranian Revolution of 1979 and its aftermath: *Islam and Dissent in Post-Revolutionary Iran* (2008); *Foucault in Iran: Islamic Revolution after the Enlightenment* (2016); and *Remembering Akbar: Inside the Iranian Revolution* (2016). He has written extensively on the topics of social theory and Islamist political thought in different journals and book chapters and is currently working on a project on *Mystical Modernity*, a comparative study of the philosophy of history and political theories of Walter Benjamin and Ali Shariati.

Mary Elaine Hegland travelled to Iran for her PhD dissertation research in June 1978 and lived in the then-village of Aliabad near Shiraz before, during and for ten months after the 11 February 1979 Iranian Revolution. This fieldwork led to articles about the Revolution and *Days of Revolution: Political unrest in an Iranian village* (2014). She made return trips in 2003 and 2018 to study change, women and education, marriage, sexuality, religion, youth, modernisation, migration and the elderly. She is professor emerita of Anthropology at Santa Clara University.

Martin Holbraad teaches social anthropology at UCL. His main empirical research is in Cuba, focusing on Afro-Cuban religions and revolutionary politics. He is author of *Truth in Motion: The recursive anthropology of Cuban divination* (2012), and co-author of *The Ontological Turn: An anthropological exposition* (2016) and *Anthropologies of Revolution: Forging time, people and worlds* (2020).

Brian Meeks is professor of Africana Studies at Brown University. Among his books are *Caribbean Revolutions and Revolutionary Theory: An assessment of Cuba, Nicaragua and Grenada* (1993 and 2001), *Envisioning Caribbean Futures: Jamaican perspectives* (2007) and *Critical Interventions in Caribbean Politics and Theory* (2014).

David Nugent is currently professor of anthropology at Emory University. His works include *Modernity at the Edge of Empire* (1997), *State Theory and Andean Politics* (with Christopher Krupa, 2015) and *The Encrypted State: Delusion and displacement in northern Peru* (2019). His interests focus on the anthropology of political and economic life. Much of his fieldwork has been conducted in the Andean region of South America, but he has also done research in East Africa and among indigenous groups in North America.

Gabriele vom Bruck is reader (associate professor) emeritus in Anthropology with reference to the Middle East at the School of Oriental and African Studies, University of London. She earned her PhD at the London School of Economics and Political Science and held teaching posts at the LSE and the University of Edinburgh. She has conducted extensive field research in Yemen and published on elites, religious movements, gender, consumption, memory and history and photography. She is author of *Islam, Memory and Morality in Yemen: Ruling families in transition* (2005) and *Mirrored Loss: A Yemeni woman's life story* (2018).

Acknowledgements

The idea for this book emerged from the international conference we organised at UCL in May 2018 entitled 'After the Event: Prospects and retrospects of revolution'. The conference was the apotheosis of our respective doctoral research and marked the closing of Comparative Anthropologies of Revolutionary Politics (ERC-2013-CoG, 617970, CARP), a five-year research project funded by the European Research Council, the aim of which was to develop an anthropological understanding of revolutions through a comparative study of revolutionary politics in Latin America and the Middle East and North African region led by Martin Holbraad at University College London from 2014 to 2019. We are in debt to him for his generosity and support as a supervisor and for his participation in the conference. We invited scholars working on revolutions across the world and asked them to focus on revolutionary posteriorities, on the afterlife, the aftermath, the aftershock and the afterthoughts, away from the historical event of the revolution itself. They obliged and delivered.

As such, we are very grateful to Igor Cherstich, David Cooper, Mary Elaine Hegland, Brian Meeks, David Nugent and Gabriele vom Bruck, who presented first drafts of their present chapters as papers at the conference, as well as Behrooz Ghamari-Tabrizi who gave the conference's keynote address. This book would not have been possible without their enthusiasm, encouragement, responsiveness and patience, which have allowed the process to run smoothly. It has been a great pleasure working with them.

We are also very grateful to Pat Gordon-Smith at UCL Press for her tremendous help and for the energy she put into this project, and to the anonymous reviewers for their insightful comments on the manuscript.

For their presence as speakers and incisive insights during the whole duration of *After the Event*, we are very grateful to Yolanda Covington-Ward, Caroline Humphrey, Bruce Kapferer, David Lan, Nicola Miller, Rafael Sánchez, Samuli Schielke, Ileana Selejan, Alpa Shah, Orin Starn, Bjørn Thomassen, Francesco Vacchiano, Piers Vitebsky, Alice

Wilson (whose thinking on the social afterlives of revolution in Darfur is also an inspiration) and Jessica Winegar. The audience also contributed to the development of our ideas by sharing their thoughts during the conference. Myriam Lamrani would like to express her gratitude to the European Union's programme Horizon 2020 for supporting her editing of this book through a Marie Skłodowska-Curie research grant (Agreement No. 101031711).

Finally, for their flawless administrative support in ensuring the smooth running of the operations, we are grateful to Pascale Searle and Suzanne Petrou. For their valuable assistance during the conference and photographic skills, we thank Yasser Kamaledin, Adryon Kozel and Jiayue Zhao. The conference that led to this book would not have been possible without their support.

Introduction

Charlotte Al-Khalili, Narges Ansari, Myriam Lamrani and Kaya Uzel

To articulate the past historically does not mean to recognise it 'the way it really was' (Ranke). It means to seize hold of a memory as it flashes up at a moment of danger.

Walter Benjamin (1969)

We seem to live in a present that is stalling, the redemptive possibilities of the future no longer lying in wait. There is without a doubt a pervasive sense of temporal 'afterness' that seems to be quite simply a manifestation of our zeitgeist and the often-invoked adage that we live in post-revolutionary times appears truer than ever. We are not only after '68, after Trotsky, Tiananmen and Tahrir, but we are being constantly reminded that we are also after truth.

To draw a straight chronology of a political struggle implies telling the story with a clear-cut beginning and a temporal endpoint. Such a narration might be, for instance, that the Jasmine Revolution started in Tunisia on 18 December 2010, with violent protests following the self-immolation of Mohamed Bouazizi, and ended on 14 January 2011 when President Zine El Abidine Ben Ali dissolved his government and declared a state of emergency. The aftermath of these events heralds the beginning of the Tunisian transition to democratic consolidation, the analysis would follow, marking the country's new status as a post-revolutionary nation. Many would recognise this as a descriptive exercise of historical narration. They may even postulate that it is only 'in retrospect' that we can understand the 'structural consequences' (Cohn, 1987: 46) of a political event such as a revolution.

While similar events across the Middle East and North Africa were taking place, quick though observers were to proclaim them as revolutionary, they were just as quick subsequently, especially with the rise of political Islam, to characterise these revolutions as failed (see Armbrust, 2019; Bayat, 2017). Yet, as reflections on the so-called Arab Spring have shown, the politics of hope and disappointment are fickle, and far from being neutral arbiters of the past, those who narrate it always access it from the point of view of the exigencies of their own current predicament.

Rosa Luxemburg reportedly said that before a revolution happens, it is perceived as impossible; yet after it happens, it is seen as having been inevitable. Hindsight is a beautiful thing indeed. But it is not the reason why we have decided to focus our attention on the aftermath of revolution in this volume. In keeping with a Benjaminian sensibility to the contingencies of time, we are interested in what happens after the 'event' because the sense that something important can be gleaned from an engagement with it resonates with us as anthropologists working within contexts where a revolution has already taken place or is ending (see Haugbolle and Bandak, 2017). In our respective field sites in Burkina Faso, Iran, Mexico and Syria, we have each had to grapple with how the passage of time actively, and continuously, shaped and reshaped the boundaries of the revolutionary experience, and the various authoritative voices that have come to narrate them. While, for example, the Iranian Revolution – its meaning, its causes, its actors, and its circumstances – has had over four decades to be 're-evaluated', 'fact checked' or 'explained' by scholars and commentators, for many who participated in it, the prospective 'spirit' of the Revolution has resisted capture by many of the retrospective treatments to which it has been subject (Ansari, 2023). Meanwhile, the verdict on the Syrian Revolution is still pending despite its Syrian actors describing it as *thawra* – a revolution. The use of the term revolution has been discussed by commentators, scholars as well as by Syrian revolutionaries, witnesses and opponents: has it been a defeated, failed or successful revolution, or rather a 'rebellion', an 'uprising' or even a 'civil war' (see Al-Khalili, 2019; 2021)? In confronting the *retrospective* impulse by distant, objective, accounts that seemed to characterise how these revolutions were made legible, we have appeared to share a common experience with many of our interlocutors for whom the revolutionary experience and its temporal boundaries and trajectories are far from settled.

Approaching revolution through its relationship to time itself, in this book we offer a critical intervention in attempts to define revolutions as bounded events that necessarily act as sequential transitions from one political system to another. Arguing that such linear analyses of revolution are inextricably tied to notions of progress and modernity, we pursue an ethnographically driven rethinking of the temporal horizons that are at stake in revolutionary processes. In this sense, we are equally interested in exploring the unexpected and unforeseen consequences of revolutionary events and actions in the Middle East, the Caribbean, and Latin America. By bringing together a wide range of ethnographic settings, this volume explores the idea that a focus on revolutionary 'afterlives' – a term we borrow from Alice Wilson (2019; 2023) – can complicate commonplace assumptions about their duration, pace, and progression, arguing that a renewed focus on the temporality of radical politics is essential to an anthropological understanding of revolution.

We thus ask: in what ways do revolutions shape people's lives in their wake, and in what manners are revolutionary pasts in turn shaped by subsequent political practice and discourse? How can we engage conceptually with the complex permutations that radical political projects undergo over time, their unexpected and sometimes perplexing consequences? Can an anthropological inquiry into the afterlife of a revolution help rethink taken-for-granted assumptions about such fundamental concerns as our understanding of political subjectivity, historical transformation and social change? These are the main questions that this volume addresses through a careful examination of the often ambiguous legacies of revolutionary projects in a range of ethnographic settings, from the Anglophone Caribbean and Cuba, Iran, Libya, and Yemen, to Nicaragua and Peru.

Our comparative choice is driven by our doctoral years within the framework of Comparative Anthropologies of Revolutionary Politics (CARP), a five-year research project led by Martin Holbraad and dedicated to developing an anthropological understanding of revolutions through case studies in the MENA, the Caribbean, and Latin America.[1] Studying revolutions ethnographically and comparatively pushed us to rethink classic conceptualisations of revolutions built around paradigms inspired by the French, American and Russian revolutions (see Al-Khalili, 2019; Cherstich et al., 2020). In this volume, we carry such a focus on regions where revolutions and their afterlives have taken shapes that do often differ from most canonical ones (see Buck-Morss, 2000).

As this book's contributions demonstrate, focusing on the aftermaths and afterlives of revolutions in these regions of the world simultaneously allows us to move away from a teleological approach to the study of revolutions as well as from the classic dichotomy that considers revolutions as either 'failed' or 'successful' (see Haugbolle and Bandak, 2017; Al-Khalili, 2023). Indeed, rather than leaving failed revolutions in history's dustbin (Scott, 2014) and letting them be erased from collective memory and history (Trouillot, 1995), we suggest looking at their effects on our interlocutors' present. The chapters of this book thus analyse revolutions' aftermaths in different temporal frames (short and *longue durée*), different domains (social life, religious practices and in the intimate sphere), and on different scales (collective and private lifeworlds).

More specifically, our comparative approach elaborates new insights on revolutionary events such as the 'de-orientalisation' of revolution (see Chapter 5) and opens the possibility of reconsidering revolutionary afterlives through the lens of 'postcolonial futures' (Chapter 7), a kind of temporality which reveals that the socio-political, economic and racial questions that we consider in this collection are quite distinct from those that started the 'notable' revolutions of this past century. This move also helps us reconsider and move away from an archetypal and very Western idea of the revolutionary 'event' (Badiou, 2009) (e.g., the bourgeois revolutions of France and America), or that of the Russian and Russian-inspired revolutions to offer valuable acumen on the uprisings that have convulsed our world in recent years, for some of the temporal horizons that we consider here have often not even been considered as revolutionary by Western observers.

The temporality of revolutionary afterlives

Engaging in an ethnographic rethinking of the scales, sites, and temporal horizons of transformations at stake in revolutionary processes, this volume proposes to focus on revolutionary posteriorities – on the afterlife, the aftermath, the aftershock and the afterthoughts of revolution – by exploring how reverberations of radical political projects extend into the present and the future. In approaching revolution through the lens of temporality – broadly understood as the lived experience of time passing (Scott, 2014) – we suggest shifting the analytical focus to those periods commonly understood as being subsequent to, and distinct from, the 'event' of revolution. This volume thus takes the experience of the afterlives of revolution as objects of study in their own right.

Here, we position ourselves against the backdrop of a scholarly tradition that has long been dominated by historians, political scientists and philosophers (e.g., Arendt, 1965; Brinton, 1965; Koselleck, 1985; Skocpol, 1979). Indeed, even though the study of political rebellion has long been a subject of interest for anthropologists (Gluckman,

1963), some observers have remarked that, until recently, there has not been a systematic canon for the anthropological study of revolutions (Thomassen, 2012; Wilson, 2019). This has changed in recent years with the publication of a number of important works which apply anthropological thinking to the general topic of revolution (Cherstich et al., 2020; Haugbolle and Bandak, 2017; Shah, 2018; Starn and La Serna, 2019; Thomassen, 2012). These publications, however, have neither focused ethnographically on the afterlife of revolution nor dedicated special analytical attention to questions of temporality raised by the process of revolutionary transformations.

If several ethnographic monographs have focused on the temporal dimensions of revolutions, they have not framed their central arguments in those terms (e.g., Verdery, 1999; Greenberg, 2014; Schielke, 2015). Moreover, although numerous publications have implicitly thematised the nexus of history and revolution (e.g., Allan, 2014; Hegland, 2014; Nugent, 1993; Piot, 2010), while the work of others explore the political, social, and philosophical dimensions of (post-)revolutionary periods in the Caribbean, Russia, and Northern Europe respectively (e.g., Scott, 2004; 2014; Ssorin-Chaikov, 2017; Krøijer, 2015), comparative anthropological works on the subject of revolutionary afterlives are still missing.

Revolutions, as we intend to demonstrate in this volume, are not only teleological destinations (Haugbolle and Bandak, 2017) spurred by radical political change. Instead, revolutions educe the kind of temporality that 'may appear finite, strictly anchored in the present, but the possibility of futurity and connections to the past continue to exist within its form' (Holbraad and Lamrani, 2021: 6). As such, they mediate different times that extend beyond the temporal window of the event of revolution (Lazar, 2014: 9; see also Ssorin-Chaikov, 2017: 4; Dalsgaard and Nielsen, 2013: 11). Historical events, Fredric Jameson (2002: 301) warns us about 9/11, 'are never really punctual … [they] extend into a before and an *after* of historical time that only gradually unfolds, to disclose the full dimensions of the historicity of the event' (emphasis ours). Here, historicity – understood in Hirsch and Stewart's (2005: 261–3) terms, not as a linear succession of tenses where the past prevails, but as framing to understand how social past and futures resonate in the present circumstances – is useful to introduce the temporal directions that this collection takes. Allowing for a conceptualisation of revolutionary time across ethnographic contexts as being 'relative, multiple, and diverse' (Kirtsoglou and Simpson, 2020: 2), in other words, as being wildly multitemporal (Chakrabarty, 2000; Munn, 1992; Ssorin-Chaikov, 2006; Bear, 2014; Birth, 2008; Pandian, 2012; Nielsen, 2014; Knight, 2014;

Shove et al., 2009; Stewart, 2017), we ask what happens when we shift our focus on temporalities *contained* in the revolutionary aftermaths?

We are simultaneously interested in locating the presence/absence of revolutionary processes in our interlocutors' everyday lives. That is, to study revolutionary transformations in 'neglected' domains of our interlocutors' lifeworlds; domains that often appear marginal to revolutionary events, having been deemed apolitical. Revolutionary transformations can thus be located in the intimacy of one's home, as much as in social and familial relations (Winegar, 2012). Moreover, they can inflect religious practices and migratory horizons, thus operating a shift in scale from the collective to the individual or vice versa (Al-Khalili, 2019; Ansari, 2023). We therefore ask: how can revolutions' afterlives, consequences and legacies be captured and described by anthropologists when these temporal unfoldings seem unrelated to 'revolutionary events'?

Analysing revolutions through such lenses leads us to conceptualise the often unimagined and unwanted consequences of revolutions. In his monograph on the forgotten (because, according to classical definitions, 'unsuccessful') Grenada 1979 revolution, David Scott develops a compelling theoretical framework and analysis to make sense of the effects of a failed revolution on time, temporality and history as well as the effects of temporality and time on revolutionary actions. Drawing on Bradley's paradox about human action in time – 'that men may start a course of events but can neither calculate nor control it' (cited in Scott, 2014: 33) – Scott argues that political action is inherently tragic, for it happens in time and therefore always has uncertain consequences. Focusing more specifically on revolutionary action, Scott writes that in this field 'the consequences of tragic collision are considerably magnified' (Scott, 2014: 34) for revolutions are organised around the idea of 'an exceptional time' and are a time of 'exceptional human beings ... whose actions are of unusual intensity and urgency' (Scott, 2014: 34).

The specific temporality of revolution thus makes revolutionary action more vulnerable to tragic endings for it rejects the past and projects itself towards an unknown future, aiming to establish a new order that is being resisted by existing powers. This analysis leads Scott to develop a concept of 'tragic consequences' – that is, uncontrollable outcomes – in relation to political and revolutionary actions. He argues that the ineradicable contingency of human action in general, and of revolutionary actions in particular, make them vulnerable to failure and often lead to tragic outcomes.

This resonates with Samuli Schielke's analysis of unexpected consequences (2015). Starting from the ethnographic description of the pursuit of grand schemes as unrealisable, Schielke draws our attention to the 'ambivalence, contradictions, and experiences of failure' rather than the 'successful ordering of social experience' (2015: 19). He thus presents failure and its unintended consequences as inherent in human actions and intentions. Moreover, Schielke diagnoses a lack of interest in, and theorisation of, consequences in anthropology, that is, 'of the uncertain and the unintended that constitutes the element of surprise and unexpected in the consequences, since they never quite fit the aims' (2015: 217). It is one of the aims of this volume to attempt to partially fill this gap by analysing the consequences of revolutions on our interlocutors' experiences, time and temporality. Hence, building on these conceptualisations of tragic and unexpected consequences, we suggest a way of grasping revolutions anthropologically and theoretically as inherently temporal phenomena that inevitably have reverberations beyond their happening, at times even counter to their actors' expectations. In this volume we enlarge this prism to include revolutions' long-term consequences in all domains of our interlocutors' lifeworlds (Al-Khalili, 2019: 31–3).

Our theoretical approach also builds on historian Fernand Braudel's concept of *longue durée* to grasp revolutions as historical processes rather than singular events creating a clear chronological before–after and a historical rupture characterised by a change of political regimes – from an 'old' one to a new one (see also Chapter 5). In doing so, we are inspired by more recent works on revolutions' 'end(ings)' (Haugbolle and Bandak, 2017) and revolutions' 'afterlives' (Wilson, 2019). We suggest seeing revolutions as open-ended processes – 'end' having both a temporal sense of closure and a sense of definite goal (see Haugbolle and Bandak, 2017). We build on Alice Wilson's work in Dhufar, Oman (2019: 133), in which she shows that political uprisings can have a 'social afterlife', leaving what she calls 'legacies' consisting in revolutionary values being upheld, even though a revolution may appear to have failed. We propose to enlarge her concept of afterlife to the entirety of our interlocutors' lifeworlds rather than limiting it to the 'social' domain.

The ethnographies gathered in this volume suggest a novel way of grasping revolutions' aftermaths across time and through the concept of (in)visible legacies. This could be read, following and transposing Yael Navaro's work on aftermath of mass political violence (2020), as a way of tracing the legacies of revolutionary processes in our interlocutors' lifeworld. This, concretely, opens up the study of the presence/absence of revolutions as traces, fragments, archives, ruins and ruinations in our interlocutors' lives (see Navaro, 2020). Such an approach is central to our volume for we aim to analyse the ways in which not only 'defeated', 'failed', erased and silenced (see Al-Khalili, 2022), but also long-passed and memorialised revolutions have effects on people's lives in unexpected and unimagined ways even long after they have happened.

In looking at revolutions through the prism of their multiple and intricate afterlives, our intention is not to ignore or dismiss other social, cultural or economic 'causes' that may contribute to the formation and unfolding of various revolutionary movements. Rather, in our view, by beginning from the vantage point of those who are subjected to and are subjects of revolutions, while resisting the impulse to impose our own temporal and theoretical frameworks, anthropology is uniquely positioned to formulate and account for the novel modes of engagement with revolutionary experience. Thus, in introducing the notion of temporality, our aim is not to bypass questions such as the role played in revolutions by, for example, gender, religion, race or class in favour of a more abstract theoretical concept. Instead, the prism of temporality is here offered as a starting point from which we can consider the very nature of the relationship between these domains of being (and becoming) a subject without assuming from the outset that we know how various realms of subjectivity affect and relate to one another.

Rethinking 'event' through revolutionary afterlives

In bringing together the collection of essays in this volume we are interested in the intersection between the temporal conditions of field research, its later representation (or presentation), and the temporality of revolution as its object of analysis. Our decision to place our focus on 'beyond the event', therefore, is to be read in a narrower conceptual and methodological sense.

If decades ago it was a preoccupation with scientific objectivity that resulted in the expulsion of time and engagement with history from anthropological discourse – as pure speculative guesswork – the introduction of historical analysis in later years also ran the risk of deploying its own ethnocentric assumptions about what is understood as history, the relationship between past and present, and the position assumed by events within these temporal frameworks.

The debates surrounding the synchronic or diachronic analysis of events in anthropology is of course not a new one. In placing our focus on the afterlives of revolutions, and their diverse manifestations in a variety of field sites, we echo earlier positions that have problematised the portrayal of non-Western cultures as static entities that exist outside the flow of history (Fabian, 2014; Trouillot, 1995). In introducing temporality as both a methodological and a heuristic question in relation to a subject that often resists definitive anchoring in the past, our concern is with the distinct contribution that the discipline of anthropology can make to the study of revolutions by exposing some of the ethnocentric analytical frameworks that have dominated their analysis. More specifically, we are interested in decoupling the historical, in its narrow universal sense, from the temporal by calling into question the assumptions entailed in the sequential framing of events as bounded units within an often linear view of history (Strathern, 1990).

In its various iterations, the 'event' has become an increasingly influential model within anthropology that allows the analysis to move beyond the static models of the social, with those who claim that one can never err on the side of rupture in a discipline as invested in continuity as ours. Our proposal to move the debate on revolutionary temporality beyond the event is not intended as a criticism undermining the work that has been done in this relatively recent paradigm (Engelke and Robbins, 2010; Holbraad et al., 2019; Kapferer and Meinert, 2015). Rather, we hope to move beyond the accounting-style counterposition of continuity and rupture as the terms in which this debate has often been conducted, and to leave behind its infinitely regressing logic in the process. To this end, we share the same approach towards the notions of discontinuity and rupture in relation to the topic of revolution as it has been advanced by the authors of *Ruptures: Anthropologies of discontinuities in times of turmoil* (Holbraad et al., 2019), who have called for a renewed interest in the study of ruptures in our discipline. As the ethnographies that follow show, revolutionary rupture, rather than an embedded condition of continuously emerging structures and ways of becoming, is often actively sought, brought about and re-imagined by various actors and in various scales and temporal trajectories of their lives.

Yet, the following chapters also highlight that these modalities of relating to revolutionary rupture are rarely bound to specific moments of transition in time, space and scale. From this perspective – namely one that seeks to decouple the notion of rupture from that of a bounded event – we see our approach, and indeed our topic, to be different to that advanced by Holbraad, Kapferer and Sauma. In bringing together topics as varied as prophetic invention, conversion, ecological disaster or jihadism, the editors of *Ruptures* successfully advance a case for an ethnographic study of discontinuity beyond the current, pervasive view of rupture as a 'constitutive element of social reality' in anthropology (Holbraad et al., 2019: 11). Yet, the treatment of the temporal dimension of ruptures explored in their volume remains predominantly within the framework of a sequential, definitive, and clear-cut transition from one set of pre-existing conditions to the next. In this volume, by proposing to focus ethnographically on revolutionary posterities, and by describing the distinctly temporal dimensions of revolutionary rupture, we seek to problematise some of the ethnocentric assumptions inherent in this coupling of the bounded event and rupture.

Taking the lead from political theories of revolution (Arendt, 1965; Badiou, 2003; Dunn, 1982; Hobsbawm, 1986), recent anthropological literature on revolution has tended to emphasise the significance of revolution as a ruptural event (Engelke and Robbins, 2010; Holbraad et al., 2019; Jansen, 2019; Robbins, 2007). Revolution in these accounts appears as an abrupt and violent suspension of the normal order that marks a transition from one political system to another. As noted earlier, our shift away from the paradigm of the event is not meant to negate the potency of discontinuity as such, or to suggest only that anthropology's traditional privileging of continuity provides a better way of understanding the complex temporality of social change. Instead, by broadening the scope of what we may consider as the revolutionary 'event', that is, its temporal boundaries and its ruptural shape and potential, we intend to open a conceptual space to examine the unexpected domains and effects of revolutionary change. This, we argue, allows us to capture alternative forms of radical transformations that take shape in various sites, scales and temporal horizons in people's lives, including religion, ethics and politics.

Drawing on these alternative views of the nexus between history and agency, the book investigates how the understanding of revolution as a bounded ruptural event is based on preconceptions about what constitutes valid revolutionary causes, actions and objectives. Emphasising the disjuncture between the liberal subject that often guides established theories of revolution and alternative forms of subjectivity emerging during revolutionary afterlives, we aim to shift our scope of analysis beyond a teleological historical framework that necessarily tends towards such notions as modernity, progress, and secularism (Ansari, 2023). This volume also stresses the gatekeeping function of this teleological understanding of history, as it delineates what counts as revolution and what can be discounted as rebellion, uprising, or mere violence.

For instance, ethnographically studying the Syrian 2011 revolution – a revolution that had long been 'invisibilised' (Trouillot, 1995) before being actively erased by the Assad regime – the anthropologist is confronted with several questions that echo Trouillot's analysis of the Haitian revolution (Al-Khalili, 2022). Indeed, if some events cannot be accepted even as they occur, how can they be assessed later? How does one write a history of the impossible (Trouillot, 1995: 73)? Building on such questions, we transpose some of Trouillot's analytical and methodological analysis of the Haitian revolution and ask: how can one do the anthropology of a revolution that is not perceived as such, a revolution that is unreadable or that has been erased from history? This suggests looking into revolutions' witnesses and survivors in order to write ethnographic stories of revolutions that appear as counter-histories and allow to 'fill the gaps' of history. Our aim, following Trouillot, is thus to render visible and readable histories of revolutions that no history book can tell or has told.

It was precisely this refusal to commit to the temporal map of Enlightenment rationalities, argues Ghamari-Tabrizi, that allowed Foucault to understand the Iranian Revolution as both 'a phenomenon of history' and 'a phenomenon that defies it' (Ghamari-Tabrizi, 2016: 2). By utilising the *prospective* momentum that characterised the revolutionary movement as a method to make sense of its ambiguous, indeterminate features, Foucault attempted to move beyond the retrospective reflections that commonly coupled the revolutionary experience and its 'outcome' (Ansari, 2023). His description of what he observed in Iran as *political spirituality* captures the non-teleological, open-ended conception of the revolutionary experience and the subject position that emerged as a result of it. It was this emergent 'movement of spirituality' which he recognised as being a characteristic of nearly all great political and social revolutions (Ghamari-Tabrizi, 2016: 124–8).

Inspired by Ghamari-Tabrizi's critique of scholars' misunderstanding of the Iranian 1979 and Arab 2010s revolutions and linking up with recent efforts to decolonise anthropological research and writing (Allan, 2014; Mogstad and Tse, 2018), our motivation is to draw attention to the broader political implications of our own knowledge practices. This entails a commitment to a form of critical recursivity that sheds light on the discipline's own liberal suppositions that have enabled some forms of radical politics to be heard while silencing others (Al-Bulushi et al., 2020; Jobson, 2020; Starn, 1991; Trouillot, 1995).

Trouillot and Ghamari-Tabrizi point out the impossibility of thinking of and conceiving revolutions that develop outside the Enlightenment frame in their full radicality. Following their caution, we thus try to push back against 'formulas of erasure' that tend to make revolutions and their afterlives – particularly those that do not fit a pre-set framework – invisible (Trouillot, 1995: 96). Placing our ethnographic focus on what happens beyond the 'event', therefore, is not so much meant to make us see that a particular revolution was inevitable all along. Rather, it is to give us renewed appreciation of the fact that the revolutions, even after they have happened, appear to have been quite impossible. That they happened nevertheless, against all historical odds, is what keeps the possibility of revolutionary futurity alive. On such a reading, the overwhelming sense of political disappointment that is palpable today appears no longer as the necessary end of politics but rather as a possible beginning for a new politics.

Outlines and rationales

Focusing on the temporality of revolutionary afterlives grants the possibility of reappraising revolution as a temporal continuum that does not stop with ideas of the revolutionary failure or success of radical political projects. Treating our interlocutors' narratives, artefacts and memories as living archives and as traces of revolutions is thus a way of broadening the field of studies of revolutions. Indeed, in paying attention to what seems peripheral, marginal and inessential in classic studies of revolutions, new theoretical and methodological avenues that challenge the very concept of time itself. Part One of this book, 'The shifting grounds of revolutionary temporality', is an ethnographic exploration of people's changing engagements with revolutionary pasts. We consider how the lingering effects of political uprisings allow for a critical ethnographic interrogation of how post-revolutionary time itself is experienced. Some of the temporal contradictions that can arise are explored in David Cooper's work on the Sandinistas in Nicaragua (Chapter 1), as some of the heirs of what many see as a finished revolution consider that revolutionary times are still ongoing. Cooper examines how a committed Sandinista community interprets polarised public opinion about the Sandinista Revolution, probing how local definitions of revolution shape perceptions of its strengths and weaknesses. In Nicaragua, the afterlife has become blurred as the revolution is still 'alive and well'.

In Chapter 2, Gabriele vom Bruck focuses on the affective dimensions of revolutionary afterlives to examine the role of photographs as memorial sites through which experiences of loss, following Yemen's 1962 revolution, are continuously reckoned with in the present. She explores how that which is manifestly absent – disappeared family members as well as photographs – might well have an agentive presence involving emotional and imaginative labour. In the aftermath of the revolution, their 'presence in absence' is central to the survivors' demands for official acknowledgement of the atrocities committed half a century ago. Meanwhile, life can stand still when young Libyan men try to 'kill' time, experiencing the heavy lid of a temporal impasse as revolutions recede from sight. In Chapter 3, Igor Cherstich highlights the contrasts between revolutionary promises and their realisation in the aftermath of the 1969 and 2011 Libyan revolutions by investigating young people's recourse to an ambivalent discourse of vitality and lethargy. Indeed, the experience of time can become one of inertia, boredom and depression. But the various experiences of the aftermath of the Libyan revolution can also contribute to the process of reinventing everyday life, a space where individuals can determine how they express their agency.

Part One closes by considering the retrospective reflections through which people revisit and re-evaluate their expectations of the Iranian Revolution from the vantage point of its outcome. Drawing on her long-term ethnographic engagement prior to, during and after the Revolution with the people of Aliabad, Iran, Mary Elaine Hegland traces the pre-revolutionary hopes, ideas and expectations of her interlocutors and their reflections, disappointments and complaints in its aftermath. Hegland's expansive account provides plenty of raw material on which to reflect on the role played by religious motifs as both 'shelters' for the practices of spirituality described by Foucault, as well as their 'restrictions' (Foucault, 2020: 124–8). In light of the recent renewed calls for a revolution in Iran, Hegland's account, with its focus on the retrospective engagements of her interlocutors with the revolutionary ideals and aspirations of 1979, invites us to reflect on the temporal dimensions of revolutionary action itself and the interaction between its prospective and retrospective momentum in such an experience.

Part Two examines the temporal logic of revolutionary afterlives from an anthropological and historical perspective, proposing novel methodological and conceptual tools to study the ways in which radical political projects remain significant in the present. David Nugent deconstructs orientalist understandings of Peruvian revolutionary history in Chapter 5, reframing what for a long time has been thought of as a revolution in its own right as the afterlife of an earlier revolution. On closer examination, revolutionary afterlives are found in retrospect as having taken place before the event itself as radical political projects. As the author argues, the revolution may have been brewing under the surface for decades before *Sendero Luminoso* (the Shining Path) sprang into action. Given the view that anthropologists have 'missed' the Peruvian revolution (Starn, 1991), Nugent's observation that revolutionary inception constitutes a *longue durée* of radical political activity in Peru is significant. In this configuration, a focus on the afterlife brings the possibility of deconstructing Western temporality. Looking at the Peruvian revolutionary uprising retrospectively upends time and de-orientalises the conceptualisation of revolution itself.

In a similar vein, Martin Holbraad explores the relationship between time and revolution in Chapter 6 by rethinking the Weberian concept of routinisation through ethnographic findings from Cuba and Soviet Russia. The perceived temporal duration of social and political struggles can condense or change course as, in Cuba, the trajectory of Fidel Castro's revolution follows its course but the cracks in the narrative, as Holbraad argues, link revolution as a rupture and its afterlife, as permanence as a 'distinguishing feature of post-revolutionary temporality'. Understanding revolutions as long-term processes, with a beginning but no endpoint, brings forward what Nugent (Chapter 5) calls a 'compression' of the revolutionary temporal horizon. The afterlife here encompasses different speed rates. It can be condensed, extended, or disjointed. So, although a straightforward definition of the afterlife supposes a survival of revolutions, we propose that it can also indicate the pre-existence of revolutionary ideas. In pinpointing the temporal category of the afterlife, the theoretical focus shifts from the revolutionary event – characterised by immediacy – towards a concept of the afterlife that acknowledges revolutionary time-shifts and the unfinished business of revolutions.

In the final chapter, based on a close engagement with the works of David Scott and C. L. R. James, as well as the rise of the Black Lives Matter movement, Brian Meeks, a historian of the Anglophone Caribbean, reflects on how tragic and romantic imaginaries respectively inflect not only our understanding of revolutionary time, but also the political possibilities of the present moment. The author's re-reading of David Scott's (2004) assessment of the tragic outcomes of the Grenada revolution, for instance, illustrates how the reappraisal of revolutions in retrospect offers new ways to think about current political movements. As the Black Lives Matter movement attests, past revolutions open the door for a new era of revolutions that can 'learn from the tragedy of history' and offer the possibility of optimism about the future of radical politics. The shift of focus towards the afterlife attends to the extension and expansion of revolution into different timeframes. Such a shift illuminates a kind of temporal collapse that exists at the heart of nationhood and mediates different understandings of revolutionary outcomes (Lamrani, 2021: 11).

Revolutionary afterlife is akin to 'a temporal shape', yet one not based on the conception of a temporally bounded event but a shape that operates across different timelines (Cherstich et al., 2020: 21). Focusing on an examination of revolutionary contexts in their afterlives illuminates the fact that revolutionary outcomes ought to be understood as being embedded in the very conceptualisation of everyday time. As Kirtsoglou and Simpson (2020: 10) elegantly put it, 'we are constantly becoming within time, within unbounded temporalities where pasts, presents and futures bleed into each other'. The foregrounding of revolutionary afterlife is a simple proposition, yet as we hope this volume demonstrates a powerful one as the remains of political struggles linger well after revolutions. In this indeterminateness of revolutionary afterlives, it is what happens as the radical revolutionary projects endure to which the authors of this volume attend.

Note

1. See https://www.ucl.ac.uk/anthropology/research/anthropologies-revolution.

References

Al-Bulushi, Samar, Ghosh, Sahana and Tahir, Madiha. 2020. 'American anthropology, decolonization, and the politics of location'. *American Anthropologist*. https://www.americananthropologist.org/commentaries/al-bulushi-ghosh-and-tahir. Accessed 25 October 2022.
Al-Khalili, Charlotte. 2019. Of revolutionary transformations: Life in displacement at the Syrian-Turkish border. PhD thesis, University College London.
Al-Khalili, Charlotte. 2021. 'Halaqas, relational subject and revolutionary committees in Syria'. *Focaal: Journal of Global and Historical Anthropology*, 21: 50–66.
Al-Khalili, Charlotte. 2022. 'Towards an anthropology of defeat: Rethinking the aftermath of the Syrian revolution'. *Condition Humaine / Conditions Politiques*, 4. https://revues.mshparisnord.fr/chcp/index.php?id=888.
Al-Khalili, Charlotte. 2023. *Waiting for the Revolution to End: Syrian displacement, time and subjectivity*. London: UCL Press.
Allan, Diana. 2014. *Refugees of the Revolution: Experiences of Palestinian exile*. Redwood City, CA: Stanford University Press.
Ansari, Narges. 2023. The prospects of change: Rituals of mediation and the emergent Shi'a subjects in Iran. PhD thesis, University College London.

Arendt, Hannah. 1965. *On Revolution*. New York: Penguin.
Armbrust, Walter. 2019. *Martyrs and Tricksters: An ethnography of the Egyptian revolution*. Princeton: Princeton University Press.
Badiou, Alain. 2003. *Saint Paul: The foundation of universalism*. Stanford, CA: Stanford University Press.
Badiou, Alain. 2009. *Logics of Worlds: Being and event II*. New York: Continuum.
Bayat, Asef. 2017. *Revolution without Revolutionaries: Making sense of the Arab spring*. Redwood City, CA: Stanford University Press.
Bear, Laura. 2014. 'Introduction: Doubt, conflict, mediation: The anthropology of modern time'. *Journal of the Royal Anthropological Institute*, 20(1): 3–30.
Benjamin, Walter. 1969 [1955]. 'Theses on the philosophy of history: VI', in Benjamin, Walter, *Illuminations*. Edited by Hannah Arendt. Translated by Harry Zohn. New York: Schocken Books, 255.
Birth, Kevin. 2008. 'The creation of coevalness and the danger of homochronism'. *Journal of the Royal Anthropological Institute*, 14: 3–20.
Brinton, Crane. 1965. *The Anatomy of Revolution: Toward a poetics of experience*. New York: Vintage Books.
Buck-Morss, Susan. 2000. *Dreamworld and Catastrophe: The passing of mass utopia in East and West*. Cambridge, MA: MIT Press.
Chakrabarty, Dipesh. 2000. *Provincializing Europe: Postcolonial thought and historical difference*. Princeton: Princeton University Press.
Cherstich, Igor, Holbraad, Martin and Tassi, Nico. 2020. *Anthropologies of Revolution: Forging time, people, and worlds*. Berkeley: University of California Press.
Cohn, Bernard S. 1987. *An Anthropologist among the Historians and Other Essays*. Oxford: Oxford University Press.
Dalsgaard, Steffen and Nielsen, Morten. 2013. 'Introduction: Time in the field'. *Social Analysis*, 57(1): 1–19.
Dunn, John. 1982. 'Understanding revolutions: *States and Social Revolutions* by Theda Skocpol; *Injustice: The social bases of obedience and revolt* by Barrington Moore'. *Ethics*, 92(2): 299–315.
Engelke, Matthew and Robbins, Joel. 2010. 'Introduction: Global Christianity, global critique'. *South Atlantic Quarterly*, 109(4): 623–31.
Fabian, Johannes. 2014. *Time and the Other: How anthropology makes its object*. New York: Columbia University Press.
Foucault, Michel. 2020. 'Political spirituality as the will for alterity: An interview with the *Nouvel Observateur*'. Translated by S. V. Bremner. *Critical Inquiry*, 47(1): 121–34.
Ghamari-Tabrizi, Behrooz. 2016. *Foucault in Iran: Islamic revolution after the Enlightenment*. Minneapolis: University of Minnesota Press.
Gluckman, Max. 1963. *Order and Rebellion in Tribal Africa*. London: Cohen and West.
Graeber, David. 2011. *Revolutions in Reverse: Essays on politics, violence, art, and imagination*. London: Minor Compositions.
Greenberg, Jessica. 2014. *After the Revolution: Youth, democracy, and the politics of disappointment in Serbia*. Redwood City, CA: Stanford University Press.
Haugbolle, Sune and Bandak, Andreas. 2017. 'The ends of revolution: Rethinking ideology and time in the Arab uprisings'. *Middle East Critique*, 26(3): 191–204.
Hegland, Mary Elaine. 2014. *Days of Revolution: Political unrest in an Iranian village*. Redwood City, CA: Stanford University Press.
Hirsch, Eric and Stewart, Charles. 2005. 'Introduction: Ethnographies of historicity'. *History and Anthropology*, 16(3): 261–74.
Hobsbawm, Eric. 1986. 'Revolutions', in Porter, R. and Teich, M. (eds), *Revolutions in History*. Cambridge: Cambridge University Press, 5–46.
Holbraad, Martin, Kapferer, Bruce and Sauma, Julia. 2019. *Ruptures: Anthropologies of discontinuity in times of turmoil*. London: UCL Press.
Holbraad, Martin and Lamrani, Myriam. 2021. 'Revolutionary circles: A morphology of radical politics'. *Focaal*, 2021(91): 1–13.
Jameson, Fredric. 2002. 'Dialectics of disaster'. *South Atlantic Quarterly*, 101(2): 297–304.
Jansen, S. 2019. 'Anthropological (in)fidelities to Alain Badiou'. *Anthropological Theory*, 19(2): 238–58.
Jobson, Ryan Cecil. 2020. 'The case for letting anthropology burn: Sociocultural anthropology in 2019'. *American Anthropologist*, 122(2): 259–71.

Kapferer, Bruce and Meinert, Lotte (eds). 2015. *In the Event: Towards an anthropology of generic moments*. New York and Oxford: Berghahn Books.

Kirtsoglou, Elisabeth and Simpson, Bob. 2020. 'Introduction', in Kirtsoglou, E. and Simpson, B. (eds), *The Time of Anthropology: Studies of contemporary chronopolitics*. London and New York: Routledge, 1–30.

Knight, Daniel M. 2014. 'Mushrooms, knowledge exchange and polytemporality in Kalloni, Greek Macedonia'. *Food, Culture and Society*, 17(2): 183–201.

Koselleck, Reinhart. 1985. 'Historical criteria of the modern concept of revolution', in Koselleck, R. (ed.), *Futures Past: On the semantics of historical time*. Cambridge, MA: MIT Press, 39–5.

Krøijer, Stine. 2015. *Figurations of the Future: Forms and temporalities of left radical politics in northern Europe*. New York and Oxford: Berghahn Books.

Lamrani, Myriam (ed.). 2021. 'Introduction: Beyond revolution: Reshaping nationhood through senses and affects'. *Cambridge Journal of Anthropology*, 39(2): 1–18.

Lazar, Sian. 2014. 'Historical narrative, mundane political time, and revolutionary moments: Coexisting temporalities in the lived experience of social movements'. *Journal of the Royal Anthropological Institute*, 20(1): 91–108.

McGovern, Mike. 2017. *A Socialist Peace? Explaining the absence of war in an African country*. Chicago: Chicago University Press.

Mogstad, Heidi and Tse, Lee-Shan. 2018. 'Decolonizing anthropology'. *Cambridge Journal of Anthropology*, 36(2): 53–72.

Munn, Nancy. 1992. 'The cultural anthropology of time: A critical essay'. *Annual Review of Anthropology*, 21: 93–123.

Navaro, Yael. 2020. 'The aftermath of mass violence: A negative methodology'. *Annual Review of Anthropology*, 49(1): 161–73.

Nielsen, Morten. 2014. 'A wedge of time: Futures in the present and present without future in Maputo, Mozambique'. *Journal of the Royal Anthropological Institute*, 20: 166–82.

Nugent, David. 1993. *Spent Cartridges of Revolution: An anthropological history of Namiquipa, Chihuahua*. Chicago: University of Chicago Press.

Pandian, Anand. 2012. 'The time of anthropology: Notes from a field of experience'. *Cultural Anthropology*, 27: 547–71.

Piot, Charles. 2010. *Nostalgia for the Future: West Africa after the Cold War*. Chicago: University of Chicago Press.

Robbins, Joel. 2007. 'Continuity thinking and the problem of Christian culture: Belief, time, and the anthropology of Christianity'. *Current Anthropology*, 48(1): 5–38.

Schielke, Samuli. 2015. *Egypt in the Future Tense: Hope, frustration, and ambivalence before and after 2011*. Indianapolis: Indiana University Press.

Scott, David. 2004. *Conscripts of Modernity: The tragedy of colonial enlightenment*. Durham, NC: Duke University Press.

Scott, David. 2014. *Omens of Adversity: Tragedy, time, memory, justice*. Durham, NC: Duke University Press.

Shah, Alpa. 2018. *Night March: Among India's revolutionary guerillas*. London: Hurst.

Shove, Elizabeth, Trentmann, Frank and Wilk, Richard (eds). 2009. *Time, Consumption and Everyday Life: Practice, materiality and culture*. Oxford: Berghahn.

Skocpol, Theda. 1979. *States and Social Revolutions: A comparative analysis of France, Russia and China*. Cambridge: Cambridge University Press.

Ssorin-Chaikov, Nikolai. 2006. 'On heterochrony: Birthday gifts to Stalin: 1949'. *Journal of the Royal Anthropological Institute*, 12: 355–75.

Ssorin-Chaikov, Nikolai. 2017. *Two Lenins: A brief anthropology of time*. Chicago: HAU Books.

Starn, Orin. 1991. 'Missing the revolution: Anthropologists and the war in Peru'. *Cultural Anthropology*, 6(1): 63–91.

Starn, Orin and La Serna, Miguel. 2019. *The Shining Path: Love, madness and revolution in the Andes*. New York: Routledge.

Stewart, Charles. 2017. *Dreaming and Historical Consciousness in Island Greece*. Chicago: University of Chicago Press.

Strathern, Marylin. 1990. *The Gender of the Gift: Problems with women and problems with society in Melanesia*. Berkeley: University of California Press.

Thomassen, Bjorn. 2012. 'Notes towards an anthropology of political revolutions'. *Comparative Studies in Society and History*, 54(3): 679–706.

Trouillot, Michel-Rolph. 1995. *Silencing the Past: Power and the production of history*. Boston: Beacon Press.

Verdery, Katherine. 1999. *The Political Lives of Dead Bodies: Reburial and postsocialist change*. New York: Columbia University Press.

Wilson, Alice. 2019. 'Invisible veterans'. *Conflict and Society*, 5(1): 132–49.

Wilson, Alice. 2023. *Afterlives of Revolution: Everyday counterhistories in southern Oman*. Redwood City, CA: Stanford University Press.

Winegar, Jessica. 2012. 'The privilege of revolution: Gender, class, space, and affect in Egypt'. *American Ethnologist*, 39(1): 67–70.

Part One:
The shifting grounds of revolutionary temporality

1
The remains of revolution: disagreements about revolutionary failure in Nicaragua

David Cooper

Revolution, dead or alive?

In April 2018, Nicaraguan politics suddenly exploded into the global news agenda after many years of journalistic non-interest. The Sandinista government was accused – in a flurry of social media activity – of brutally repressing student protests against planned pension reforms. As reports of student deaths spread, the unrest escalated, and protesters against the government set up roadblocks across the country. Further reports told of clashes between police and those manning the roadblocks, and of government-sponsored paramilitaries working to systematically put down the protests. Within a few months hundreds had lost their lives, and hundreds more had been arrested. Once the government had succeeded in eliminating the roadblocks, many of the student activists who had led protests were imprisoned on terrorism charges.

This resurgence of international news attention caused many who had celebrated and supported the Sandinista revolution during the 1980s to suddenly try to catch up with the political developments of the intervening decades. Forming a view on these events required people to sort out their stories of the revolution's trajectory.

In doing so, they had two basic narratives available to them. The first narrative – which has been consistently developed by the overwhelming majority of Nicaraguan intellectuals and political commentators, and which most Nicaraguanist scholars find persuasive – tells of the death of the Sandinista revolution. The utopian dream of transforming society was gradually worn down during the 1980s. The United States had sponsored a counter-revolutionary war, which gradually ground down public support for the revolutionary project. In 1990, general elections were held, and the revolutionary Sandinista government, to their bewilderment, lost the vote to a conservative opposition coalition. In the years since that electoral defeat, the 'gains' of the revolution were almost completely undone. The Sandinista National Liberation Front (henceforth the 'FSLN', or the 'Sandinistas'), gradually shifted from being a party of genuine revolutionaries to being a machine for the personal enrichment of party leaders and their cronies.

This is a story, then, of the revolution's utter defeat, and Nicaragua's slide back towards tyranny, authoritarianism and the dictatorial rule of strongmen. Among scholars and commentators, the notion of history repeating itself – the re-emergence of an entrenched political culture of populism, clientelism and caudillismo (strongman politics) – has become a frequent trope in attempts to synthesise these developments (for example Baltodano, 2009; Hoyt, 2004: 18; Sierakowski, 2012: 324–5). With the president's wife Rosario Murillo now holding the formal role of vice-president, and at least one of his sons seemingly being groomed for high political office while other relatives hold significant public positions and own much of the country's media (Gutiérrez and Ocampo, 2019), there is a sense that another dynasty is in the making. And from this perspective, of course, reports of a dictatorial government brutally repressing protesters seem entirely plausible.

The second narrative is about revolutionary continuity. It finds voice in the speeches of the president, in the daily radio broadcasts of the first lady and vice-president, and in the writings of some 'international solidarity' activists who remain loyal to the FSLN. On this view, while the revolution was defeated electorally in 1990, this is best understood as a temporary shift in the balance of power within Nicaragua between the political forces of the Left and the Right. The narrative tends to rely on a Manichaean political imaginary that opposes 'Left' and 'Right', the interest of the 'People' and those of 'Imperialism', and sees politics as an enduring struggle between 'Socialism' and 'Capitalism' – a struggle which, in Nicaragua, maps onto the struggle between the FSLN and its 'US-backed' opponents. The Right's ascendancy came to an end with the FSLN's electoral victory in 2006. The return to power of the Sandinistas indicated a return to political dominance of the Left, and allowed the revolution to enter a 'second stage'. From this perspective, it seems clear that all those reports of government repression were a part of a systematic disinformation campaign, part of a 'coup' attempt by 'the Right'. And if the great majority of scholars and journalists depict Ortega's regime as brutally repressive, this is taken to reflect naive reliance on a narrow sector of Nicaragua's elite for information, who will do anything to undermine a government that governs in the interests of the poor.[1]

Revolution as national event in historical time

So, the Sandinista Revolution died, or the revolution lives on. This metaphor of life and death seems to work well, and it is often drawn on explicitly by those who narrate the revolution's trajectory. It suggests itself because of the way these opposing accounts, despite their incommensurable differences, each position the revolution as *a national event in historical time*. By doing so, they establish the terms of revolutionary failure.

As an event in historical time, the revolution *began* at a particular moment, and everyone agrees when that was: it was the moment of revolutionary triumph in July 1979, when the old regime was finally defeated, when President Somoza finally lost his family's decades-long hold on power, and the Sandinistas stormed into the capital city and, soon after, became a governing party. At that moment, Nicaragua became 'Sandinista Nicaragua'; a phrase which provided a title for countless scholarly studies. Nicaraguan society became 'revolutionary society'. The sense is of the political regime governing life within a nation suddenly and dramatically changing. The national polity, coinciding with the political territory, was, all of a sudden, undergoing revolution. Old, 'pre-revolutionary' Nicaragua, became revolutionary, Sandinista Nicaragua. The impression is produced by these pithy descriptors that everything was swept up, all together. Nicaraguans might have been *for* the revolution or *against* it, but they were, without question, involved in it, part of it, *within* it. With the revolution cast as an event in national historical time, sheer presence within the territory of the nation was enough to guarantee involvement.

And the failure of revolution – on this model of an event in historical time – necessarily has to do with duration and continuity. Within the collective sweep of national history, the revolution either failed because it finished, or didn't fail because it hasn't finished. It either came to an end, because its 'gains' were overturned, or continues, because its achievements are entrenched, enduring and ongoing. The disagreements about the current state of politics I have sketched above revolve around divergent views of whether or not the country's incumbent leaders really are revolutionaries any more. *They* say they are. Most, and with good reason, are of the view that they are not.

Conceiving the Sandinista Revolution as a collective political event, then, relies on a sense of a singular starting point at some time in the past. It carries with it a sense of the nation as a political container conditioning life for everyone within it. And it tends towards the assumption that the end of revolution would coincide with the end of government by genuine revolutionaries, and the resulting dismantling of the changes the real revolutionaries put in place. It can be observed that while the opposed perspectives in the polarised dispute contesting the interpretation of Nicaragua's political present disagree as to whether this shift has taken place, they nevertheless share the conceptual foundation of linear national time on the basis of which it is asserted.

These disagreements about the Nicaraguan revolution's temporal trajectory share some notable conceptual features with the way questions of time and temporality have played a role in the arguments put forward by anthropologists who have studied revolutions more broadly. Anthropologists have explored the ways in which the putative sociopolitical ruptures proclaimed by revolutionary discourse might conceal continuities; attending to the way older, even 'traditional' political forms play out in a new contexts (Cherstich et al., 2020: 1–17; Wilson, 2019). While revolutionaries themselves might proclaim a radical break with the old society, anthropologists have been alert to the ways in which longstanding social and cultural forms find new expression within revolutionary contexts. An underlying question here is whether a given 'society' was really transformed absolutely, or whether some aspects of it remained the same. Nicaraguan leaders talking the talk of revolution, while doing the politics of traditional Latin American clientelism, seem to exemplify just the kind of awkward political continuity that anthropologists have observed in numerous other post-revolutionary contexts.

The line of analysis to be developed in this essay will revolve around an examination of the above ways of thinking about revolutionary continuity in the light of several quite different ways of conceiving revolution I encountered during fieldwork with a community of government supporters in the Nicaraguan countryside, and will explore the distinctive forms revolutionary durability takes when revolution is locally understood as land, as development, and as *mestizaje* (racial and cultural mixing). The treatment of each topic will necessarily be brief, and I have developed more extended explorations of each of them elsewhere (Cooper, 2015; 2018; 2021). The aim here is to think though their implications in relation to this collection's theme of revolutionary afterlives. The simple argument I will develop is that the revolution was not always understood, among my rural interlocutors, as an event in national historical time. As a consequence, what it meant for the revolution to fail was not always a question of continuity, and revolutionary durability took multiple, divergent forms, even within a single location. We will see that the temporal horizon of revolutionary participation emerged in varying, sometimes contradictory ways, in relation to specific local ways of conceptualising and engaging with revolution. Rather than asking broad questions about whether society in general was truly transformed, the perspective taken here suggests that the temporal parameters of revolution – and as a result, what it means for revolutions to continue, or to fail – always emerge in relation to specific ways of attempting to enact the possibility of transformation.

Presence and absence in the imagined community

In order to pursue this line of analysis, it will be useful to draw on Benedict Anderson's (1991) classic account of the emergence of a nationalist 'imaginary'. Anderson's work investigates how 'print capitalism' facilitated the emergence of new and distinctive ways of thinking about sovereign collectivities: shifts facilitated by novel ways of thinking about the simultaneous coexistence of a national constituency within the flow of time. Indeed, his theory of nationalism focuses on just the temporal coordinates described above, those which underpin the conception of revolution as an event in linear national time. We will see as the discussion proceeds that the range of divergent ways revolution came to be conceptualised and engaged with in rural Nicaragua raise a number of questions about the role of presence, absence, and governmental efficacy in Anderson's model.

I want to highlight two components of Benedict Anderson's analysis of the way the narration of collective national experience becomes thinkable, which will be helpful points of comparison in the discussion to follow. Firstly, note the way he draws on a depiction of territory in his contrast between pre-modern and modern conceptions of sovereignty. The comparative characterisation is captured in the following observation:

> In fundamental ways 'serious' monarchy lies transverse to all modern conceptions of political life. Kingship organizes everything around a high centre. Its legitimacy derives from divinity, not from populations, who, after all, are subjects, not citizens. *In the modern conception, state sovereignty is fully, flatly, and evenly operative over each square centimetre of a legally demarcated territory.* But in the older imagining, where states were defined by centres, borders

were porous and indistinct, and sovereignties faded imperceptibly into one another. Hence, paradoxically enough, the ease with which pre-modern empires and kingdoms were able to sustain their rule over immensely heterogeneous, and often not even contiguous, populations for long periods of time. (Anderson, 1991: 19; emphasis added)

Older monarchies and empires were able to operate discontinuously, because of a distinctively pre-modern mode of conceptualising the basis of sovereign power, which inhered in the relationship of monarchs and nobles to divinity. As the relationships constitutive of the political order weakened, sovereignty dissipated accordingly. Sovereignty, as a result, had no necessary relationship to a given territory; a zone could stand outside the relationships constitutive of sovereignty without compromising the divine basis of sovereignty itself. It was, then, at least theoretically possible to live in close proximity to centres of power without having anything to do with a polity. The result is a view of sovereignty that maps discontinuously onto territory and there is the possibility of gaps. The modern conception of a national territory as Anderson depicts it, in contrast, recalls an atlas's image of a neatly divided political map, in which, to reiterate the point, 'state sovereignty is fully, flatly, and evenly operative over each square centimetre of a legally demarcated territory'. The political map, we might note, has no shading or half-colours; no indistinct border zones where jurisdiction is unclear or ambiguous, no territories left unfilled. Congruent with the depictions of 'Sandinista Nicaragua' referred to above, all populations living within a given nation-state are, by the modern notion of national sovereignty, equally and uniformly 'within' it.

In relation to the 'pre-modern' model, Anderson gives us a very brief sense of the relationship between the way sovereignty is conceptualised, and the role of effective governmental capacity. Since the polity was mediated by relationships between nobles, which in turn were thought to mediate a relationship with divinity, the broader political order stood as a hierarchically ordered amalgam of localised social systems. Centralised governmental capacity of whatever kind – either in the form of military force, or in any redistributive capacity or role in the provision of services or the construction of infrastructure – was simply not a necessary ingredient in this configuration. A legitimate king could, in theory, hold a polity together on the basis of allegiance alone. In the modern conception, however, Anderson's analysis, while focused on the conceptualisation of sovereignty, implicitly relies on the idea that there is some kind of correspondence between the 'flat' conception of territorial hegemony, and the practical capacity of states to exert governmental influence of some kind within that territory. Modern ideas about the role states should play depend, at least in part, on the premise that states are able to act, to enact governmental will, to 'do' something or other within the territory putatively governed. Everyone is 'within' the modern nation, at least in part, because modernity brings with it states that actually have the capacity to intervene in the lives of their citizens.

The second of Anderson's observations I wish to highlight emerges from his key argument about the emergence of modern 'simultaneity' through the symbolic premises of novels and newspapers; symbolic effects which, he suggests, enable the possibility of thinking of the nation as a singular community jointly traversing the linear flow of time. In the case of novels, Anderson focuses on the ways in which particular descriptive details are cast as typical of a distinctive national type. In relation to newspapers, he teases out the temporal implications of the basic logic of presenting a diverse array of happenings that take place on a given day as having anything to do with each other. It is the idea that they take place within or in relation to an ongoing national experience that this eclectic arrangement of fragments makes sense. Together, these allow for the very possibility of thinking of an event in historical time as having any coherent empirical referent:

> The idea of a sociological organism moving calendrically through homogeneous, empty time is a precise analogue of the idea of the nation, which also is conceived as a solid community moving steadily down (or up) history. (Anderson, 1991: 26)

In Anderson's analysis, the nation emerges as part of the imaginative work by which the reader-citizen interprets an observed instance in relation to an imagined collectivity of similar instances, 'a world of plurals', with the collectivity itself – the imagined community – constituted by the reader's recognition of shared characteristics. The national context can never be encountered directly, because it inevitably exceeds the capacity for direct perception of any given observer, but it emerges from the interpretative move by which those observed particularities that do indeed fall within the range of a viable viewpoint are framed as belonging to a typical form. The idea of a nation as a singular 'sociological organism', then, operates as an absent schema fixed onto that which is accessible and present; an interpretative framework brought to bear on direct observation by the nationalist subject. It emerges by weaving tangible particularity into the intangible generality of shared characteristics.²

The imagined community of Anderson's modern nation, then, constructs a sense of a shared collectivity moving through time together, jointly undergoing a common trajectory of temporal experience. And this sense of common temporal trajectory mutually conditions a sense of national territory as itself fully saturated by the national experience, in contrast to the discontinuous nature of pre-modern polities. At first glance, dramatic political events definitive of national history – events such as revolutions – might appear to be phenomena that crystallise the mode of nationhood Anderson is concerned to theorise. The divergent ways in which revolution was understood in rural Nicaragua, however, raise questions here. If an implicit set of claims regarding governmental efficacy accompanies Anderson's account of the 'flat' quality of modern sovereignty, the material explored below prompts the question of what happens when modern governments are incapable of action, and when there is little in the way of infrastructural or service provision to accompany the idea of statehood. Similarly, what happens to Anderson's notion of a national imaginary when the tangible referent of collective identity (the typically Mexican prison, in one of his examples) is absent; when that which is putatively definitive of the national experience is in short supply, inaccessible, out of reach, ruined, or simply non-existent? What happens, in other words, to the imaginative work of weaving the generalised position of a national frame of reference from the particularities of tangible instances … when those instances are themselves also missing? We shall see that each of the three themes explored below introduces a distinct dynamic of presence and absence which demands that these questions be addressed, and which, as a result, give rise to forms of revolutionary durability distinct from those that might obtain for a singular 'sociological organism moving calendrically through homogeneous, empty time' (Anderson, 1991: 26).

The remains of revolution in an agrarian reform community

The village of Gualiqueme was established in 1984, as part of the founding of Rigoberto Cruz Cooperative, a new 'Sandinista Defence Cooperative', which was a collectivised and militarised agricultural organisation established on expropriated land. Prior to the revolution, this region within the Segovian mountains had been a zone of extensive haciendas that produced coffee and raised cattle. Small hamlets existed on the peripheries of the haciendas with residents sometimes providing seasonal labour during coffee harvests. Many rural people also lived within hacienda-owned lands, relying on sharecropping arrangements with landlords to grow subsistence crops, frequently with the requirement that every few years a new patch of forest be cleared in order to open new land for expanding dairy herds. Several local landlords had close ties with the Somoza regime, and fled the country when the Sandinistas took power, leaving their estates unoccupied. The incoming government soon appropriated these lands. After an initial policy of converting these estates into state farms, collectivised cooperatives were established, in line with the view that intensive, mechanised, large-scale production in the countryside would be essential in order to fund the revolution's objectives (Baumeister, 2012; Enríquez, 1991; Kaimowitz, 1986; Martí i Puig and Baumeister, 2017).

Rigoberto Cruz was founded at a time when the 'Contra' war was at its height, and the new cooperative was expected to operate as a military outpost in an area of considerable insurgent activity. Founding members had almost all been displaced from their previous homes by Contra attacks on villages perceived by the counter-revolutionaries to have developed strong ties with the FSLN. After a period of time living as refugees in a nearby town, the prospect of a position in a new cooperative offered founding members the chance to return to life in the countryside. Early years saw fully collectivised production under the direction of an elected leadership, but production was made difficult by the fact that the institution was operating in a warzone. Many agricultural activities were performed by women, since men and many boys had been drafted into the Sandinista army. Those men who remained in the community served in a militia that kept constant guard in case of Contra attack, but even so, the women working the fields carried arms, just in case. On several occasions the militia successfully defended the cooperative from Contra attack, but not without suffering numerous casualties.

By the time I first visited Gualiqueme, the agricultural land of the cooperative had long since been informally de-collectivised, but the institution itself remained in existence, serving to provide residents with an avenue to commercialise their individual production through membership of a coffee-exporting cooperative. Serious tensions in relation to land tenure – which remained legally the collective property of the cooperative – had flared up over the years. The sale of land to outsiders, technically prohibited but increasingly common, was widely viewed as a problem. Most families, however, retained access to cooperative land; and produced coffee for export, along with maize and beans for both sale and consumption (for detailed accounts of land division in the community see Cooper, 2015; 2018). A series of non-governmental organisations had been active in the area over the years, offering small-scale development programmes, loans and infrastructure projects, among other interventions, and residents generally placed great value on their work. Migration to Honduras was easy, requiring no documentation, and was common for young men during the coffee season. Costa Rica was harder to get into, but was also a popular destination. Nobody from the community had made it as far as the United States, though young men swapped heroic stories of less long-distance border-crossings, and cultivated fantasies of one day making the trip to the United States. In general, while residents recognised themselves as being very poor, they viewed their access to modest parcels of land as placing them in a more secure economic position than those they knew in towns and cities. In the cities you have to buy everything, people would often tell me; and if you do not have any money, you starve.

Revolution as land

Residents of Gualiqueme frequently stated that the whole point of the revolution had been the land. In the years prior to 1979, Sandinista guerrillas venturing out of a nearby training camp had told some of the founding members that the revolution would take land from the rich and give it to the poor. And most members of the cooperative had long understood this as a promise that referred to the eventual delivery of personal plots of land. In Gualiqueme, as in collectivised cooperatives across Nicaragua, after a few years of faltering collective production, the land started to be divided out informally. First, small parcels were shared out within the cooperative's coffee-producing areas. Then areas which had once been used for pasture were allocated to members to raise modest parcels of maize and beans of their own. When the war ended, and it became safe to go into the more mountainous zones of the cooperative's territory, members began to claim more parcels there. At a time when other nearby cooperatives had legally disbanded and fully divided out lands, the idea emerged among many members that each of them should have the right to a full share of the cooperative's whole territory. Children of members, looking to start independent households of their own, claimed parcels too, arguing that they were claiming part of the share that their parents were entitled to. People claimed parcels by marking out perimeters, by visibly working the land, and by planting crops and trees. If someone began to work a parcel, others recognised it as their property, even if they disputed the legitimacy of the claim. Almost all the land within the cooperative was eventually claimed in this way.

People told me that they would always support Daniel Ortega, because he had given them the land. They also told me that they had won the land themselves at the cost of many lives. They contrasted their current lives with those they had lived before the revolution. Before, they had had to work at the beck and call of the rich, all day, for almost no money. But now, they had land. Thanks to the land, they were no longer quite so poor, they said.

But if the revolution was about land, and if the land in question was a share of the cooperative's fragmenting collective territory, it was not quite the case that they 'had' the land. Though there was hardly any unclaimed land left, most residents only owned part of what they considered to be their entitlement. The idea of a full, fair share hung over them as an unrealised promise. And so, if the revolution had always been the promise of land, then it was hardly something that came about, all together, at a single point in the past. The revolution's gains had been partly realised, but they also partly stood as a potential that was yet to materialise.

Many residents talked about the prospect of a full, legal division of land in the future, in which everything which had been grabbed would be measured out, and those who had grabbed too much would be made to hand it back. But people also pointed out that much land had been sold, illegally, to outsiders. Would they be made to give it back? How would the full territory be shared out if part of it had already been lost?

What it might mean for the revolution to fail was conditioned by this conception of revolutionary gains as the realisation of a share of land. As individuals claimed personal plots – illegally, as far as the municipal Sandinista government was concerned – they understood themselves to be asserting their right to the revolution's promised gift of land. The ways in which ownership was locally recognised and secured became ways in which the revolution's gains were shored up. The ways in which property could be lost became ways in which the revolution, in turn, could be lost. Just as important, ways in which the prospect of obtaining those unclaimed, potential entitlements to a share of land might be weakened or undermined, became ways in which the revolution's full promise could wither away.

Towards the end of my fieldwork, a prosperous potato farmer rented a few parcels within the formerly collective territory that had been claimed as personal property by one cooperative member. He paid Gualiqueme residents to do the ploughing, the planting, the tending and the harvesting. He began to expand his enterprise, buying neighbouring plots from other cooperative members. Some appreciated the paid work, which was not normally available so close to home. Others saw the defeat of the revolution in the potato farmer's success. This was how it happened before, the cooperative's president told me. Haciendas encouraged the peasantry to fall into debt, then claimed their lands as repayment. Peasants became landless labourers. The loss of the revolution would be the repetition of the historical process by which the land was lost before.

Revolution as development

If land was one important way in which Gualiqueme residents thought about the gains of revolution, another had to do with economic and infrastructural development. When the Sandinistas had been out of power between 1990 and 2006, I was told, the 'Liberal' governments had done nothing to help the poor. The return of the Sandinistas to power – the return of the revolution, as my interlocutors framed it – brought with it a whole series of poverty-reduction programmes and infrastructural projects (Spalding, 2009). Ongoing revolution, as my interloctors saw it, meant road construction, electrification, and government programmes like Plan Techo – 'the Roof Plan' – which distributed sheets of corrugated zinc to needy households. It meant a government that would weave rural communities into a national infrastructural network, and which would provide services and afford a basic level of welfare to rural constituencies.

Revolution, then, meant improvement of the lives of the poor. It meant a government that took the poor into account, and which worked to improve their conditions of life. The revolution was seen to be still under way when government trucks arrived in Gualiqueme to repair dirt roads worn down by years of rainfall. Its gains were known through the various rounds of Plan Techo delivered to residents. And with the revolution understood in this way, its viability, success and ongoing vitality were related to how infrastructural and poverty-reduction programmes were actually accessed. The possibility that the revolution might fail, on this model, came to revolve around the ways in which access, inclusion and eligibility to state services and infrastructural development came to be threatened.

In general, in abstract proclamations of support for their Sandinista government, Gualiqueme residents affirmed that by these criteria, the revolution continued apace. Daniel Ortega, unlike the 'neoliberal' governments who preceded him, was in the process of delivering countless projects, building countless roads, constructing countless houses and allocating them to ordinary Nicaraguans. Everyone was familiar with the litany of infrastructural improvements recounted each day on the first lady's daily radio broadcast, and had heard the lengthy lists of names of beneficiaries recited by the president at political events. The imagery and rhetoric of governmental delivery was a theme endlessly repeated, day after day, on the media sources consumed in this community.[3] Improvement was happening everywhere, and the revolutionary project continued.

But as with land, it was not the case that revolutionary development was something that necessarily stood available, here, for me. Development may have been happening to 'Nicaragua', but the nation's abstract improvements did not seem to carry everyone along. It was noted earlier that conceiving of the revolution as an event in historical time results in a depiction of Nicaraguan territory as a kind of political container; everyone was necessarily carried along with an event that filled the nation. But if the hope for revolutionary development in Gualiqueme gave rise to any sense of the nation as a container, it must have been something like a colander: it was full of holes, and there were many ways of being left behind.

Indeed, there was a real sense of anxiety regarding the ways in which revolutionary development was accessed. Many in Gualiqueme felt that their eligibilities had been overlooked. They felt that some members of their cooperative had managed to manoeuvre themselves into privileged positions, enjoying close relationships with local politicians and gathering up all the benefits of the revolution for themselves. A clientelistic imaginary informed these evaluations. Governmental support was understood as a kind of gift, and it was assumed that personal relationship was the medium through which revolutionary benefits could be realised. When access to state projects was not forthcoming, many came to the conclusion that the problem was a problem of personal relationship. The government, the president and the party were all unable to see them or recognise their needs, and the possibility of mutual encounter was lacking. The people who should have been working to serve as political intermediaries were failing to make the pressing needs of residents adequately known to powerholders. People felt cut off. The viability of revolutionary gains, from this perspective, depended upon the prospect of recognition, and upon a kind of visibility which would make political relationship a possibility.

I noted previously that accounts of the revolution as an event in historical time tend to assume that the Sandinista revolution lived on for as long as true revolutionaries held political power. Society was revolutionary society as long as it was revolutionaries who governed. That assumption relies on the simple premise that government and society are in contact. Government works upon society. Governments with a transformative agenda transform society, or at the very least try to, and if they fail it has to do with the extent to which society resists that will to transform, or perhaps emerges as a result of the way planners and politicians misread the reality of local conditions. Everyday life, and the transformative work of government, push against each other. There might be 'friction' here (Tsing, 2005), but at the very least there is contact.

The way Gualiqueme residents experienced themselves as being cut off from the relations which enabled development, however, gives rise to a very different sense of the relationship between government and everyday life. The work of revolutionary government was assumed to be out there, in general, but making sure you remained an object of that transformative work was a problem. Rather than revolution saturating a uniform national territory, revolution became something contingent upon an elusive state of political connection. Revolution came to be something which some people managed to grab more of than others; something which only some people, by dint of the relationships they had managed to establish, were able to benefit from. Revolutionary failure, on this model, became the absence of the right kinds of relationship.

Revolution as *mestizaje*

The final theme I will discuss emerged through the intersection of ideas about revolutionary transformation with the ambiguous and stigmatised status of ethnic identity for Gualiqueme residents. Recent historical scholarship of Nicaragua – primarily that of Jeffrey Gould (1993; 1996; 1998) – has critically documented a pervasive 'myth of *mestizaje*', a broad cultural claim that ethnic particularity in Pacific Nicaragua was a thing of the past. Gould argues that discursive disavowal of the existence of Indian communities within Spanish-speaking Nicaragua – at a time when in fact many such communities retained a viable institutional existence – stood as a primary causal factor underpinning the actual disintegration of these indigenous communities throughout the nineteenth century, as communal lands were privatised and large haciendas expanded into formerly indigenous territories. These arguments are of pressing relevance to the region under consideration here. Lands traditionally belonging to Chorotegan Indians had been appropriated by the region's haciendas, and overlap with the land reform title granted to the Gualiqueme cooperative. A neighbouring land reform cooperative was almost entirely located within such lands. And, as documented by Monachon and Gonda (2009), the *Comunidad Indígena de Telpaneca* (Telpaneca Indigenous Community) – a political organisation representing this historic indigenous community – has been involved in a continuing political struggle aimed at gaining recognition of jurisdiction over this territory, and an accompanying right to receive the traditional rent for which those occupying the land would be liable.

As Monachon and Gonda make clear, the historic disintegration of communal lands led to a weakening of subjective indigenous identity throughout the area. Nobody in Gualiqueme identified in any positive sense as indigenous. But ethnic descriptors were frequently employed by others when describing Gualiqueme villagers in general, or sometimes certain individuals in particular. Physical attributes such as height, skin colour, and less commonly individual traits such as gait or style of speech were singled out as evidencing an ethnic status of either '*indio*' (Indian) or, much less commonly, '*indígena*' (indigenous). These ethnic terms were almost universally disavowed within the community as terms of self-identification, except in very occasional situations of confidence and trust – and even then in an ambiguous and distanced fashion. In open and casual usage, it was almost always other people who were the '*indios*'. Despite this, ethnic terms were continually referenced in everyday life. Sometimes they indexed technological or cultural simplicity. 'Indian soap' referred to traditional handmade soap, rather than the commercially produced varieties that were seen as superior. 'Indian chickens' were hardy native breeds rather than the commercially bred hens that were much more productive but required expensive feed. At times *indio* was used to mean 'poor' in an economic sense. On one occasion I had been speaking to a pair of young men in Gualiqueme and they mentioned that people in the adjacent village of El Poso referred to Gualiqueme as *indios*. But that was nonsense, they both argued, because people there were even poorer: 'we have land, but they have nothing', they insisted. Nevertheless, the local potency of the category had to do with both this intense stigma surrounding it, as well as its ambiguous reference in relation to local people themselves. The security of always situating Indianness elsewhere, for many Gualiqueme residents, was continually threatened by the possibility of being identified with the stigmatised category. It was all too easy to recognise, in the connotations of backwardness and simplicity, signs of the material conditions that continued to mark local lives.

This possibility of troubling identification, however, was countered by the assurance that the revolution had effected a fundamental transformation. The most consistent feature picked out by Gualiqueme residents when characterising and defining actually existing *indios* was a startling inability to speak. One of my hosts during fieldwork, Wilber, articulated this idea starkly after he had chastised his mother for using a word that he considered to be too *indio* to be used in polite company. She had referred to her belly as a *barriga*, and Wilber had immediately interrupted her, insisting that *barriga* was meaningless, a senseless 'Indian' word that conveyed nothing.[4] The correct term to use was *'estómago'*. The thing about *indios*, he explained, is that they are stupid. They do not understand anything. Our ancestors that lived here before, he went on, just like the *indios* that still live in some remote communities, were unable to speak. They might try and say 'left', but the word 'right' would come out of their mouths. If they tried to say 'son', they would say 'daughter'. And so on. They couldn't communicate, and their words were jumbled and backwards in relation to their referents.

This depiction of confusion and communicative inability caused by unwitting lexical inversion functioned as a standardised image of indigeneity among Gualiqueme residents, one that was frequently drawn upon when people wanted to characterise present-day Indians living elsewhere. Crucially, however, this unfortunate condition had – for Gualiqueme residents at least – become a thing of the past. While *indios* still existed, still beset by these cultural disadvantages, for Gualiqueme residents a cultural gulf had been opened up between them and their ancestors. Wilber was forthright in explaining how this transition came about. The revolution is what happened, he stated. With the revolution came groups of teachers – student participants in the Literacy Crusade – who taught people to read and write. As a consequence of the revolution, schools were established that people could attend for free. Indeed, for many older residents of Gualiqueme the first experience of being able to write came about through their experiences participating in Literacy Crusade classes. Though some individuals who have been involved in administrative elements of cooperative organisational work have retained literacy levels gained during those classes, in many cases the skills older rural people acquired did not progress very far, and were later lost through lack of practice in the years that followed. But the ability to sign documents yourself is widely taken by participants in the Crusade in Gualiqueme to indicate a categorical shift between a prior state of unchanging ignorance, and the transition to a state of progress, however gradual. This amounted to a sense that the Literacy Crusade and more recent state provision of education had been responsible for a profound shift in the kind of people Gualiqueme residents were, effecting a transition from uncivilised *indios* to proper members of the category of 'the poor'. Within such claims is conveyed the sense that any deficiencies attributable to ethnicity have been overcome and eliminated through the progress made possible by the revolution.

In relation to this way of conceptualising revolutionary transformation, once again, what it means for revolution to fail takes a form quite different to that of an event coming to an end. With revolutionary transformation framed as a kind of progressive ethnic development – an overcoming of a deficient indigenous identity that previously conditioned ways of speaking and comporting oneself in the world – revolutionary failure came to be seen in moments of ethnic slippage, moments that made a transition away from ethnicity and towards citizenship seem partial or incomplete, such as when Wilber saw in his mother's choice of words a painful recognition that an indigenous heritage might not be entirely in the past, but could also be carried along in the present within words, minds and bodies.

Revolution, dead *and* alive

Revolution is not only an event, then, and as a result, a revolution's failure is not always a matter of ending. There is certainly nothing surprising in the idea that the nature of revolutionary durability depends on what revolution itself is understood to mean, a statement that verges on tautology. Nevertheless, the implications of the observation can be hard to square with an abiding imperative to relate revolution in the form of a story. Revolutions and their aftermaths compel public affirmations of loyalty, approval, opposition and critique, and in doing so they give rise to the demand for narrative. And this impulse to depict the trajectory of revolution within narrative time, as an event undergone by a national collectivity in the course of history, stands in tension with the varied temporal forms produced by the different conceptions of revolutionary transformation explored above.

To return to our initial set of propositions that emerged from treating revolution as a national event in historical time: we saw that conceiving revolution as a collective political event implies a singular starting point, some time in the past. But for residents of Gualiqueme, the close association of the revolution's gains with partially unclaimed land unsettled any such sense of a singular beginning. The revolution was a promise that had still only partially been fulfilled. Some of the revolution's gifts remained to be given, and everyone needed to make sure they seized what was due to them. To concede that the revolution had come to an end carried the implication that this claim of outstanding debt might also be relinquished, and that the full share of cooperative land which many saw as their due would never be realised. Claims of revolutionary continuity, in other words, were also active claims regarding local entitlements and ownership, not simply diagnoses of the state of national politics.

Similarly, the idea that the revolution was something that had already happened, and that its transformations had already been effected, was drawn upon in negotiating an ambiguous set of ideas about the revolution's role in overcoming stigma-laden ethnicity. Moments where ethnic markers re-emerged unbidden, or where the connotations of ethnic categories seemed to uncomfortably index the conditions of the present, also unsettled any such sense of a singular originary revolutionary moment. Instead, revolutionary transformation became something that needed to be produced and maintained through a careful choice of words, and through efforts at cultivating standards of living that marked people out as having moved beyond the life of 'Indios'. Claims that the revolution's gains had been overturned had to contend with a firm sense that the schooling and education now widely available to primary-age children (Muhr, 2013) had permanently solidified this shift away from the indigenous lives of 'ancestors'.

We also saw that conceiving revolution as event carries with it a sense of political territory as a container conditioning life for everyone within it. Anderson's account of a 'modern' view of nationhood smoothly saturating a national territory captured this well. A substantial literature has critically examined the ways in which an undifferentiated sense of a national revolutionary process led FSLN leaders in the 1980s to overlook the profound cultural, political differences that exist within Nicaragua, most significantly in relation to the Atlantic coast; elisions which resulted in profound political ruptures with Miskitu communities (Hale, 1996; 2017). The ways Gualiqueme residents depicted the revolution as having to do with land and development point towards the ways in which uniform, unitary notions of involvement and participation similarly efface notable forms of exclusion that continue to condition the experiences of those living within communities supposedly at the heart of the original revolutionary process, and which remain part of the 'base' of core FSLN supporters whose electoral support is unwavering. With the revolution defined as land or development, partaking in the revolution's gains became contingent on specific forms of ownership, entitlement and inclusion. Revolution becomes something distributed unevenly between individuals and between communities – it becomes something 'patchy' (Tsing, 2015), which might easily fall away, but which you can strive to recover and retrieve.

Two comments regarding Anderson's analysis emerge here. Firstly, the fact that fellow citizens jointly participate in the sense of shared membership in a polity forged on the basis of the common temporality of 'events' does not tell us much about the material underpinnings of a sense of citizenship and national belonging. Another way of putting this would be to observe that it is possible to be a full participant in the discursive construction of a national polity without having any corresponding access to state-provided services, infrastructure, or welfare provision. To the extent that these infrastructural correlates of a putatively revolutionary project were viewed by rural Nicaraguans as definitional of revolution as such, their experience of the 'second stage' of the revolution set unitary notions of an ongoing national event against the local specifics of unmet demands for land and state-provided services. Secondly, the prospective and subjunctive quality of the signs by which revolutionary transformation was gauged in Gualiqueme contrasts with the sense of national belonging Anderson analysed in nationalist novels. Anderson focused on the way nationalist consciousness interprets particular instances of observed reality as typical of a generalised national type. The way Gualiqueme residents defined the revolution as a series of demands, many of which remained unmet, however, suggests a form of political consciousness focused on absences rather than observed instances. That which was taken to be typical of the ongoing event of national revolution – abundant state services, and the continual transformative work of an active government – was often out of reach. In this context, the act of weaving specifics into a generalised national context became not just an interpretative move constitutive of national consciousness, but the assertion of a rightful place in the imagined community.

Finally, we saw that the sense of revolution as national event tends towards the assumption that the end of revolution would coincide with the end of government by genuine revolutionaries. Each of the examples we have explored, however, gives rise to quite different criteria of revolutionary failure, and makes clear that the notion the revolution is continuing opens up a quite different set of evaluative criteria for the ordinary Nicaraguans who find it persuasive. When Gualiqueme residents found the FSLN's claims that the revolution was continuing persuasive, in other words, they were not engaged in the same kind of evaluation of the governing party as scholars who have charted the FSLN's trajectory. Their assertions of revolutionary durability were woven through with fractious land claims, assertions of full national citizenship as opposed to ethnicised exclusion, and efforts to secure the elusive protections of a viable welfare state.

It is notable, in this regard, that Gualiqueme residents seemed quite comfortable to combine their stated support of Ortega and their commitment to the notion that the Sandinista revolution was ongoing with a nuanced moral appraisal of Ortega as an individual. The opposed narratives recounted at the start of this chapter presented morally coherent, internally consistent stories regarding the relationship between the revolution and its leaders, with Ortega figuring as marked by either virtue or vice depending on whether the narrative casts his role as that of true revolutionary, or self-interested traitor to the revolution's aims. Those I knew in Gualiqueme did not seem to need to purify their political and historical narratives in this way, and I frequently heard the same individuals who proclaimed lifelong loyalty to Ortega also criticise him as greedy and corrupt. They were familiar with critiques relayed by the political opposition along these lines, and were troubled by the extent to which Ortega had enriched himself and his family by means of his political position. But these observations did not lead them to switch between poles of the dichotomous, mutually incompatible accounts of the revolution's life or death that marked public political debate. Ortega, they assumed, could be a problematic individual and a force for good at the same time. Appreciating the varying, overlapping, and contradictory temporal forms revolution took in rural Nicaragua – and the way the temporal coordinates of revolution emerged through a range of practices in addition to that of telling a story – allows us to understand why.

Notes

1. The many online writings of solidarity activist John Perry since April 2018 provide a good English-language sense of these arguments (for instance Perry, 2019), which, within Nicaragua, have been promoted through government-controlled media outlets (with the increasingly sophisticated propaganda output of the Sandinista Youth playing a major role on YouTube and Twitter; see, e.g., https://www.youtube.com/channel/UC9eaNdd1t64xLogaRVmGrow), and in the writings of intellectuals who remain loyal to the FSLN.
2. Anthropologists, along with nationalist novelists, contend with the rhetorical affordances and analytical pitfalls of the interplay between specific instances and generalised types. To make long-term fieldwork with a fairly limited pool of individual interlocutors speak to categorical constituencies – 'Malay villagers', 'rural Nicaraguans', and so on – requires the descriptive work of making observed instances stand for, or in some way speak to, sociological categories that can never be perceived directly. Anderson's interests here, as a result, resonate with

discussions within the discpline about the role of 'example' and typicality in both ethnography and anthropological analysis (Højer and Bandak, 2015).
3. Ownership and control of media has been a key strategy pursued by the governing family. Critical scholarship and civil society activists in Nicaragua have charted a steady accumulation of ownership of television and radio channels by the president himself, along with his family members. Critical and non-partisan analysis of the government makes no appearance on these channels, which exclusively develop themes aiming to promote support of the FSLN.
4. The word does not derive from an indigenous language, but its informality in Spanish perhaps prompted Wilber to identify it as 'Indian'.

References

Anderson, Benedict R. 1991. *Imagined Communities: Reflections on the origin and spread of nationalism*. London: Verso.
Baltodano, Andrés P. 2009. 'La cultura política nicaragüense y el FSLN: De la utopía al pragmatismo', in Close, D. and Martí i Puig, S. (eds), *Nicaragua y el FSLN (1979–2009): ¿Qué queda de la revolución?* Edicions Bellaterra, 137–67.
Baumeister, Eduardo. 2012. 'The politics of land reform', in Close, D., Martí i Puig, S. and McConnell, S. A. (eds), *The Sandinistas and Nicaragua since 1979*. Boulder, CO: Lynne Rienner, 245–68.
Cherstich, Igor, Holbraad, Martin and Tassi, Nico. 2020. *Anthropologies of Revolution: Forging time, people, and worlds*. Berkeley: University of California Press.
Cooper, David. 2015. Productive dilemmas: Assistance and struggle in a Nicaraguan agricultural cooperative. PhD thesis, University College London.
Cooper, David. 2018. 'Grounding rights: Populist and peasant conceptions of entitlement in rural Nicaragua'. *Social Analysis*, 62: 128–48.
Cooper, David. 2021. 'Revolutionary abandon: Circles and machines in Sandinista Nicaragua'. *Focaal*, 2021(91): 31–49.
Enríquez, Laura J. 1991. *Harvesting Change: Labor and agrarian reform in Nicaragua, 1979–1990*. Chapel Hill: University of North Carolina Press.
Gould, Jeffrey L. 1993. '"¡Vana ilusión!": The highlands Indians and the myth of Nicaragua mestiza, 1880–1925'. *Hispanic American Historical Review*, 73: 393–429.
Gould, Jeffrey L. 1996. 'Gender, politics, and the triumph of mestizaje in early 20th century Nicaragua'. *Journal of Latin American Anthropology*, 2: 4–33.
Gould, Jeffrey L. 1998. *To Die in This Way: Nicaraguan Indians and the myth of mestizaje, 1880–1965*. Durham, NC: Duke University Press.
Gutiérrez, Fernando and Ocampo, Alejandro. 2019. 'Latin America: From media censorship to media ownership', in Mishra, S. and Kern-Stone, R. (eds), *Transnational Media: Concepts and cases*. Hoboken, NJ: Wiley, 97–106.
Hale, Charles R. 1996. *Resistance and Contradiction: Miskitu Indians and the Nicaraguan state, 1894–1987*. Stanford, CA: Stanford University Press.
Hale, Charles R. 2017. 'What went wrong? Rethinking the Sandinista Revolution, in light of its second coming'. *Latin American Research Review*, 52(4): 720–7.
Højer, Lars and Bandak, Andreas. 2015. 'Introduction: The power of example'. *Journal of the Royal Anthropological Institute*, 21: 1–17.
Hoyt, Katherine. 2004. 'Parties and pacts in contemporary Nicaragua', in Close, D. and Deonandan, K. (eds), *Undoing Democracy: The politics of electoral caudillismo*. Oxford: Lexington Books, 17–42.
Kaimowitz, David. 1986. 'Nicaraguan debates on agrarian structure and their implications for agricultural policy and the rural poor'. *Journal of Peasant Studies*, 14: 100–17.
Monachon, David and Gonda, Noémi. 2009. '¿Cómo lograr una gestión concertada y sostenible de las tierras indígenas chorotegas en un contexto de presión y de liberalización comercial que afecta a los recursos naturales?'. *Intercambios*, 105. Accessed 15 December 2022. https://www.academia.edu/1987730/_Cómo_lograr_una_gestión_concertada_y_sostenible_de_las_tierras_indígenas_chorotegas_en_un_contexto_de_presión_y_de_liberalización_comercial_que_afecta_a_

Muhr, Thomas. 2013. 'Optimism reborn: Nicaragua's participative education revolution, the citizen power development model and the construction of "21st century socialism"'. *Globalisation, Societies and Education*, 11: 276–95.

Perry, John, 2022. 'A year after Nicaragua coup attempt, the media's regime-change deceptions are still unraveling'. *Grayzone*. Accessed 2/12/2022. https://thegrayzone.com/2019/07/15/a-year-after-nicaraguas-coup-the-medias-regime-change-deceptions-are-still-unraveling/.

Sierakowski, Robert James. 2012. In the footsteps of Sandino: Geographies of revolution and political violence in northern Nicaragua, 1956–1979. PhD thesis, UCLA.

Spalding, R. J. 2009. 'Las políticas contra la pobreza en Nicaragua', in Close, D. and Martí i Puig, S. (eds), *Nicaragua y el FSLN (1979–2009): ¿Que queda de la revolución?* Edicions Bellaterra, 351–81.

Tsing, Anna L. 2005. *Friction: An ethnography of global connection*. Princeton: Princeton University Press.

Tsing, Anna L. 2015. *The Mushroom at the End of the World: On the possibility of life in capitalist ruins*. Princeton: Princeton University Press.

Wilson, A. 2019. 'Revolution'. *Cambridge Encyclopedia of Anthropology*. Online. https://www.anthroencyclopedia.com/entry/revolution. Accessed 25 October 2022.

2
Picturing absence in post-revolutionary Yemen

Gabriele vom Bruck

Introduction

In 1962 the age-old Yemeni imamate was overthrown by so-called 'Free officers' with the support of Egypt, and a republic established.[1] Half a century later, visual artefacts related to that period continue to reveal Yemenis' diverse political locations: portraits of revolutionary heroes displayed by the detractors of the old elites glorify those whom others regard as their tormentors. Their display in the domestic sphere may generate instantaneous interaction, tacit understandings, the articulation and sharing of memories, as well as expressing political commitment. Analysing the relationship between visual imagery, agency, and revolutionary violence,[2] I focus on the modalities of remembering that are being created around images of the past buried in people's albums or exhibited in their diwans ('reception rooms').[3] I explore how (post-) revolutionary subjectivities are mediated by photographs and how these social artefacts often speak to a past that is experienced and understood in the present tense (Morton, 2015: 268). Susan Sontag (1977: 70) draws our attention to photography's inherent link with human mortality, documenting 'the vulnerability of lives heading toward their own destruction … this link between photography and death haunts all photographs of people'.[4] The poignancy of this haunting quality is heightened when we gaze at images of people who died untimely or violent deaths. What kind of historical, moral or cultural claims are made by these displays? As noted by Lucie Ryzova (2015a: 161), photographs capture a complete likeness of persons in tandem with other acts and practices, notably by being acted upon, managed and circulated in unpredictable ways.

Here I am interested in photographs that changed hands by being forcefully appropriated during revolutionary unrest or stored and displayed in the survivors' homes in its aftermath. Practices such as those indicated above attest to the agency of photographs and the ways in which they operate as affective spaces that embody the debris of lived experiences and unfinished pasts. They offer clues as to how attachments, rejections and sensibilities of various sorts are formed. 'Affective spaces' are conceived of in terms of emotive, interpretive, and performative sites for engaging with and negotiating ruptured pasts (Behrouzan, 2016: 9), whereby the personal and the political are closely intertwined.[5]

In what follows, revolutionary afterlife is studied through both present and absent (reimagined) images. They are conceived of as texts rather than illustrations of a text. Photographs, which form part of quotidian socialities, reveal the minutiae of personal loss and fractured lives, as well as hopes for 'progressive' politics and social mobility. They acknowledge 'absence', whether of disappeared relatives or of revolutionary transformation that has remained a distant dream, and engagement with them shows that there is often more than one story found in them (Batchen, 2009: 33). One of my concerns is with 'that which is absent but nevertheless experienced as a presence' (Fowles, 2010: 25), an endeavour which must include an inquiry into how 'absence' is marked, dealt with, and acknowledged. Attending to the problem of absence is not just about conceiving of absence as the antonym to presence (Bille et al., 2010: 13), but as something that may have an agentive presence by virtue of being absent. Since Roland Barthes's (2000: 87, 99–100) characterisation of the photograph 'as a certificate of presence' and his auto-ethnographical notes centred on a personal image which conveys a presence that is immediately submerged by a sorrowful absence, the issue of the presence of the dead and disappeared generated via visual representation has been problematised.[6] Dealing with the vexed issue of presence and the problem of continuity and discontinuity on a more general level, the social historian Eelco Runia has provided a novel reading of metonymy that is not limited to the discursive realm. Metonymy is understood as a trope of 'presence in absence ... in the sense that in the absence ... that *is* there, the thing that isn't there is still present'. By presenting an absence, metonymy is a 'transfer of presence'. The author's analysis includes artefacts such as the photographs illustrating the novels of W. G. Sebald and the Berlin Wall (Runia, 2006: 1, 5–6, 15, 29).

While it has been widely acknowledged that photographs do not truthfully represent the past (Batchen, 2009: 33), in recent writings they have been appreciated for their relational quality and agentive capacity. Centred on the notion of 'distributed personhood', these aspects of Alfred Gell's anthropological theory of visual art have inspired work on photography, though he himself dealt with the subject only peripherally.[7] Gell (1998: 102) claims that the agency of the person that is represented in an image is impressed on the representation. With respect to the photographic image – unlike someone's painted portrait – the emphasis is solely on the person *qua* object (the index) rather than on the 'maker' (the photographer), who in the case of a painting is visible only via his works (for example, Leonardo da Vinci).[8] In other words, the person appearing in a photograph is not merely 'a secondary agent'; rather, the prototype is the cause of the index (1998: 35, 50). It may indeed be argued that the visual image of the person represents the relational qualities of the 'material' *par excellence*. Gell insists that *'images* of something (a prototype) are *parts* of that thing (as a distributed object)' (1998: 223, emphasis his).[9] The parts that perceptible objects give off themselves are incorporated by the onlooker in the process of sensual perception. A person and a person's mind consist of various biographical events, as well as of 'a dispersed category of material objects, traces, and leavings, which can be attributed to a person'. Persons 'are' the sum total of all indexes that testify to their biographical existence (1998: 222–3).[10]

Establishing a well-conceived theory of object agency, Gell (1998: 222) argues that the opposition between 'mind' (the internal person) and the external person (who is the sum of their relations with other persons) is only relative. Elizabeth Edwards, whose work on photography and the production of history has been inspired by Gell, maintains that engagement with photographs provides evidence of this blurring of distinctions between the internal and external person, and that their capacity to distribute personhood has significant implications for the telling of histories. According to her, this is so because it is through the agency of photographs and relations with them that they are historically entangled (Edwards, 2006: 32, 34). Thus, Edwards links Gell's notion of relational agency to the modalities of making visual images legible, arguing that this process is relevant to the articulation of histories. Against the backdrop of nineteenth-century colonial photography of Australian *indigènes* more generally (Edwards, 2001: 131–55; Peterson, 2003), she finds evidence of this 'distributed personhood' in statements by their descendants when they were presented with the photographs taken of their forebears. Benjamin Smith (2003: 15), who carried out research on the subject, was told by his interlocutors that their forebears were 'looking at us' from those photographs. Edwards writes within a genre that raises questions regarding the kinds of histories that can be composed if we start from the photographic image as the basis of a lived experience rather than a representation (Geismar and Morton, 2015: 231). She is especially interested in the ways in which it provides a resource for the production of alternative historical knowledge and operates as 'conduits of historical consciousness'.[11] 'Photographs allow people to articulate histories in interactive social ways that would not have emerged in those particular figuration [sic] if photographs had not existed. Photographs become a form of interlocutor. *They literally unlock memories*' (Edwards, 2006: 29, 39; emphasis mine).

This chapter explores how Yemeni men and women who experienced the 1962 revolution relate to the visual artefacts preserved by them. Rather than focusing attention on the 'event' per se, it will consider the resulting burden of remembering its traces and its inscription into the present (Behrouzan, 2016: 30). I raise questions about the extent to which photographs serve as memory's prosthetics, and whether 'telling histories' via photographs is a kind of straightforward storytelling. I suggest that if we want to research photographs as 'memory images' (Gell, 1998: 228) that might inspire the historical imagination, as Edwards does, practices of viewing necessitate elaborate scrutiny.[12] One of the issues that interest me in this regard concerns the ways in which images become catalysts for the articulation of memories when their owners are *not* confronted with direct questions by anthropologists about their provenance and identity ('histories'). I argue that their capacity for performing as agentive artefacts can by no means be taken for granted and requires consideration of context and ambiguity. Without denying that memory is encoded in photographs, let me stress that we must also pay attention to remembering in terms of something performed through specific acts or doing things with visual artefacts (Ryzova, 2015a: 165), such that the emphasis is on unpredictability and contingency.[13]

Afterlives

Exploring the affective trajectories of the North Yemeni revolution ethnographically, I present three vignettes related to the photographs kept or re-imagined by Yemenis who lived through that revolution as children or young adults, beginning with the story of a man of humble background who, after studying abroad, became a banker.

Case 1: Waiting for the revolution: 'Ali b. Muhammad

'Ali's paternal grandfather served as a headman (*'aqil*) of one of the quarters of Sana'a. With the exception of his father, who worked as an army clerk, prior to the revolution 'Ali's paternal relatives were mostly soldiers. His father listened regularly to an Egyptian radio service with an anti-monarchical bias, the *Sawt al-'Arab* (Voice of the Arabs).[14] He was a friend of Iraqi-born Jamal Jamil who served as an officer in Imam Yahya's army but turned against him in 1948.[15] The father's portrait, dating from the late 1950s, shows him wearing a suit which he had borrowed from his uncle (Figure 2.1). In those days, the Yemeni leadership wore traditional, non-European clothes only, and he apparently wanted to make a statement of siding with the 'progressive' forces that opposed Western imperialism and the Arab monarchies. He considered the ruler of his time, the imam, a despot (*zalim*).[16]

A picture from the mid-1950s depicts 'Ali's father and grandfather wearing traditional garments, the young 'Ali in their midst wearing an Egyptian-style uniform during *'id* (religious festival) (Figures 2.2 and 2.3).[17] He is particularly proud of this image for it presents him in the spirit of revolutionary effervescence. One of the images that greet visitors entering his diwan is a photo of 'Ali's baby grandson Qasim. Whilst I was complimenting him on this cute looking child, 'Ali hastened to explain that he was

Figure 2.1 'Ali b. Muhammad's father, 1950s. Image re-photographed by the author and reproduced by permission of 'Ali bin Muhammad.

Figure 2.2 The young 'Ali (centre), his father (left) and grandfather (right), 1950s. Image re-photographed by the author and reproduced by permission of 'Ali bin Muhammad.

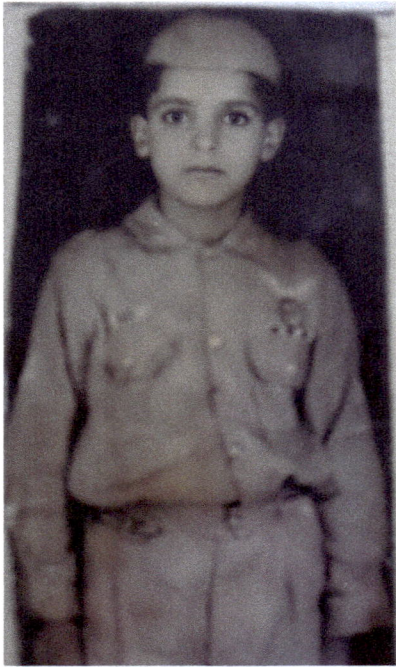

Figure 2.3 'Ali b. Muhammad wearing an Egyptian-style uniform a few years before the Egyptian army entered Yemen in 1962. Image re-photographed by the author and reproduced by permission of 'Ali bin Muhammad.

named after Qasim Amin, the nineteenth-century Egyptian lawyer who had been one of the founders of the Egyptian national movement.[18]

Another photograph shows one of 'Ali's relatives, 'Abdullah Barakat, when he was a student at the military academy of Sana'a a few years prior to the revolution. He continued his studies at the police academy in Cairo, and later played an important role in the first republican government as Chief of Police of Sana'a and minister of the interior in the mid-1960s. Barakat possessed a camera and the photograph was taken at his house, using a self-timer (Figure 2.4). Hadi 'Isa, one of his companions who is also depicted in the photo, served as the head of the National Guard (*al-haris al-watani*) during the revolution and was responsible for the death of a large number of those accused of 'despotic rule' (Serjeant, 1979: 100) who had been declared enemies of the revolution.[19] All those pictured were students of the military academy of Sana'a during the 1950s and were trained by Major Jamal Jamil.[20]

According to 'Ali, these men spearheaded the movement for revolutionary change and were helping to implement it. Barakat was considered to have brought fame to the family, and it was always he who initiated marriage proposals on behalf of its members. The very ordinary

Figure 2.4 Students at the military academy of Sana'a, 1950s. Image re-photographed by the author and reproduced by permission of 'Ali bin Muhammad.

snapshot of jovial cadets during a break, emphasising male camaraderie (Figure 2.4), permits those looking at it to ignore the atrocities subsequently committed by some of them. However, with hindsight, contemporary viewers who suffered profoundly during the revolutionary period find the grinning of Hadi ʿIsa, the future executioner, disturbing.

The visual images on display in ʿAli's diwan celebrate historical rupture. They demonstrate the family's desire to confine the imamate to history. Because *qat* chews are 'minipublics' (Wedeen, 2008: 113) open to anyone who wishes to attend, the images which adorn ʿAli's diwan are a public endorsement of the portrayed men's actions and an enduring commitment to the principles of the 1962 revolution. They operate as performative sites of revolutionary history in line with official interpretations according to which the imams were autocrats and opposed to political and social reforms (see note 1). ʿAli's family was gratified that their country had joined the Arab republics. Their enduring revolutionary subjectivity manifested itself in regular defamatory remarks about the old hereditary elite, the *sada* (sg. *sayyid*) – explaining that they hated Hadi ʿIsa – and approval of the permanent exile of the surviving members of the imam's House.[21] They defended the execution of government officials, arguing that the creation of a new state necessitated such measures and that negotiations with them would have been futile.

On another level, however, the photographs in ʿAli's diwan are also testimony to an unfulfilled past and present in the wake of the militarisation of society and politics. Besides celebrating the revolution, the exhibition in the late twentieth and twenty-first centuries of the image of the cadets may also have been intended to send a tacit message of disapproval of future republican regimes that claimed the legacy of the revolution for themselves but had – in ʿAli's view – failed to deliver. ʿAli attributed some of the murders of politicians he had admired to the regime of ʿAli ʿAbdullah Salih (r. 1978–2012), who had claimed to be 'one of the sons of September' but had played no role in the revolution.[22] By displaying the picture in a prominent place while declining to exhibit one of the president, which was customary among regime loyalists, ʿAli denied the former president ownership of the revolution and fashioned the present rather than the past as a site of contention. Thus, the image might have been put to new uses by telling a story of 'real' revolutionary heroes – those who leapt into the dark half a century ago and who in the eyes of their admirers still rightfully wear the revolutionary mantle. Seen in this light, remembering via photographs is as much an engagement with absence as it is for those targeted by the revolution.

The display of the images of revolutionary heroes in ʿAli's household, which endorse the elimination of the imamate's ruling elite, contrasts with those that speak of the 'lost presence'[23] of beloved relatives who have been 'disappeared'. In the early 1960s, the disappeared became an important mobilising point for instating the Yemeni nation-state as a 'progressive' and pan-Arab space. The violations inscribed on their bodies and the revolutionary rhetoric around them enabled the imagination of a militarised state granting inclusive citizenship.

Case 2: Jalila's disappeared husband

Jalila Agha, wife of Hamud al-Wushali, governor of Taʿizz province (naʾib al-imam) from 1950–62, provided the following testimony:[24]

> When they killed my husband, my youngest daughter was about three months old. I had been married for seven years. When the revolution started, the children and I did not leave the house for a month. The house was continuously watched by soldiers. My husband was taken away in an armoured military vehicle on the first day of the revolution. *Khalas* (that's it). We had no knowledge of what had happened to him, we were cut off from everything (*ghalaqu ʿalayna*). No one was permitted to enter the house.[25] Then they allowed my brother to enter with one of the soldiers who had been watching our house. My brother told us that my husband had been taken to Sanaʿa to see the president. I do not know what happened thereafter [her voice falters]. For a week I didn't know that they had killed him. *Taʿibt* (I was weary). My three children were still small. They did not know their father. My youngest daughter was only three months old. I was married for only seven years, five, six, seven … the revolution came and we were done, that was the end of it. Then they removed us from our house and stole things … furniture, clothes, gold, anything they could find. I was stressed out. They took us to another house.

Jalila and her children stayed at the house of a poet whose daughter had been Hamud al-Wushali's first wife. The poet suffered a breakdown and went blind after witnessing the execution of Jalila's husband and other friends.[26]

Figure 2.5 Sayyid Hamud al-Wushali, early 1950s. Image re-photographed by the author and reproduced by permission of Jalila Agha.[27]

> We lived there for fifteen years, fifteen ... Soldiers came to see us from time to time, in the morning or evening, and asked us questions, but we didn't know anything ... they asked us who had escaped, who had joined the royalists ... we told them no one had escaped, we didn't escape and didn't join the royalists.

The portrait of Jalila's disappeared husband (Figure 2.5) is prominently displayed in her diwan and is testimony to arbitrary revolutionary violence. During our conversation, she told the history of what is absent from the photograph without referring to it. Our encounter took place beneath it, but she did not seem conscious of it. While she provided an emotional account of a life overshadowed by revolution, her intimate memory of her husband may have been detached from his photograph in her diwan. I was unable to make out how she related to it; she may not have wished to comment upon her engagement with the image in my presence.

The new reality forced Jalila to become her family's provider, a role she had not been prepared for. Her husband's loyal soldier ('*askari*) who acted as a guard and whose photo is placed opposite the governor's, had undertaken to look after his family on the day he was taken away.

Figure 2.6 Ahmad Qa'id. Image re-photographed by the author and reproduced by permission of Jalila Agha.

> He [Ahmad Qa'id, the ʿ*askari*] stayed with us, he never let us down. They took him, they jailed and beat him, but he refused to leave us. They handcuffed him and flogged him and asked him not to return to us, but he always did. All those who did bad things to us during the revolution have passed away. *Yalla* [with a sigh, her intonation revealing a modicum of pain].[28]

The governor had asked Ahmad Qa'id (Figure 2.6) to look after his family during his absence, and he honoured his promise. Various members of Jalila's family expressed their gratitude to the soldier for demonstrating loyalty, bravery and unfailing commitment.[29]

During my conversation with Jalila, I asked her how her neighbours treated her after her husband had been taken away, and whether they provided help:

JA: Nobody helped us. No single soul. *Khalas, ʿashna* [we eked out a living] … I never took any money from either of my two brothers or my uncle. After al-Hamdi took power, he returned our assets and property to us and we went back to our house.[30] He was a great man. There was hardly any support. We had very little to live on, but we were patient. Al-Hamdi helped us, and I had some inheritance from my father. Life improved slightly when Ahmad [her son] grew up. I was patient.

GvB: How were the children at that time?

JA: *Al-hamdu li-llah* (praise be to God), they studied. Ahmad attended high school and then studied in Cairo. Nafisa graduated and Sukayna [her daughters] graduated from the United States, *al-hamdu li-llah* (praise be to God).[31] They studied, and I taught them myself. I did everything I could for them as if their father were alive [inaudible words follow], but I refused to get married again. People used to come [and asked for her hand], but I stayed with my children ... *khalas* [with very low voice, almost inaudible] I refused for the sake of my children.

Thus, although Jalila uses the language of victimhood, this should not lead us to deny her agency with which she inhabits her experience of loss. She refused all future marriage proposals in order to nurture her children. Rather than becoming a dependant, she acted as her family's provider while Ahmad Qa'id continued to guard the house and carried out tasks that convention prescribed as male, such as running errands in the market.

GvB: Did the children often ask about their father?

JA: They grew up knowing only me and the soldier who was staying with us. They didn't know their father. I used to provide them with everything, good food, nice clothes, and school uniforms, they didn't lack anything. I provided them with everything, so they didn't feel their father was missing. *Khalas*. When they grew up, there was no father. When they were young, they did not understand what it means to have a father or not to have a father. When they grew up, they began to understand.

GvB: Did you explain it to them?

JA: Yes, I talked to them, and they learned about what happened from their schoolmates and from the neighbours ... they were told they didn't have a father, but this was children's talk at the school.

GvB: Did you learn anything about your husband's burial site?

JA: No, no I did not learn anything about that. We do not know where he is buried – [with raised voice] *ma-fī ayyi haja* (nothing whatsoever). We did not speak to the authorities [about this matter] nor to anyone else. People are scared, no one dares to ask, so there's no one to talk to and I had no one [with low voice]. *Khalas*, they killed him, they took him ... [with low voice, after a brief pause] what can we do, who should we talk to, there is no one to talk to. *Yalla* [sighs and pauses].

Over the years some government officials who approved of the revolution became critical of the way in which it was instituted. One of them reflected on his encounter with Jalila's husband, Hamud al-Wushali, in his early adolescence:[32]

> Our school was besieged by the imam's soldiers. The imam sent the governor, Hamud al-Wushali, twice to convince us to abandon the strike. I was among three students who shouted when al-Wushali was talking to us. Later I graduated with distinction and asked the governor for a job. However, he remembered me from those days and told me to ask 'Abd al-Nasser [the Egyptian president] for a job instead. I was about sixteen years old when the revolution broke out. In those days we hoped that al-Wushali would be killed. [When some fifteen years ago I told him that al-Wushali left behind a young widow and three children, he was almost tearing up. When we spoke again in the spring of 2020, he explained that in those days the value of a human being was not on the students' minds.] Al-Wushali never committed any wrongdoing. He was truly a very humble man. *Allah yirhamuh* (May God bless him). He was killed because an army commander had his eye on his house in the Jahmaliyya quarter of Ta'izz.[33] This was one of the big mistakes of the new regime. It killed many innocent people without a trial. None of those who were executed were given the opportunity to declare whether they were with or against the revolution.

Case 3: Revolutionary timescapes: Umhani al-Shaybani

Like Jalila, Umhani al-Shaybani, daughter of a senior official who served in Imam Yahya's and Ahmad's governments, was forced to abandon her home in 1962. After her father was arrested and one of her brothers executed, the family was ousted from their house and had to live in cramped conditions in a much smaller one. The soldiers who had entered their house after their departure stripped it of everything: valuables, doors, electrical wires, books and photographs.

> After soldiers had looted our house, we were taken by night to another. We had to leave at night because the women had no *sharshaf* (outdoor garment) left. They covered themselves with bed sheets. There were times when there were forty women and no men in the house because all were in jail.

When the revolution began, Umhani's father's soldiers (who acted mainly as guards) ran away. Later the family found one of their photographs in the house of the soldier who had acted as her father's office messenger. The soldier's acquisition of the family's personal photographs gave him access to what had always been hidden from the sight of unrelated men.³⁴ Appropriating them was a means not only of maintaining control over the family but also of humiliating them. In spite of discovering a precious artefact deemed lost, a potential heirloom, Umhani's sisters, dismayed at this violation of their privacy and the soldier's disloyalty, tore it up: a symbolic act of removing the shame that resulted from a male stranger's gazing at unrelated women via their images.³⁵ Their concern can be conceptualised in accordance with Gell's terms: indexes, including photographs, borrow their agency from an external source, in this case the women who were always hidden from the soldiers' sight (Gell, 1998: 36). This performative act, minor in comparison to other forms of violence meted out to the family, permits us to envisage history as partly determined by struggles occurring at the level of the visual (Pinney, 2005: 265; Kalantzis, 2019: 9).

After Umhani's house (referred to by the family as the *bayt al-kabir*, the big house) had been taken over by Egyptian officers and army barracks were set up in their garden, the soldiers were shown films on a large screen at night as a distraction from the war. The house the family occupied at that time was in close proximity to the old one. As soon as Umhani's father was asleep, the women of the house switched off the lights and, also seeking a diversion from reality, watched the movies through the window of their new quarters, which were nearby. The Yemeni republican army's foreign auxiliary forces and the victims of the revolution unwittingly found themselves sharing the films – a crossing of spatio-temporal boundaries. Umhani's introduction to a hitherto unknown public culture constituted an accidental fallout from the revolution.³⁶ Much later she and I saw one of the films together on television and the story came out.

The albums that had been stolen by soldiers after the family was forced to leave their home have gained a life of their own in Umhani's memory world. The reimagined pre-revolutionary albums and the one that contains images of more recent times have shaped her post-revolutionary self in equal measure, whereby loss is felt across temporal horizons. The material images that disappeared are being evoked in the process of memorisation. Umhani visualises herself sitting on a horse; her father and other officials on special occasions; herself wearing cross-gender clothes at 'fancy dress parties' (*hafalat tanakuri*), photographed by her brother Isma'il in the garden. Those visuals constitute an imaginary geography of pre-revolutionary life without being romanticised. Because republican soldiers took them along with other artefacts, Umhani does not possess a photo of her brother Ahmad who was executed. In view of the analogous materiality of the body and the image (or 'personhood' in Gell's terms [1998: 222]), Ahmad's body vanished twice. Creating 'absence', the hand that removed his image from his house also eradicated his body, never to be made available for burial.

Umhani reasoned that Ahmad's son Hamza may have salvaged a photograph of his father. For years I have been wondering about this photo's life cycle, assuming that Hamza had rescued it from the house before the family was forced to depart from it. When I finally managed to speak to Hamza, I learnt that in the 1950s his uncle Khalid, who served as a diplomat abroad, took photographs of Ahmad and other family members that are now in Hamza's possession. While visiting Khalid in 1962, Hamza sent a picture taken of him with his uncle to his father on the occasion of 'id al-adha (a major religious festival) (Figure 2.7). He did not obtain confirmation that he received it, and never asked his mother whether he had. This uncertainty is another form of troubling absence for him. Hamza remains in exile where some of those photographs are on display in his study.[37]

The plastic folder where Umhani keeps her photographs (which I refer to as her 'album') does not contain any photographs from the 1960s, the period of revolutionary turmoil and civil war. There is a

Figure 2.7 Yemeni boy visiting his uncle abroad shortly before the revolution. Image re-photographed by the author and reproduced by permission of Umhani al-Shaybani.

marked discrepancy between her memories and what the images represent. The album does not mirror her family's fragility and precariousness in the early post-revolutionary period, unsure about their location in republican Yemen. In fact, it testifies to the success story of a family that was closely affiliated with the *ancien régime* but was in favour of reforms and understood the new zeitgeist early on. Some of the young generation, born in the late 1930s, had already left the country before the revolution in search of modern education. Even while suffering profound discrimination after the revolution, they were determined to accommodate themselves to the new order and to prosper. However, the sensibilities harboured by Umhani speak to scarred memories of both the more distant and recent past. The photo taken of the old house well over a decade after the revolution reminds Umhani of the hardship endured during the early revolutionary years rather than the dawn of a brighter future during the era of President al-Hamdi.[38] Contemplating her sister-in-law's accident, the photograph of her brother Muhsin and their children, now bereft of a wife and mother, and the one depicting her and her mother who suffered from illness for decades, she remains silent and invokes God.

The images are neither placed in a specific order nor do they have captions. Umhani struggles to identify persons, places and time frames. She shows me a photo of her mother.

U: She was lovely, she was already sick (*ta'bana*) then.
GvB: Who took the photo?
U: My sisters took it in Aden or some place like that. And this is my brother Ibrahim and I in Prague [where he studied]. Look at this photo, I resemble my mother, [taken] some fifteen years ago, when I was in America. [Showing me another one, she asked me to guess who is shown.] This is me [making me laugh]. She is dressed like a *qabili* [countryman].[39] This was the *haflat al-tanakuri* [a fun event dedicated to girls' gender cross-dressing sometimes taking place before weddings].[40] This is my brother Khalid, my uncle ['*ammi*] Muhammad al-Mansur ...[41] This is ... she died ...

Her voice being suppressed by grief, I barely understood the name she uttered. She is again talking about Fatima, her brother Muhsin's wife who had died in a car accident not too long before I came to visit. 'See, how lovely [she was] ... oh, I've become so weary of troubles (*ta'iba*). This is me in the big house, my brother took it.' This was probably one of the first photographs taken in that house after it had been returned to the family in the 1970s. When I asked Umhani how long she had stayed in the small one, she answered with a high-pitched voice. 'Five years, after the revolution'. It seemed to me that she did not like to remember those days. 'After the revolution we moved to the small house which is now the house of my brother 'Ali, we left the large one'. She mentioned the forced evacuation repetitively and remained resentful of it throughout her life. 'They [the revolutionaries] took the big house and everything else. The Egyptians were living in the big house, the devilish military (*al-shaytan al-'askariyya*)'.

On another day, when we were not looking at photographs, Umhani shared other pertinent memories of the time following the family's expulsion from their home. Following the detention of her brother 'Abd al-Karim, who graduated from the Police Academy where he had subsequently been employed, Umhani took it upon herself to save his life.[42]

During the *ayyam al-masriyyin* ('the time of the Egyptians'), as Umhani calls them, 'Abd al-Karim was arrested on the orders of 'Abdullah Barakat, the Chief of Police. 'Abd al-Karim was imprisoned in a house that had been confiscated from one of the imam's daughters, and he was in danger of execution. 'I wrote to Barakat that 'Abd al-Karim's nanny was going to visit him and bring him food.' Umhani dressed like an old, frail woman and went to see her brother. She had stuck a note under his food explaining his escape route via a large tree in the garden. Then they jailed all the other brothers, and the small house was inhabited mainly by women. While narrating these events, she handed me his picture, clasping her thigh (Figure 2.8).

Figure 2.8 Graduate of the Police Academy, 1963. Image re-photographed by the author and reproduced by permission of Umhani al-Shaybani.

When I visited Umhani after having purchased copies of photographs produced by Ahmad ʿUmar al-Absi, a Yemeni photographer who had taken pictures of Imam Ahmad in the 1950s, she was keen to inspect them. In northern Yemen executions had been photographed since the early 1940s. Looking at the images of executed men, Umhani believed these were killed in 1962. 'Who executed them? The imam? Oh …!'[43] The images caused her to reminisce about the autumn of 1962, which had brought disaster to her family. 'They killed them all, the elders (*al-awwalin*; forebears). My brother was only thirty years old when they killed him. They killed the Chief of Staff (*amir al-jaysh*, ʿAli Ibrahim), all of them'. On coming across Sayyid Hamud al-Wushali's photograph (Figure 2.5), she blurted out how handsome he had been (*jamil, jamil, jamil!*), then became upset. 'He was just like my brother Ahmad, he was very handsome, he had three daughters and a son'. Umhani was with her father when he received news of his son's execution. He shouted his name and lost consciousness. Like Jalila, Umhani lives in the emotional residues of the revolutionary upheaval of the 1960s. Her emotive performance created a link between the photograph and her own memories of the revolution. Without further explanation, her rather conventional exclamation ('how handsome he was!') would have betrayed the hardship and grief she had endured. As noted by Batchen et al. (2012: 177), in light of the viewer's retrospective knowledge, such ordinary photographs (for example Figure 2.5, Sayyid Hamud al-Wushali photographed sitting on a chair) can become 'photographs of atrocity'.

According to Umhani's brother Ibrahim, after the arrest of his brother and father, the soldier who was ordered to kill both refused to execute the father because of his age. Umhani's brother Ahmad had been keen on change and was willing to cooperate with the new government. After the imam's palace was attacked on 26 September 1962, he had declined an offer by his friends to take him to a safe place in the countryside. During those days Umhani was listening to Muhammad al-Zubayri on the radio declaring that her father and brother, ʿAli Ibrahim, and Hamud al-Wushali were dangerous men.[44] She made me consider that her father had only one guard in front of his house and, like all ministers, went out in the evening without any. Around the time ʿAli b. Muhammad was photographed in his Egyptian-style child's uniform, Umhani's father already had a sense that the state he was serving was about to be overthrown. He advised his family to be unassuming and among 'the people' and objected to hiring more than one housekeeper so as not to project an ostentatious lifestyle.

On coming across a picture of Colonel 'Abdullah al-Sallal (r. 1962–7) (Figure 2.9), the first republican president who had shelled the imam's palace in 1962, Umhani threw it onto the floor and pointed her finger at it as if she wanted to shoot him.[45]

Her subjective engagement with this photograph, involving tactile interaction, moves it from the level of mere representation to an affective one. Divested of the verbal articulation of memories, her interaction with this evocative artefact was saturated with visceral sensations and projections – the impact of the revolution on her family; her brother's execution; her father's humiliation by the republican authorities. In the absence of either her slain brother's body or his image, her handling of Sallal's portrait suggests that she was taking symbolic revenge on his behalf. Here 'bearing witness' is decoupled from her own intimate representational domain of family photography and centred instead upon the colonel under whose watch the executions were carried out, her brother's 'presence' affirmed by memories such as her father's exclamation of his name after learning about his killing. The bouleversement of 1955 passed her by and only when seeing the images related to it, she realised that executions had occurred during the years preceding the revolution, carried out by the head of state her father had served (see note 43).

Figure 2.9 Colonel 'Abdullah al-Sallal, leader of the Yemeni revolution. Image re-photographed by the author and reproduced by permission of Umhani al-Shaybani.

Irrespective of who exercised it, she conceived of state violence against opponents as atrocious. The images of men executed in 1955, demonstrating the vengeance Imam Ahmad took on his adversaries a few years before the revolution swept away the imamate, dismayed her. Her father had discussed the event with his older sons, officials, and friends at afternoon *maqayl* (*qat* chews, see note 3) but never talked to her about it.

Discussion

The photographs kept or reimagined in novel contexts by the women and men featured in this chapter are the 'traces' of their lived experiences and memories of the revolution of 1962.[46] Their memories attest to the revolutionary years as a plural, contested past. Some of the photographs and narratives dealt with in this chapter speak to each other, negotiating the terms of the revolution. For example, Umhani's engagement with Hamud al-Wushali's portrait elicited memories of her executed brother. Speaking about the revolutionary years, she referred to 'Abdullah Barakat, the minister of interior who had detained one of her brothers and whose portrait decorates 'Ali b. Muhammad's interior. Whilst Barakat provides 'Ali b. Muhammad's family with kudos, he is represented by others as their *bête noire*.

For those who represent themselves as victims of the revolution, photographs of disappeared family members constitute memorial sites that are managed within kinship relations. As affective spaces, they are locations of generational memories and scarred pasts. In the eyes of others, such as 'Ali b. Muhammad who welcomed the revolution, the images of its protagonists who turned the wheels of history in a new direction represent their dream of joining other Arab republics. His childhood portrait in an Egyptian uniform (Figure 2.3), produced several years before the revolution, symbolised his family's firm commitment to a new order. He explicitly endorses violence as a means of instating it. Prominently mounted in his reception room to the present day, the image conveys this message to visitors to his house, among them republican dignitaries. The portrait presaged the emergence of novel notions of the male subject and the new state's commitment to strong military and security institutions run by some of the people depicted in another photo in 'Ali's diwan (Figure 2.4). However, reading across diwans, as it were, it emerges that 'Abd al-Karim al-Shaybani's portrait as a police officer does in fact conform to this idealised male subject. It is unlikely though that Umhani's decision to place it in her diwan had a political rationale. For her, 'Abd al-Karim's outfit did not stand for the person; it remained an empty shell inhabited by him for particular reasons during the revolutionary years. By contrast, as already indicated, for men such as ʿAli the exhibition of images showing him wearing a uniform or in the company of well-known republican figures, is a way of pledging loyalty to or demonstrating kinship with them ('doing politics with images').[47] Such photographs can also be found in the houses of former imamate officials who escaped execution and are eager to convey the same message.

Revolutions, whose time span tends to be contested and is contingent on political frames and individual subjectivities, lend themselves particularly well to an analysis that does not seek to make photographs or other artefacts legible through a single moment, focusing instead on disjunctions and ruptures (Pinney, 2005; Ryzova, 2015a: 161–2; Nikro, 2018: 203; Kalantzis, 2019: 9). Thus, the revolutionary temporality inhabited by Umhani does not have a definite ending. I have contextualised her experience of arbitrary revolutionary violence within an emotive register of past experiences of suffering rather than characterising it as the only event in her life, though it was surely the most devastating.[48] Within the affective configuration of her memory work, the 'event' encapsulates other instances of severe distress and loss such as her sister-in-law's accident, which Umhani experienced as a violent death. In other words, rather than conceptualising her memory images as a juxtaposition of disconnected temporalities, each of which brought new suffering, I conceive of them as shading into each other.[49] Umhani's remembrance communicated a mode of 'being' in the historical present that revealed itself in daily emotive performances centred on being *ta ʿiba* (troubled and weary). In relation to the photographs she had cherished, both the acts of looking at those contained in her album and reimagining the lost ones constitute processes by which absence is understood and commemorated. Reassembling the stolen albums imaginatively and linking them to the collection of photographs she had begun in the 1970s created interlocking memories as well as a sense of continuity that was predicated upon a condition of loss.

Regarding the issue of 'viewing' and 'narrating', as noted above, Edwards makes a strong argument about the mutuality of memory and visual imagery. Taking her cues from Gell's theory of art and agency, she centres her analysis on the affinity between the relational agency of visual artefacts such as photographs and acts of narration. Her study is based on photographs that circulated within 'a community' of Australian *indigènes* while being shown, exchanged and displayed (Edwards, 2006: 35).[50] She argues that as relational objects which partake in the making and enunciating of histories, they excavate memories (Edwards, 2006: 36, 39). My data show that they certainly have this potential, but the relationship between memory and the materiality of the image cannot be determined in an *a priori* fashion.

A few years after Umhani's family's eviction from their house, her brother ʿAbd al-Karim found himself incarcerated in a restricted space, and his life was in danger; she went to considerable lengths to rescue him. The day she and I looked at her album and came across a photograph of him, she passed over it. It did not stir a memory of her bold and risky rescue plan. Her mind was focused on the images we shared at the same time, of Fatima who had died an untimely death and of her long-suffering mother. Whenever we spent time in the room where the large portrait of the uniformed young man is displayed, she never offered to tell the story of her rescue mission. The materiality of built-up spaces rather than the visual image provided the context for Umhani's transmission of this pivotal experience to me. She began talking about rescuing her brother after accessing spatial memories of the enforced departure from the house where she and her siblings were born and raised. Why would the forced displacement rather than his photograph generate memories of his incarceration? Considering the specific emotional register within which she recounted the biography of the *bayt al-kabir*, the large house, Umhani may have established a link between different homes that were expropriated in 1962 and subsequently used as prisons and garrisons. It can thus be inferred that histories which are embodied in artefacts such as photographs may not immediately be narrated by our research subjects.

Anthropologists' common use of photo elicitation can easily lead to an overemphasis on the centrality of photographic images in mnemonic practices. It is important to appreciate the place of photographic cues in everyday life rather than in orchestrated encounters. A staged event such as the presentation of images at interviews in the expectation of being offered a comprehensive narrative may only be half of the story.[51] In other words, the nature of remembering deserves as much attention as its contents (Stoler and Strassler, 2000: 9), as does 'the unsayable' (Das, 2007: 90) in interviews, an aspect I cannot elaborate on here. My findings indicate that memories are neither in decay once they become fixed to material objects as argued by Michel de Certeau,[52] nor are they inevitably triggered by artefacts such as photographs. The cases of both Jalila and Umhani suggest that routinised viewing of photographs limits their agency as catalysts of memory in everyday life. During my conversation with Jalila, she did not interact with her husband's photo in any obvious way, and Umhani related the story of coming to her brother's rescue only when recounting her family's eviction from their home. Unlike Jalila, who is familiar with her husband's portrait in her domestic surroundings, Umhani's interaction with it generated an intense emotional response. Thus, portraits that are part of quotidian socialities, which somehow 'stand in' for persons, may have limited impact on the way in which absence is experienced. Whether we are dealing with images of kin who fell victims to political violence or were exalted as revolutionary heroes, it cannot be taken for granted that specific 'affective demands' (Ryzova, 2015a: 165) are being placed upon them.[53] Nor are they intended to provide the young generation with *aides-mémoire* for understanding the family's past. For example, Hamza's children do not raise questions about the photographs in his study, nor does he encourage discussion of them. According to him, *for them the past is a different chapter*. Perhaps they wish to shield themselves from engaging with the agonising details of their family's recent history, wishing to remain aloof from practices of bearing witness. Hamza's comment on his mode of engagement with the portraits of his late father and other family members (*what can you do?*) reveals an ambiguous aloofness that betrays the emotional burden of living with injurious memories.[54]

In relation to Runia's notion of a 'transfer of presence' via commemorative objects, my encounters with Jalila did not offer clues as to the way her husband's photograph hanging on the wall of her diwan was constitutive to occasioning 'presence'. Runia's analysis of metonymously informed subject–object relations is intriguing but based on assumptions that would seem to require more empirical research. This would focus specifically on the beholder's subjectivity, giving attention to discursive and non-discursive forms of knowing, affective resonance, projections and desire. 'Presence' as analysed by Runia does not leave room for the agentive power of absence (see, for example, Crossland, 2002; Domanska, 2006; Fowles, 2010; Nikro, 2019). Umhani's brother's absent image had no less hold on her than those of her other brothers that she had preserved. This 'presence in absence' (Runia, 2006: 6) may thus be as powerful as that mediated by material objects. Moreover, as in the case of Hamza's children, there may not be a 'desire' or 'need for presence' (Runia, 2006: 5; Roth, 2009: 87).

Reconstructing Jalila's framing of her reminiscences, on the one hand there is a sense of her husband's absent presence whereby the temporal separation of past and present is irrelevant. On the other hand, the frequent use of terms such as *khalas* (that's it), revealing distinct emotions and intentions, are meant to indicate the pastness of the past.

The present is entwined with the past and yet discontinuous from it. In this context the past that is preserved as if frozen must be distinguished from the past dedicated to motherhood, a period during which Jalila provided for her children in such a way that they would not feel that *their father was missing*. The ambiguity of the past that is not absent, as evinced by Jalila's gendered performance of early widowhood, has been dealt with by Ewa Domanska in her work on the disappeared in Argentina in the 1970s and 1980s. She conceives of the 'non-absent past' as constituting 'the liminal space of "the uncanny"' – a past that 'cannot be so easily controlled or subject to a finite interpretation ... The missing body possesses a kind of *power of absence*' (Domanska, 2006: 346, emphasis hers). However, the non-absent past is also testified to by the still-present body that witnessed heinous acts. The bodies of those who did – such as Hamud al-Wushali's father-in-law who went blind thereafter – became surfaces on which the revolutionary credo was to be written and read.

It seems to me that Jalila's husband's photograph, which is a semi-public testimony of his disappearance, is a focus of both personal remembrance and a claim for accountability. Because no republican government has to date acknowledged the atrocities committed during the revolution of 1962, the disappeared remain officially 'unremembered' (Baer, 2000: 51). The presence of the image makes visible an absence that still requires elucidation. Jalila resented that *there is no one to talk to* about her husband's execution and his burial site. The affect that underlies her intense resentment serves to uphold moral claims about historical injustice. The absence of the disappeared body is meaningful in terms of a demand for admission of the extra-judicial killings that took place in the 1960s. Reading 'presence' thus also links the personal and private domain that dominated Barthes's photographic studies with the political. The regime's shunning of 'the affective' (Stoler, 2004: 17) by not giving the families of the disappeared a public platform is a way of maintaining its own truth-claims and control.

I suggest that studies of (post-)revolutionary subjectivities fashioned by the present absence of people portrayed in domestic photography should place more emphasis on processual, situational analysis. Viewing practices should be problematised such that more weight is given to contextualisation and contingency, exploring how visual artefacts mediate absence in a variety of mundane locales, including the non-verbal domain. Projecting our gaze onto them as part of knowledge-making practices is always potentially ambiguous, circumstantial, interpretive and routinised.

Notes

1. The right of the scholar-jurists who had governed the imamate for more than a millennium was enshrined in the Zaydi-Shi'i doctrine which stipulates that the office of the supreme leader, the imam, be reserved for those able to demonstrate descent from the Prophet Muhammad and outstanding erudition. Republican leaders depicted the *ancien régime* as 'reactionary', and specifically opposed the dynasty that had prevailed since the early twentieth century and was accused of autocratic governance. During the revolution, key members of the regime were eliminated. For the most part, the newly established republican state was characterised by military rule.
2. Due to the 'Arab Spring' uprising of 2011 and counter-mobilisation efforts by some Gulf states that culminated in military intervention in Yemen in 2015, I have been unable to continue researching the subject dealt with here and some data remain scant (especially regarding Case 1). With respect to Cases 1 and 3, surnames have either been omitted or pseudonyms used to protect the identity of persons who are still alive. The vernacular Arabic used by some research participants has been maintained in the text. I am grateful to Paul Basu and Susanne Küchler for comments on an earlier draft. This chapter was previously presented as a paper at a Middle East Studies Association (MESA) panel organised by Marieke Brandt on 'The birth of modern Yemen: Internal views of the 1960s civil war' (San Antonio, November 2018).
3. Depending on who is present, these places are multi-purpose rooms that are constantly refashioned. They are neither unambiguously private nor public, and gendered only when inhabited by 'strangers' (i.e. non-*mahram*, according to *shari'a* law all those who in theory are eligible marriage partners). During the afternoon dozens of either men or women participate in *qat* chews that are by no means always marked by class divisions (Vom Bruck, 2000).
4. Alluding to Sontag's argument, Judith Butler (2010: 98) attributes this haunting quality to the capacity of photographs to act upon us partly because they outlive the lives they document. They 'establish in advance the time in which that loss will be acknowledged as a loss' (see also Barthes, 2000: 97; Baer, 2002: 181–2; Belting, 2011: 121).
5. Reminiscent of Yael Navaro-Yashin's (2007: 95) study of governmentality in the self-styled Turkish Republic of Northern Cyprus, when placed in specific social relationships with persons photographs, like documents, have the potential to be experienced as 'affectively charged phenomena'. However, unlike Navaro-Yashin (2009: 15–16) I am disinclined to analyse affective spaces in terms of 'spatial melancholia' which has had questionable attachments throughout European history.
6. See, for example, Azoulay, 2008; Deger, 2008; McKay, 2008; Wright, 2013; Nikro, 2019.
7. See, for example, Smith, 2003; Edwards, 2002; 2006; 2009; Hirsch, 2004; Vom Bruck, 2013. While Gell's argument about 'distributed personhood' is a powerful one, and has found resonance in several disciplines, in ethnographic contexts of looking at photographs, vital questions still need to be addressed as to the multiple and atomised performances in which the 'abduction' of agency from an index occurs (Gell, 1998: 222). Gell comes closest to dealing with this issue in his analysis of Malagan carvings (Gell, 1998: 223–8).
8. I have noted elsewhere (Vom Bruck, 2013: 159) that the role of photographers who choose the objects they are about to create (the indexes) and arrange the 'scenes' at studios and imprint their creations by touching them up has been unduly neglected in Gell's work.
9. Gell (1998: 34, 67) draws attention to (Christian) devotees who in past centuries submitted to the power of icons and to cults of idols of living Hindu goddesses, but does not explore this issue in relation to photography. For example, the subject of devotees having their picture taken in front of photographic reproductions of statues of gods which can act as a medium for encounters with the divine (Pinney, 1997: 110) constitutes an understudied domain of agency.

   Photographs of Yemeni women, which are attributed as much agency as human actors (in terms of their capacity to stir desire), are conceived of as potentially perilous objects of exposure that must never be shared with non-*mahram* (for this reason, none has been reproduced here; *mahram* are close relatives who are legally disqualified from becoming partners in marriage). Analysing the prototype as the source of the index, Gell deals with the index as a person ethnographically only with respect to deities and Malagan statues (1998: 67, 223–8). The photographs of Yemeni women are treated as persons well beyond their deaths (Vom Bruck, 2013: 147).

10. This interpretation is reminiscent of Barthes's (2000: 80) notion that 'the photograph is literally an emanation of the referent'.
11. Edwards, 2006: 29, 37. For a moving example of photograph-based storytelling in a Middle Eastern context, notably Palestine, see Musleh-Motut (2012; 2015).
12. The term 'memory images' was originally coined by Kracauer (1993 [1927]: 425, 428, 433).
13. For a more general discussion of the vexed relationship between photography and memory, see Batchen, 2004.
14. This transnational Arabic-language broadcasting service began spreading the message of the Egyptian Revolution to other parts of the Middle East in 1953. Attacks against imamate rule were stepped up by the service after the break-up of the union between Egypt, Syria and Yemen in 1961 and a poem written by Imam Ahmad (r. 1948–62) against the Egyptian president Jamal 'Abd al-Nasser's Arab socialism (Dresch, 2000: 86). During the 1950s 'Ali b. Muhammad's uncle spent time in Cairo and had his photographs developed there.
15. Major Jamal Jamil, a Kurd, was a member of the Iraqi military mission to Sana'a (1940–2) who, after the departure of his fellow officers, stayed behind. At the height of the constitutional movement against the imam in 1948 he shot dead two of his sons.
16. At that time, a cautious effort was being made to build a police force and national army, the latter of which provided a humble income for 'Ali's father. Several Yemeni students were sent for training at the military academy of Baghdad, while others were trained as pilots in Rome. However, neither commercial activities nor membership of these institutions carried much prestige, and there were few avenues for social mobility for people like 'Ali's father.
17. Like in countries such as Syria, Lebanon and Iraq, in Yemen there was enthusiasm for Jamal 'Abd al-Nasser, who was appreciated as an opponent of imperialism and advocate of pan-Arabism. During his adolescence 'Ali greatly admired him. Consequently, children like him were keen to wear those uniforms. Although even the Yemeni crown prince Muhammad al-Badr had sympathies for Nasser, most of the political elite saw him as a threat. Buttressing the coup in 1962, Nasser sent an expeditionary force to Yemen, tying up more than a third of his army there (Vatikiotis, 1980: 403; Ferris, 2013: 36).
18. Conventionally in Zaydi-Shi'i socialities, children called al-Qasim were named after the Zaydi Imam al-Qasim b. Ibrahim (d. 860). The name derives from *qasama* (to break, shatter). Some old elite families idealise it by attaching religious meanings of 'dividing truth from falsehood (*bayn al-haqq wa- l-batil*)' to it.
19. Hadi 'Isa studied in the USSR and Cairo and worked as a translator for the crown prince al-Badr. After having been accused of having ties with the royalists and subsequently sentenced to death in 1966, his corpse was dragged through the streets of Sana'a (Qasim al-Wazir, personal communication, July 2018).
20. *Below right* (from right): 'Abdullah Barakat (student), Hadi 'Isa, Muhammad al-Habury, Husayn al-Daf'iy (minister of defence in 1964, later ambassador to Moscow), Ahmad al-Haymi ('Ali's maternal uncle who studied sociology in Cairo and later worked in the ministry of education until 1962).
    Above from left: Muhammad al-Haymi, Muhammad Tilha (?), Lt. Muhammad al-'Ulufi, Lt. 'Abdullah al-Luqayya (both took part in the attempt on Imam Ahmad's life in 1961), Muhammad al-Wasi'i (?).
21. The *sada* represent themselves as descendants of the Prophet. During the imamate, many of the educated ones worked in the service to the state, and some continue to do so. However, for reasons explained elsewhere (Vom Bruck, 2005: 59–61), many of the 'Free Officers' were *sada*, among them 'Ali Qasim al-Mu'ayyad, who announced the revolution on the radio.
22. 'Ali 'Abdullah Salih referred to the revolution that started on 26 September 1962. Until his death in 2017, he claimed he would not abandon three things: the revolution, the republic and the unity (of Yemen).
23. I borrow a term used by Naomi Leite (2007: 11) in a different context.
24. Jalila is the daughter of Ahmad Hasan Agha, a merchant of Turkish origin.
25. In the context of Morocco, Laura Menin (2018: 27) has described this state-inflicted experience of waiting as one of the most invisible and subtle forms of violence that produce fear and suffering.
26. The poet, who I met at his home in Ta'izz in the mid-1980s, was Ahmad b. Muhammad b. Husayn Sharaf al-Din. On that occasion the family did not reveal the cause of his blindness because there was always hesitation among the victims of the revolution to speak about such

issues during a researcher's first visit. However, it was later confirmed by his relatives (Sharaf al-Din family, personal communication, July 2018).
27. The photo was taken at a photographic studio in Ta'izz where British influence was greater than in Sana'a because of the city's proximity to Aden. In Sana'a European-style furniture was uncommon. After Imam Ahmad had put down the constitutional revolt in 1948, he moved his government to Ta'izz and appointed al-Wushali head of the *diwan al-maliki*, the royal court, before he became governor of the Ta'izz region. Imamate officials were not used to being photographed and did not attach significance to having their photographs taken and disseminated. For this reason, his posing was not particularly statesmanlike and almost casual.
28. Here *yalla* (let's go, come on) takes on the meaning of 'one has to let go'.
29. Like in other revolutionary contexts, former household employees' expressions of loyalty towards the families they had served were resented by the new leadership, eager to see those families socially isolated and unable to provide for themselves. The image of the soldier who had remained loyal to the dependants of officials who were portrayed as 'reactionaries (*raj'iyyun*)' was an embarrassment to the revolutionary authorities in Yemen.
30. President Ibrahim al-Hamdi (r. 1974–7) tried to reconcile Yemenis after the civil war and to unite the Yemen Arab Republic (YAR) with the People's Democratic Republic of Yemen (PDRY) which had been established after the departure of the British. On discovering that many Yemenis were still deprived of basic facilities when inaugurating development projects in the mid-1970s, he asked on several occasions 'where is the revolution?' ('Ali Muhsin Hamid, personal communication, 26 March 2021).
31. Ahmad runs an engineering and construction company in Sana'a. Nafisa has been teaching at Sana'a university.
32. Interview, 18 April 2020.
33. He was Dirham Abu Lahum, the commander of Ta'izz. Abu Lahum was ousted from his post a year after Ibrahim al-Hamdi – who opposed the power of the tribal leaders (shaykhs) – had become president.
34. That is, all those who do not fall into the category of *mahram* (see n. 3).
35. Women's photographs are considered intimate belongings that must be shared only with *mahram* or female friends (Vom Bruck, 2013; see also n. 9).
36. A considerable number of films were produced in Egypt from the late 1920s onwards, playing an instructive role in the construction of the country's nationalism and its relationship with other Arab-speaking ones (Armbrust, 2000: 292–3). During the imamate, such films were inaccessible to Yemenis unless they had travelled to places such as Egypt and Iraq (during British rule and the monarchy). After 1962 cinemas were built in Sana'a and Ta'izz.
37. Interview, 27 July 2020.
38. In the same way al-Hamdi helped Jalila Agha, he transferred funds to Umhani's father to help him take care of his large family. However, rather than providing him with a monthly stipend, he channelled the funds through one of his friends. Most likely he was concerned not to be accused of supporting those officially labelled 'reactionaries'.
39. *Qabili* (pl. *qaba'il*) is a term customarily used to refer to arms-bearing settled agriculturalists. Many migrated to the cities after the revolution and took prominent positions in the state and the commercial sector. Until the late 1980s they were looked down upon by the Sana'anis.
40. See also Ryzova's analysis of Egyptian women's cross-dressing photographic performances during the interwar period (2015b: 239–40, 242–3). I am disinclined to characterise the *hafalat* [pl. of *hafla*] *tanakuri* as a 'transgression of patriarchy' (2015b: 244) because at those occasions Umhani was often photographed by one of her brothers who apparently regarded those sessions as fun. Neither her father nor her brothers disapproved of the cross-gender dressing.
41. Although she does not have a close kin relationship with him (other than tracing descent to the Prophet like him), she fondly refers to the eminent scholar Muhammad b. Muhammad al-Mansur (d. 2016) as her 'uncle', indicating affection and respect.
42. His portrait, produced in 1963, provides the visual sub-text of his breaking with his family's tradition. From the mid-1950s onwards, many urban young men like him were striving to pursue alternative professional pathways beyond religious scholarship. In any case, when he enrolled at the academy after the revolution this kind of education was no longer thriving. He may also have wished to demonstrate that he was willing to serve the newly established state.

43. The images relate to a minor revolt against Imam Ahmad staged by his brother 'Abdullah in 1955. The rebellion collapsed and 'Abdullah, his brother al-'Abbas and a few of their supporters were beheaded. Like the photographs of executions by Iranian photographers in the late nineteenth century, these attested to new photographic practices, and 'thanks to photography this spectacle of death could be extended indefinitely' (Schwerda, 2015: 183). In both cases, the images demonstrated the inscription of the rulers' power on the bodies of those deemed traitors and criminals (Vom Bruck, 2018: 50, 83–4).
44. Al-Zubayri was a poet who was part of the opposition movement against Imam Yahya in the 1940s. He spent time in Cairo in the early 1950s and in 1954 began broadcasting a weekly programme on Yemen on *Sawt al-'Arab* (Douglas, 1987: 176–8).
45. Al-Sallal's uniform clearly transformed his self-image (he came from a lower-class background of blacksmiths). Looking into the camera almost seductively, he projected confidence but also a sense of vulnerability.
46. I refer to 'traces' as part of a dispersed category of varied contents that testifies to a person's agency during their lifetime and even after their death (see Gell, 1998).
47. The ubiquitous gold-framed portraits of 'Ali 'Abdullah Salih that were displayed in private and public spaces until the beginning of the 2011 uprising can also be seen in this light.
48. As discussed earlier, I am here using a processual definition of 'event'.
49. Thus, my interpretation diverges somewhat from Siegfried Kracauer's dictum that 'one must rid oneself of the delusion that it is the major events which have the most decisive influence on people. They are much more deeply and continuously influenced by the tiny catastrophes which make up daily life' (Kracauer cited by Levin, 1993: 422).
50. A similar method was used by Christopher Wright (2013) in his study of photography's entanglement with perceptions of past and present on the Solomon Islands. Deger (2016) analysed the production of family portraiture based on the use of image technology among northern Australian *indigènes* who shared their photographs created by their mobile phones with her.
51. The potentially diverse modalities of viewing with respect to hitherto unknown images and those that decorate homes have not been given attention by either Edwards or MacDonald (2003) whose ethnography of Australian *indigènes* provides the context for part of the former's analysis. Pinney's *Camera Indica* (1997) includes observations of people's interactions with photographs without having been asked questions, but he does not analyse them in terms of the epistemological status of methods.
52. Cited in Forty (2001: 7).
53. An interesting aspect of studying photographs in quotidian environments is an exploration of the circumstances in which photographs that tend to be given minor or no attention (by virtue of their constant presence) become 'visible' again and stir the beholder's emotions.
54. Interview, 7 August 2020.

References

Armbrust, Walter. 2000. 'The golden age before the golden age: Commercial Egyptian cinema before the 1960s', in Armbrust, W. (ed.), *Mass Mediations: New approaches to popular culture in the Middle East and beyond*. Berkeley: University of California Press, 292–328.
Azoulay, Ariella. 2008. *The Civil Contract of Photography*. New York: Zone Books.
Baer, Ulrich. 2000. 'To give memory a place: Holocaust photography and the landscape tradition'. *Representations*, 69: 38–62.
Baer, Ulrich. 2002. *Spectral Evidence: The photography of trauma*. Cambridge, MA: MIT Press.
Barthes, Roland. 2000 [1981]. *Camera Lucida*. London: Vintage Books.
Batchen, Geoffrey. 2004. *Forget Me Not: Photography and remembrance*. New York: Princeton Architectural Press.
Batchen, Geoffrey. 2009. 'Seeing and saying: A response to "incongruous images"'. *History and Theory*, 48: 26–33.
Batchen, Geoffrey, Gidley, M., Miller, N. K. and Prosser, J. (eds). 2012. *Picturing Atrocity: Photography in crisis*. London: Reaktion Books.
Behrouzan, Orkideh. 2016. *Prozak Diaries: Psychiatry and generational memory in Iran*. Redwood City, CA: Stanford University Press.

Belting, Hans. 2011. *An Anthropology of Images: Picture, medium, body*. Princeton: Princeton University Press.
Bille, Mikkel, Frida Hastrup and Tim Flohr Sørensen. 2010. 'Introduction: An anthropology of absence', in Bille, Mikkel, Hastrup, F. and Soerensen, T. F. (eds), *An Anthropology of Absence*. New York: Springer, 3–22.
Butler, Judith. 2010. *Frames of War: When is life grievable?* London: Verso.
Crossland, Zoë. 2002. 'Violent spaces: Conflict over the reappearance of Argentina's disappeared', in Schofield, John, Johnson, W. G. and Beck, C. M. (eds), *Matériel Culture: The archaeology of twentieth-century conflict*. London and New York: Routledge, 115–31.
Das, Veena. 2007. *Life and Words: Violence and the descent into the ordinary*. Berkeley: University of California Press.
Deger, Jennifer. 2008. 'Imprinting on the heart: Photography and contemporary Yolngu mournings'. *Visual Anthropology*, 21: 292–309.
Deger, Jennifer. 2016. 'Thick photography'. *Journal of Material Culture*, 21(1): 111–32.
Domanska, Ewa. 2006. 'The material presence of the past'. *History and Theory*, 45: 337–48.
Douglas, Leigh. 1987. *The Free Yemeni Movement 1935–1962*. Beirut: American University of Beirut.
Dresch, Paul. 2000. *A History of Modern Yemen*. Cambridge: Cambridge University Press.
Edwards, Elizabeth. 2001. *Raw Historis: Photographs, anthropology and museums*. Oxford and New York: Berg.
Edwards, Elizabeth. 2002. 'Material beings: Objecthood and ethnographic photographs'. *Visual Studies*, 17(1): 67–75.
Edwards, Elizabeth. 2006. 'Photographs and the sound of history'. *Visual Anthropology Review*, 21(1–2): 27–46.
Edwards, Elizabeth. 2009. 'Photography and the material performance of the past'. *History and Theory*, 48: 130–50.
Ferris, Jesse. 2013. *Nasser's Gamble: How intervention in Yemen caused the six-day war and the decline of Egyptian power*. Princeton: Princeton University Press.
Forty, Adrian. 2001. 'Introduction', in Forty, A. and Küchler, S. (eds), *The Art of Forgetting*. Oxford and New York: Berg.
Fowles, Severin. 2010. 'People without things', in Bille, Mikkel, Hastrup, F. and Soerensen, T. F. (eds), *An Anthropology of Absence*. New York: Springer, 23–41.
Geismar, Haidy and Morton, Christopher. 2015. 'Introduction'. *Photographies*, 8(3): 231–3.
Gell, Alfred. 1998. *Art and Agency: An anthropological theory*. Oxford: Clarendon Press.
Hirsch, Eric. 2004. 'Techniques of vision: Photography, disco and renderings of present perceptions in highland Papua'. *Journal of the Royal Anthropological Institute*, 10: 19–39.
Kalantzis, Konstantinos. 2019. *Tradition in the Frame: Photography, power, and imagination in Sfakia, Crete*. Bloomington: Indiana University Press.
Kracauer, Siegfried. 1993 [1927]. 'Photography' (translated by Thomas Y. Levin). *Critical Inquiry*, 19(3): 421–36.
Leite, Naomi. 2007. 'Materializing absence: Tourists, surrogates, and the making of "Jewish Portugal"', in Robinson, Mike (ed.), *Things That Move. The material worlds of tourism and travel*. Leeds: Centre for Tourism and Cultural Change, 1–21.
Levin, Thomas Y. 1993. Foreword to Kracauer, Siegfried, 'Photography' (translated by Thomas Y. Levin). *Critical Inquiry*, 19(3): 421–36.
MacDonald, Gaynor. 2003. 'Photos in Wiradjuri biscuit tins: Negotiating relatedness and validating colonial histories'. *Oceania*, 73(4): 225–42.
McKay, Deirdre. 2008. 'Ghosts of futures present: Photographs in the Filipino migrant archive'. *Visual Anthropology*, 21: 381–92.
Menin, Laura. 2018. 'A life of waiting: Political violence, personal memories, and enforced disappearances in Morocco', in Nikro, Norman S. and Hegasy, Sonja (eds), *The Social Life of Memory: Violence, trauma, and testimony in Lebanon and Morocco*. New York: Palgrave Macmillan, 25–54.
Morton, Christopher. 2015. 'The ancestral image in the present tense'. *Photographies*, 8(3): 253–70.
Musleh-Motut, Nawal. 2012. 'Negotiating Palestine through the familial gaze: A photographic (post)memory project'. *Topia: Canadian Journal of Cultural Studies*, 27: 133–52.
Musleh-Motut, Nawal. 2015. 'From Palestine to the Canadian diaspora'. *Middle East Journal of Culture and Communication*, 8: 307–26.
Navaro-Yashin, Yael. 2007. 'Make-believe papers, legal forms and the counterfeit'. *Anthropological Theory*, 7(1): 79–98.

Navaro-Yashin, Yael. 2009. 'Affective spaces, melancholic objects: Ruination and the production of anthropological knowledge'. *Journal of the Royal Anthropological Institute*, 15: 1–18.

Nikro, Norman S. 2018. 'ReMemory in an inter-generational register: Social and ethical life of testimony', in Nikro, Norman S. and Hegasy, Sonja (eds), *The Social Life of Memory: Violence, trauma, and testimony in Lebanon and Morocco*. New York: Palgrave Macmillan, 195–217.

Nikro, Norman S. 2019. 'Memory within and without the photographic frame: Wadad Halwani's *The last picture ... while crossing*'. *Memory Studies*, 12(3): 279–93.

Peterson, Nicolas. 2003. 'The changing photographic contract: Aborigines and image ethics', in Pinney, Christopher and Peterson, Nicolas (eds), *Photography's Other Histories*. Durham, NC and London: Duke University Press, 119–45.

Pinney, Christopher. 1997. *Camera Indica: The Social Life of Indian Photographs*. London: Reaktion Books.

Pinney, Christopher. 2005. 'Things happen: Or, from which moment does that object come?', in Miller, Daniel (ed.), *Materiality*. Durham, NC: Duke University Press, 256–71.

Roth, Michael. 2009. 'Photographic ambivalence and historical consciousness'. *History and Theory*, 48: 82–94.

Runia, Eelco. 2006. 'Presence'. *History and Theory*, 45: 1–29.

Ryzova, Lucie. 2015a. 'The image sans Orientalism: Local histories of photography in the Middle East'. *Middle East Journal of Culture and Communication*, 8: 159–71.

Ryzova, Lucie. 2015b. 'Boys, girls, and kodaks: Peer albums and middle-class personhood in mid-twentieth-century Egypt'. *Middle East Journal of Culture and Communication*, 8: 215–55.

Schwerda, Mira. 2015. 'Death on display: Mirza Riza Kirmani, prison portraiture and the depiction of public executions in Qajar Iran'. *Middle East Journal of Culture and Communication*, 8: 172–91.

Serjeant, Robert B. 1979. 'The Yemeni poet Al-Zubayrī and his polemic against the Zaydi Imāms'. *Arabian Studies*, 5: 87–130.

Smith, Benjamin. 2003. 'Images, selves, and the visual record: Photography and ethnographic complexity in Central Cape York Peninsula'. *Social Analysis*, 47(3): 8–26.

Sontag, Susan. 1977. *On Photography*. New York: Farrar, Straus and Giroux.

Stoler, Ann L. 2004. 'Affective states', in Nugent, David and Vincent, Joan (eds), *A Companion to the Anthropology of Politics*. Oxford: Blackwell, 4–20.

Stoler, Ann L. and Strassler, Karen. 2000. 'Castings for the colonial: Memory work in "New Order" Java'. *Comparative Study of Society and History*, 42(1): 4–48.

Vatikiotis, Panayiotis. 1980. *The History of Egypt from Muhammad Ali to Sadat*. Second edition. London: Weidenfeld and Nicolson.

Vom Bruck, Gabriele. 2000. 'A house turned inside out: Inhabiting space in a Yemeni city', in Robbins, Derek (ed.), *Pierre Bourdieu*. London: Sage, 244–56.

Vom Bruck, Gabriele. 2005. *Islam, Memory, and Morality in Yemen: Ruling families in transition*. New York: Palgrave.

Vom Bruck, Gabriele. 2013. 'Self-similarity and its perils', in Marsden, Magnus and Retsikas, Konstantinos (eds), *Articulating Islam: Anthropological approaches to Muslim worlds*. Dordrecht: Springer, 139–69.

Vom Bruck, Gabriele. 2018. *Mirrored Loss: A Yemeni woman's life story*. Oxford: Oxford University Press.

Wedeen, Lisa. 2008. *Peripheral Visions: Publics, power, and performance in Yemen*. Chicago: Chicago University Press.

Wright, Christopher. 2013. *The Echo of Things: The lives of photographs in the Solomon islands*. Durham, NC and London: Duke University Press.

3
Smoking, praying, killing: the politics of boredom in post-revolutionary Libya

Igor Cherstich

Dissonances

Modern Libyan history has been marked by two revolutionary occurrences. In 1969 Colonel Muʿammar al Gaddafi led a coup against the king of Libya, abolishing the monarchy and establishing one of the most perdurable socialist governments of the twentieth century. Forty years later, a revolution broke out against Gaddafi, determining the sudden collapse of the socialist state. In this chapter I will examine the aftermaths of these two uprisings. In so doing, I will show that in spite of their antithetical character – one revolution brought Gaddafi to power, the other put his rule to an end – both events were characterised by a similar, fundamental discrepancy. More specifically, I will demonstrate that in both cases the revolutionaries claimed to have brought about a completely new phase in Libyan history: a novel era marked by an unprecedented sense of vitality and dynamicity. Equally, I will show that the insurgents attained exactly the opposite of what they aimed to achieve: rather than precipitating an age of effervescence and movement, they generated an age of stasis. A stagnant state of affairs where Libyans could not help but feeling stuck, lethargic, and bored.

Naturally, in suggesting that these uprisings failed to inject Libyan society with fresh dynamism, I am not implying that they had absolutely no positive impact on the lives of Libyans. Besides, it is important to remember that the tendency to misfire is a recurrent feature of many revolutionary endeavours, and it is an aspect of these phenomena that does not necessarily testify to their propensity to fail (Dunn, 1989: 246) – as with the cases I am analysing – but also to their creative power: a capacity to produce unintended outcomes that might better society, thus exceeding the expectations of revolutionaries themselves (Graber, 2011: 4, 11–66). Rather, my aim is to investigate the relation between boredom and miscarried projects of radical change.[1] More precisely, my intention is to explore the possibility that the profound sense of tedium and stuckness that I have often witnessed amongst my Libyan friends was the by-product of a specific contradictory experience: the condition of being presented with prospects of unparalleled advancement and vibrancy, while, at the same time, being confronted with the unfulfillment of these prospects.

This particular way of looking at boredom has a precise genealogy, and it is essential for me to outline the roots of my approach, so that I can better contextualise my investigation of Libyan post-revolutionary scenarios within the relevant debates. The main inspiration for my line of argument comes from Yasmine Musharbash's analysis of Aboriginal Australia. In her persuasive study Musharbash argues that amongst the many personal and sociological factors that might push individuals to feel bored or stuck there is also a distinct element of dissonance. In particular, Musharbash shows that ennui tends to arise when people are expected to orientate their life in accordance with certain values, but they live under circumstances that do not allow them to actualise such values. Musharbash describes this occurrence as a process in which 'ways of being in the world and the world jar' (2007: 315): the emergence of a distance between discourses and experiences that pushes subjects to feel apathetic and listless, because they are faced with the disorienting – if not impossible – task of living in a particular way, without having the instruments to do so. Bearing this in mind, one might propose – expanding on Musharbash's argument – that the state of boredom closely resembles the so-called 'double bind': a befuddling psychological condition famously described by Gregory Bateson (2000: 206) in which a person receives a request, but concurrently is placed in a position where this request cannot be satisfied.[2]

Why is it helpful to consider this dissonant nature of ennui? And why is it illuminating to do so with reference to Libya? Because I am under the impression that when recent anthropological analyses have identified a discord between 'ways of being in the world and the world' in revolutionary contexts, they have highlighted the existential features of this discrepancy over its political dimension. To clarify this point let me briefly consider my second source of inspiration, one that more closely parallels the cases I am examining: Samuli Schielke's study (2015) of the Egyptian Revolution of 2011. In his compelling body of work Schielke documents the contrast between the experiences of boredom that often characterise Egyptian everyday life, and the expectations of improvement that are presented by revolutionary discourses. In particular, Schielke shows that Egyptians read their lives in the light of the promises of sudden progress and unmatched happiness that are entailed in revolutionary narratives. Nonetheless, when faced with their unchanging daily monotony, they also find themselves bored, existentially jammed, and prone to deploying repetitive ways of killing time that contradict such promises (Schielke, 2015; 2008: 262).[3]

Schielke thus demonstrates that, while it is true that revolutionary events produce new subjectivities and approaches to life (Badiou, 2003: 55–65), it is also true that this process is often marked by contradictions and complexities (Holbraad, 2014). Furthermore, his work adeptly describes the sharp incongruity that, as we have seen, lies at the heart of boredom: the clash between what is expected of people and their concrete circumstances. Yet, in my view, Schielke's analysis also features an unspoken tension, and it is in relation to this element that I want to situate this chapter. In particular, Schielke argues that his informants were bound to experience a misalignment between revolutionary discourses and their everyday dimension, because the grand narratives that human beings use to organise their lives – 'revolution' being one of them – tend to be marked by a sense of 'purity and certainty which life can never have' (Schielke and Debevec, 2012: 10). At the same time, however, Schielke seems to suggest that this misalignment takes place only under certain conditions. In the case of Egypt, for instance, his study shows that political activists framed the revolution through the lens of two discourses: Islamic revivalism with its focus on the rewards that the faithful will enjoy in the afterlife, and capitalism with its obsession for betterment.[4] Such notions widened the gap between revolutionary narratives and people's experiences, because they encouraged Egyptians to constantly imagine a better life for themselves, thus pushing them to approach their daily existence with dissatisfaction and boredom (Schielke, 2009a; 2015: 23, 105, 122).

Doubtless, Schielke's shrewd investigation can help us understand the Libyan context. However, as a way of highlighting the difference between his analysis and mine, I believe it is important to emphasise that Schielke's examination ultimately features a combination of two potentially conflicting readings of ennui. On the one hand, his work is informed by an existential approach, one that identifies the root of boredom in the fact that meta-narratives such as 'revolution' are always, as Sartre would say, 'in perpetual incompletion' (1992: 220): they are discourses that can never be fully put into practice, as they aim at 'pursuing ... perfection in an imperfect world' (Schielke, 2015: 4). On the other hand, Schielke simultaneously adopts a contextual approach, one that articulates tedium not as the product of an unfillable chasm between over-arching projects and one's experiences, but as the effect of specific political settings that create a discrepancy between life and the way life is expected to unfold. Incidentally, these two positions resonate with broader discussions in philosophy and in anthropology on whether boredom is an inherent aspect of the human condition (Heidegger, 1995: 78; Kierkegaard, 1995: 51; Toohey, 2011), or the upshot of particular socio-historical factors (Sahlins, 1972: 38; Healy, 1984; Klapp, 1986; Conrad, 1997: 46; Benjamin, 1999: 108; Goodstein, 2005: 18; Ralph, 2008; Lefebvre, 2011: 195).[5] Now, unless I misunderstand Schielke's approach, I believe that he implicitly privileges the former perspective.[6] In this chapter, however, I will champion the latter. Or at least I will favour the contextual aspects of Schielke's analysis over its existential implications.

More specifically, I will argue that the issue with boredom is not so much that individuals are expected to live in a certain way – the 'right way' so to speak – but they inevitably fail to meet this expectation because such is the pattern of human existence. Rather, quoting Theodore Adorno's famous pronouncement, the issue is that 'the wrong life cannot be lived rightly' (Adorno, 2005: 39). In other words, the problem with the two Libyan revolutions is not that they were informed by unattainable discourses of dynamicity that were destined to remain unfulfilled because all meta-narratives seek to pursue perfection in an imperfect world. Rather the issue lies in the fact the revolutionary leaders declared that they were going to build a new and dynamic Libya, but then, out of convenience, they created instead a static nation. A country plagued by nepotism where only a few had access to a truly vibrant life, while the majority felt the pressure to be actors in the revolutionary process and, at the same time, was excluded from this process. It is by concentrating on this political incongruity, and not by looking at a supposedly inescapable existential mismatch between life and discourses, that the root of Libyans' sense of dullness is to be found.

In order to shed light on this state of affairs, I will explore the ways in which the inhabitants of the capital city of Tripoli faced their boredom during the years of Gaddafi's rule, and in the aftermath of his dethronement. More specifically, I will concentrate on young males that I have met during two fieldwork experiences, between 2006 and 2008, and in 2012.[7] In analysing the lives of these individuals, I will demonstrate that their ennui stemmed from political contradictions, and especially from the fact that they were encouraged to embody the spirit of motion of the revolution, and, simultaneously, forced to live under stagnant conditions. Additionally, I will show that, at times, these contradictions were so intense that they pushed my informants to find equally intense, and even violent ways of confronting their monotony. Finally, in the last part of the chapter, I will offer a broader ethnographic critique of the view held by Schielke that an existential gap always occurs between discourses and experiences. In particular, I will suggest that, while it is true that the static circumstances of young Tripolitans contradicted the revolutionary narratives – and this dissonance fuelled their ennui – it is also true that other grand narratives, particularly some of a religious nature, helped my informants to contextualise their sensation of stuckness and to look at boredom with a sense of prospective. Rather than generating unrealistic expectations of amelioration, therefore, these narrations assisted my interlocutors in experiencing a strong alignment between life and discourses, as opposed to a disparity between the two.

When motion becomes stillness

We begin our examination of the political nature of post-revolutionary boredom by concentrating on the first Libyan uprising. The so-called 'al-Fatah' revolution, whose name derives from the date of its launching: the first day, the 'opening' or 'al fatah', of the month of September. On this date Colonel Mu'ammar al Gaddafi left his mark on Libyan history by deposing King Idris as-Sanusi, who had been made monarch with the help of Britain in the aftermath of the Second World War. Gaddafi's coup was informed by a mixture of Nasserian socialism, anti-colonial sentiment and pan-Arabism. Even though mapping the role that each of these components played in the Colonel's revolutionary theory exceeds the purposes of this chapter, it is important to focus on one aspect of his socialist thought: his vision to establish the purest form of direct democracy. In order to implement this notion, in 1979, the Colonel turned Libya into a *jamahiriya*, a 'state of the masses', or 'peopledom' (Anderson, 2014: 264): a system that comprised popular assemblies where Libyans would meet and take all the decisions pertaining their country. Peopledom was designed to be the only true democracy in the world. Yet, in reality, the system was actualised in ways that completely contradicted the ideas that inspired it.

As explained by Gaddafi in his political manifesto, *The Green Book*, the assemblies, or 'Basic People's Congresses', communicated their decisions through secretaries, whose task was to meet in a 'General People's Congress', and organise the pronouncements of the assemblies into coherent proposals. Once formalised, the proposals were sent back to the 'People's Congresses' to be re-discussed, and, if approved by a majority, they were executed by the 'People's Committees': congregations whose members were also chosen by the assemblies (Gaddafi, 2005: 16–19). In peopledom, therefore, every decision had to 'travel' from the lower assemblies to the higher one, and then back to the lower ones for approval. Interestingly, this kinetic quality of the *jamahiriya* – its propensity to entail a constant movement of proposals between the assemblies – was mirrored by Gaddafi's speeches, as the Colonel often clarified that the new, revolutionary age was an era of movement, one that 'advances rapidly' (Gaddafi, 2005: 26) and 'excites the emotions' (Gaddafi, 2005), as opposed to a previous era where the monarchy had generated 'stumped growth and regression' (Gaddafi, 1982).[8] The stress was on the literal meaning of the word 'revolution' – 'thawra', an Arabic term whose root refers to the idea of 'rising up', or 'being excited'[9] – and the emphasis was on Libyan society to 'wake up and rise' (Gaddafi, 1995). The Colonel, it seemed, had finally reactivated the engine of Libyan history. On a closer look, however, one realised that his kinetic rule was nothing more than a form of stasis.

My contacts in Tripoli regularly took part in the system devised by Gaddafi, and almost unanimously praised the democratic principles that inspired the 'State of the Masses'. During my fieldwork, for instance, I would frequently witness my friends postponing our appointments because they had to participate in the assemblies. Nonetheless, my interlocutors also clarified that they mainly attended these gatherings because failing to do so would have prompted Gaddafi's secret service to come knocking at their door. Furthermore, as I have observed on many occasions – and as documented by Libyan sociologists and political scientists (Obeidi, 2001; Al-Werfalli, 2011) – many showed distrust and apathy towards the system. More specifically, my informants explained to me that even though the assemblies succeeded at resolving some local issues, they had practically no power at a national level, because it was Gaddafi and his entourage who ultimately decided how to manage the country. Such a dynamic was epitomised by the fact that the Colonel often appeared on television and communicated his decisions in the form of security measures that had been finalised without being discussed by the assemblies.

The kinetic nature of peopledom thus acquired a circular quality. Proposals did 'travel' from one assembly to another, but they seemed to go around in circles ceaselessly. While the masses spent their time discussing how to run the country, the country was effectively run by the *hukuma*, the 'government': a word that Tripolitans invariably used to describe Gaddafi, his close associates or the secret service. Doubtless, my friends often stressed that in the first decades after the revolution, the system worked in a very efficient manner, as it allowed Libyans to enjoy an unprecedented degree of control over their nation and their lives. Nonetheless, during my stay, every Tripolitan I met specified that, over the years, the situation had become paradoxical, because the people who were supposed to govern themselves were in fact governed by their revolutionary leader.

Interestingly, this paradox was embodied in the figure of Gaddafi himself, as the Colonel was exempted from all the obligations that peopledom imposed on common Libyans. Even though, according to the rules of the *jamahiriya*, every citizen over eighteen years of age was obliged to participate in the assemblies, the Colonel and some high-profile members of this government never did, thus reinforcing the idea that, in the end, power resided outside the system. This notion was also strengthened by the fact that the closer one was to this external source of power the easier it became to navigate Libyan society. This was true at the highest level, where individuals related to Gaddafi through relationship of kin or tribe played central roles in key areas such as the oil industry and the military.[10] However, this was also true at a lower level, where being acquainted with friends who had good political connections made it easier for Tripolitans to find a job in the administration, or to open a business. In a way, this aspect of the *jamahiriya* forced my informants always to be active and inventive, as it constantly pushed them to find ways of cultivating their *wasta*, 'relationships of patronage', or 'connections' (Brown, 2008: 448; Egan and Tabar, 2016; Lackner, 2016). Nonetheless, this feature of peopledom also inevitably produced an inert society, one where inequalities were never challenged, but rather reproduced at every level.

Frequently, Tripolitans with the best political connections found better paid and less demanding occupations – even when they did not have the necessary qualifications – and this gave them the opportunity to organise their lives between work and free time. As for those with good, but not excellent levels of *wasta*, they tended to have desk jobs that allowed them to bend the rules of the workplace, and to use their working hours for other purposes if they so wished. Those without strong connections, however, were inevitably forced to have multiple petty jobs, usually a few hours here and there, often oddly spread during the week. A condition that left them unoccupied for the majority of their time, and that pushed them to rely heavily on Gaddafi's welfare system: the only efficacious facet of the Colonel's government that furnished every Libyan family unit with basic goods such as flour, olive oil and tea, as well as with subsidies on fuel, and benefits for dependants.

There were, of course, noticeable exceptions, some of which will be discussed later in the text. But the general situation in the capital, and more broadly in the country, was characterised by inequality, immobility and joblessness. With youth unemployment reaching 48 per cent in a population of 6 million, Libya's labour force around the time of my fieldwork comprised only about a third of the resident population – 2.6 million – 50 per cent of whom were foreigners: sub-Saharan and Egyptian migrants that were assigned manual labour and factory work, and skilled foreign professionals that held the most specialised occupations, often working as consultants for the government.[11] Given this state of affairs – and given that, in the majority of cases, women were forced to take care of all the activities related to the keeping of the household[12] – many male Tripolitans were left with considerable periods of time to fill. And they spent at least some of this time in a desperate attempt to kill time.

Seven teas and seventy cigarettes

To exemplify this fundamental contradiction – that of a dynamic nation whose population largely led a stationary existence – I will now document a day in the life of my friend Mansur, a twenty-six-year-old man with a sophisticated sense of humour and a love of languages. Mansur – a pseudonym, like all the names mentioned in this chapter – studied computer science. But having failed to find work in his field due to lack of political connections, he helped his father selling goods in various street markets three days a week. At times, Mansur attempted to study Italian – an activity that, he told me, helped him to appreciate Italian football better – but he spent the rest of his time doing very little. Typically, Mansur would come to my house in the late morning, with two espresso coffees in paper cups. I would invariably try to convince him that I had work to do. But then, inevitably, I would agree to go with him, which was when our repetitive routine began.

Mansur drove unhurriedly – often due to the capital's notorious traffic – sipping his espresso with everlasting slowness, and, obviously, we smoked. At the time you could buy unpackaged cigarettes in Tripoli and stopping by a cigarette shop felt like attending a buffet. Habitually, each of us would purchase some twenty Marlboro Red, by far the most popular brand in Tripoli, fifteen Lucky Strike, and around ten national brand cigarettes, *Riadhy*, 'sporty': a rather hazardous inclusion on the menu, given that, despite their name, the strong 'sporty' cigarettes severely limited our ability to breathe. Following this habitual daily ritual, we would buy another espresso or a cup of Turkish coffee from a local café, and then sit somewhere in the city centre, chatting and smoking copiously until lunch time.

At around one o'clock we would make our way to Mansur's house to eat food that had been prepared by his mother. We ate, smoked, took a nap and then, at five in the afternoon, we drank our first tea of the day. Then, without fail, we would go to see Mansur's friends, which meant gathering in the lethargic space of someone's guest room, or *marbu'a*. Four of five more teas followed (at this point we had had about six strong teas and two coffees). Needless to say, we watched television, zapping from one channel to the next, and we smoked until the room was filled with a thick fog. Noticeably, only a few shows were watched in silence, and that included replicas of the popular Syrian historical soap opera *Bab el Hara*, and football. Another tea and about twenty-five cigarettes later it was dinner time. After food – and tea – we would go to an internet café (many Tripolitans had no internet access at home), and we would smoke some fifteen, twenty cigarettes until Mansur, or someone else, decided it was time to go home. Mansur and I had our last communal smoke of the day in front of my door. One, or more, solitary smoking sessions followed, as Mansur confirmed to me, for a daily count of seventy to eighty cigarettes or more.

Doubtless, the routine I described was in some respects pleasant, as it allowed us to engage in relaxed conversations that covered a variety of topics, ranging from personal issues to football and world politics. But there was also something undeniably depressive about this way of living. Naturally, as with other ethnographic contexts (Achilli, 2015: 174–5), my informants differentiated between good ways to kill time and bad ones. For instance, Mansur and his friends did not perceive tea-drinking and cigarette-smoking as malign activities. Conversely, they considered the consumption of alcohol and hashish – items that were not accessible to the average Tripolitan due to the strict control exercised by the government over intoxicants[13] – as more despicable ways of passing time. However, when commenting on people's daily patterns, Mansur and his friends described both moral and immoral activities as having the same function: that of *yaqsar el waqat*, 'shortening time'. These actions were therefore perceived as attempts to condense an otherwise intolerably long sequence of hours, days and weeks. More importantly, my interlocutors depicted these forms of behaviour both as actions that helped them to avoid feeling bored, and as operations that, due to their inherently repetitive nature, increased the level of boredom. As expected, it was young Tripolitans who felt the urge to abbreviate time most strongly.[14] A similar attitude, however, could also be observed with older people, as they too attempted to 'shorten' their hours by engaging in similar, though often less tobacco-infused, versions of Mansur's schedule.

Contradictions and black things

Now, much like with the Egyptian case analysed by Schielke, my friends' experience of boredom had an existential dimension. In some cases, it was melancholic reflections on the meaning of the human condition, or the realisation that life never unfolds the way one would like it to that pushed Tripolitans to pursue a dull routine, often in an attempt to escape these unsettling thoughts. Furthermore, my informants often lamented that their monotonous reality negatively influenced all aspects of their existence, throwing them into a spiritual, psychological and physical torpor.[15] As with Khalifa, a thirty-year-old unemployed accountant who often told me that he felt as if a 'black thing' – *haja soda* – weighed on his chest: a feeling that Khalifa ascribed not only to the effects that chain smoking was having on his lungs – 'this shit is killing me, ya Igor' – but also to a sensation of heaviness that pervaded his body and soul, preventing him from doing anything other than smoking and watching television. Significantly, when Khalifa detailed the effects that the 'black thing' had on him, he offered descriptions of ennui that resembled illustrious existential depictions of boredom as 'the root of all evil' (Kierkegaard, 1995: 51); a 'silent fog' (Heidegger, 1995: 78) that – like the black thing weighing on Khalifa's chest – 'weighs like a lid on the groaning spirit' (Baudelaire, 2006: 100). Yet, at the same time, in contrast with Schielke's analysis, my interlocutors classified existential unwellness as an effect of boredom, not as its cause.

Even though my friends recognised that human existence is inevitably characterised by a degree of unfulfillment and unresolvedness, they also stressed the contextual nature of their sufferings. In particular, my informants frequently recognised a link between their feelings of tedium and the political contradictions that, as I have previously shown, characterised Gaddafi's peopledom. For instance, in tracing the roots of the 'black thing', Khalifa clarified that, even though the government preached socialism and equality, he could not find a job because he belonged to a tribe that was not on good terms with Gaddafi. Khalifa thus located the origin of his ennui in a specific discrepancy: a gap between the state of stuckness in which he found himself as a result of his lack of political connections, and the emphasis on dynamicity that characterised Gaddafi's revolutionary discourses.

This mismatch coloured many aspects of Khalifa's life, but it found its clearest expression in a specific phenomenon: the fact that the 'black thing' seemed to deprive him of his energy and prevented him from partaking in actions that he recognised as beneficial, such as exercising and playing football. As every Tripolitan knew, the Colonel had devoted a whole section of *The Green Book* to argue that 'sport, like power, should be for the masses' (Gaddafi, 2005: 80). More specifically, Gaddafi had declared that 'the multitude which crowds the stadium to watch a game is a multitude of fools who are incapable of practising sports themselves … sports need to be practised, not watched' (Gaddafi, 2005: 81). Nevertheless, in contrast with these statements, the 'black thing' forced Khalifa to lie down in his living room, watching sports on television. In a similar vein, the Guide of the Revolution had invited all Libyans to be heroic protagonists of their existence rather than mere spectators, specifying that 'those who make their own life do not need to see how life takes its course through watching the actors on stage' (Gaddafi, 2005). Yet, Khalifa spent his days commenting on the attractiveness of Hollywood actors and actresses while watching romantic comedies and action films with his friends. In short, my informant felt the pressure to live as an active revolutionary, but he also experienced the impossibility of doing so.[16]

Interestingly, Khalifa also clarified to me that he and his friends inevitably fuelled each other's sense of boredom, because they pushed each other to smoke and stay indoors compulsively: a condition that, in his view, had to do with the fact that his friends had the 'black thing' pressing on their chests too as a result of the issues characterising the *jamahiriya*. Khalifa thus described a complex process, one in which individuals bored each other, and where the political inconsistencies of peopledom featured as the very engine of this vicious cycle. In so doing, Khalifa traced a picture of the mechanics of boredom that closely parallels some philosophical reflections on the collective dimension of tedium.

In particular, my informant's statements echo the notion articulated by Deleuze that human beings have a fundamental capacity to affect each other, arousing in each other sensations of joy or sadness that excite or depress them, thus increasing or decreasing their ability to be active in the world: their capacity, one might say, not to be stuck (Deleuze, 1978; Deleuze and Guattari, 2004: 287; Freydberg, 2017: 63; Ruddick, 2010).[17] Such view of ennui and stuckness as the products of constant interactions between individuals illuminates the social, and therefore necessarily political – rather than purely existential – nature of boredom (Deleuze and Guattari, 1986a: 4; 1986b: 17; Massumi, 2004: xiv; 2015; Negri, 2003: xxiii; Legg, 2018). More specifically, this reflection helps us to understand that my informants influenced each other in a chain of depressive affections, one that developed along the route of their social patronage connections, and that ultimately linked all Libyans together, including the very source of their apathy, the Colonel himself. Though they had never met, Khalifa had been affected, in a Deleuzian sense, by the Libyan leader. The latter had decreased the former's capacity to act, and the weight of the disparity between Gaddafi's discourses and Khalifa's life was literally squashing my friend's chest.[18]

Time stands still, life stands still

Having shown that my interlocutors stressed the political quality of boredom over its existential connotation, I should also clarify that not all Tripolitans could afford to spend their days lying in a living room as Khalifa did. In the words of cultural historian Joe Moran, and paraphrasing Patricia Meyer Specks' analysis of boredom, 'ennui is more likely to be experienced by those who can delegate the tedium of mundane tasks to their wives ... and have the leisure time to dwell on unfulfilled promise' (Moran, 2003: 169; Spacks, 1996: 101). Such reflection proves particularly true in the case of Tripolitans, given that women of all ages, including Khalifa's mother, were continuously engaged in cooking, cleaning, childcaring and – in the case of those who had a job or studied – trying to balance between housekeeping and keeping their job. Even so, women too often described their lives as being monotonous. Moreover, in their case too one could notice a strong connection between their sense of boredom and the incongruous political actions of the government.

For instance, it was common knowledge amongst my informants that Gaddafi's policies in terms of women's employment were based on the notion that 'driving a woman to do a man's work is an unfair aggression against the femininity that is naturally bestowed upon her' (Gaddafi, 2005: 72). Such a view was also reinforced by traditional perceptions of gender roles. Yet, like everything else in Libya, the definition of femininity – and the degree to which wives and daughters were bound to stay home – varied according to the quality of one's political connections. Consequently, most female Tripolitans were frequently discouraged from finding jobs that clashed with their domestic duties, while those who were close to the government were not. As in the case of ʿAysha al-Gaddafi, a public figure in Libya, who, being Gaddafi's daughter, held the military rank of Lieutenant Colonel, collaborated with the United Nations and worked as a lawyer – 'manly' and dynamic professions that were completely inaccessible to the vast majority of Libyan women.[19]

Like women, male café owners, taxi drivers, and shop keepers also worked all day. But they too experienced ennui as a result of Libya's political inconsistencies. Under Gaddafi Friday and Saturday were rest days. There were also various public holidays, such as the anniversary of the revolution. Yet, the need to sustain their children – and the lack of rule enforcement that regulated the work hours – pushed some to keep their shops always open, day in and day out, constantly enacting the same, repetitive, and often boring routine.[20] Furthermore, in order to keep their business permits, shop owners had to engage with state bureaucracy on a regular basis. For those who did not have strong connections, this meant waiting in long queues outside state offices, filling this time with cigarettes and tea, receiving news that the clerk who was going to process their documents had decided not to come to work, making phone calls to ask that cousin about that person who might help and, maybe, discovering that the person in question was the clerk who had stayed home that day.[21] At times this process proved extremely lengthy, and some of my informants had to wait several months before receiving their work permits: an experience that confirmed the contradictory nature of their theoretically dynamic – but effectively static – nation.

It is also important to highlight that the sense of immobility I am describing affected the most intimate aspects of my interlocutors' lives, regardless of whether they had a busy working schedule or not. Certainly, my friends' monotonous dimension was punctuated not only by repetitive actions, but also by special occasions such as marriages and funerals – occurrences that allowed Tripolitans to break from their dull routines. Nevertheless, even on these occasions my friends were reminded of the political contradictions that generated their stationary condition; a phenomenon that I witnessed in a particular marriage celebration. On that occasion guests had calmly gathered in the groom's home, as customary practice dictates. Yet, at some stage, one of the attendees had produced a foam spray, and had proceeded to sprinkle the groom with coloured foam. Though practical jokes are to be expected at wedding parties they tend not to be directed against the groom, the reason being that, as I was often told, a man on his wedding day should be treated with the respect due to a sultan. The flamboyant gesture, therefore, broke the protocol. Later on, however, I was told that the man with the foam spray was a close relative of Gaddafi, and this explained why the groom had taken it quietly. A forced smile on his face. Frozen on his chair. Embodying a sense of immobility that contradicted and negated his 'sultan' status.[22]

With reference to the subject of marriage, one should also consider that Tripolitans were aware that the static nature of peopledom was increasingly affecting their ability to forge meaningful relationships, and especially their capacity to get married. For instance, due to their precarious working lives, several of my informants could not afford to buy a house – an absolute prerequisite for marriage. Furthermore, many were not willing to rent as resident foreigners did, because they perceived this to be a disreputable option: one that clashed both with traditional notions of masculinity – the expectation that a real man should own his home – and with the revolutionary theories expressed in the Green Book, which stated that 'a person living in another person's house in return for rent, or even without rent, is not a free person' (2005: 38). As a result, many lived in a perpetual state of sentimental inertia.

Some were betrothed to a girl they fell in love with while they were at university, but their engagement had drawn out for months or years, and they were endlessly worried that her parents might get tired of waiting for their potential son-in-law to find economic stability. Others were continuously looking for the right companion, and for the right conditions that would make them marriable. Yet others, tired of waiting, accepted their incapacity to get married, but elaborated intricate plans that would allow them to spend time alone with their fiancées. Maybe even going as far as engaging in intercrural or anal sex with them, but always restraining themselves. Never free to enjoy the intimacy they desired fully for fear that unwanted pregnancies might affect their reputation, force them into a reparation marriage, and prevent them from creating the respectable family they dreamed of. In some cases, my informants restrained themselves even if they did not want to, because worries and frustrations had depressed their interest in sex, producing in them a sort of erotic ennui.[23]

Naturally, this does not mean to say that all Tripolitans passively accepted their all-encompassing state of inaction. As with other, similarly stagnant ethnographic settings (Durham, 2000; Ralph, 2008; Marlovits, 2013), some of my informants faced their situation with creativity and strategy; an approach that helped them to circumvent the obstacles that prevented their lives from moving forward. In my fieldwork I witnessed many examples of such an attitude. For instance, some Tripolitan families bent the traditional rules of marriage arrangement and agreed to reduce the provision paid by the groom to the bride, thus facilitating the stipulation of marital contracts in the absence of strong economic means. In other cases, some used the surplus time they had as unemployed individuals to study for a second degree, taking advantage of the fact that the government provided university education for free to all Libyans.[24] Even amongst those who engaged in perpetual smoking and television watching, some approached these activities with a sense of purpose, using communal tea-drinking sessions to encourage each other to think positively: a phenomenon that resembles other cases studied by anthropologists (Mains, 2012; Masquelier, 2013).

These instances shed light on a dormant – but fundamentally present – capacity for agency that characterised my interlocutors in spite of their difficulties. In the end, it was precisely this capacity that unfolded in 2011, when Libyans decided to revolt against Gaddafi's incongruous style of governance, and managed to end his rule.[25] In the following section, I will explore this second revolutionary occurrence. Given that I was able to visit the country only for a short time after the fall of peopledom, I will not investigate its aftermath with the same degree of detail with which I have surveyed the Colonel's era. Nevertheless, I will highlight some elements that marked the collapse of the regime. In particular, I will show that Tripolitans embraced this event as the advent of a long-awaited chance to act and move: an opportunity for Libyans to achieve the advancement and dynamicity that Gaddafi had failed to bring about. However, I will also show that eventually many of my informants fell prey to political contradictions that closely resemble those I have described in the context of the *jamahiriya*. Contradictions that pushed them, once again, to feel bored and stuck.

Killing time, time to kill

Before I elucidate the role played by boredom in my informants' lives after the breakdown of peopledom, I will briefly present the landscape of post-Gaddafi Libya as I observed it in 2012, a year after the revolution. Upon my return, Tripoli felt like a completely different city. Gaddafi had been brutally killed.[26] A transitional national government had been formed with charismatic politician Mustafa 'Abdul Jalil acting as chairman.

Revolutionary militias – groups that had spontaneously emerged during the uprising, acting as the protagonists of the revolt – filled the streets with parades and tanks. Many of these militiamen sported long hair, unkept beards, and improvised uniforms: the distinguishing marks of the *thwar*, 'revolutionaries'. Even though the presence of these armed groups reminded Tripolitans that the past months had been marked by violence and civil war, the leaders of the militias constantly released interviews on television, reassuring the population that their allegiance lay with chairman ʿAbdul Jalil and with the transitional government. The general atmosphere, therefore, was one of effervescence, motion and hopeful transition. Yet, at the same time, the inhabitants of the capital also experienced a sense of tension: a tangible feeling of apprehension that cast doubts on whether the time had truly come for the nation to leave its past condition of immobility behind and enter a new age of movement.

Even though the anti-Gaddafi rebellion had originated as a popular insurrection, the uprising had largely succeeded due to the involvement of Western powers. In the initial weeks that had followed the revolution my informant had already started to realise that France, Italy and other nations were demanding a reward for their support, asking the new government to facilitate their access to Libya's oil and gas resources, and pushing the country to re-enter the global neo-liberal market hastily after months of inactivity. Furthermore, my friends had begun to spot Saudi and Qatari militaries, oil consultants and religious preachers operating in the capital, a proof that Gulf countries were also becoming involved in Libyan affairs. The most unsettling consequence of Libya entering the world stage, however, was the fact that – in contrast with their official commitment to the new government – militias had begun to strike their own independent deals with foreign powers and with international Islamist networks. This contradictory behaviour on the part of revolutionary groups paralleled the spreading of a familiar kind of dissatisfaction and boredom in the population. A form of alienation and apathy that was certainly related to the existential distress that the tragedies of war and the uncertainties of the future had produced in Tripolitans, but that was also deeply rooted in the ambiguities that were increasingly affecting post-Gaddafi politics.

The alliances that militias had forged with Gulf nations and transnational jihadi groups were mainly made along religious lines, as a number of Libyan militiamen showed a strong, though often vague, sympathy for organisations such as Al Qaeda or what was to become the Islamic State of Iraq and Syria (ISIS).[27] Others took a more visibly political form. In both cases, however, militias had started to pursue their own agendas, even opposing the transitional government whenever its pronouncements clashed with their plans or with those of their foreign allies. Therefore, a fundamental contradiction was taking place. The militiamen – the heroes of the revolution, those who had presented themselves as the proponents of a *new* order of things – were acting in ways that were recognisably *old*. These groups had fought to create a Libya for Libyans, but they behaved as if they were agents of external forces: partaking in political schemes that – in striking similarity to the way in which Gaddafi had run the country – took place neither with the consent nor with the participation of the larger population. As a consequence, many Tripolitans had started to feel a profound sense of powerlessness. Even those who had initially enthusiastically joined the militias – my friend Khalifa, whom I have previously mentioned, being one of them – had decided to leave these groups. This had led them to spend most of their time at home; away from the public sphere; disillusioned with the revolutionary movement; worried and prone to ennui.

This was certainly the main inconsistency that characterised the new Libya, particularly in light of the fact that militiamen often publicly encouraged the population to be active participants in the state-building process, while effectively forcing them to disengage with politics. However, this was not the only incongruity that marked the presence of the revolutionary groups. In the aftermath of the uprising, the militias had also begun to act as a police force. Even though this meant that Tripolitans received protection from thieves and other criminals, it also meant that the capital had turned into an utterly chaotic space. Given that, as I have explained, militiamen had different political and religious leanings, they exercised different, and often contrasting, interpretations of justice, so that, effectively, the situation in Tripoli was one of lawlessness. Some areas were under a crude version of shari'a law, while others had different sets of rules, or no rule at all. Having no access to a coherent justice system, my informants were forced to fulfil their needs and solve their everyday issues using old means: building political connections – a phenomenon that, very much like in the days of peopledom, inevitably produced immobility and inequalities.

Some managed to befriend members of the transitional government and influential militiamen, and this move allowed them to get on with their lives. Others, however, had to fend for themselves. Now, during the uprising, the revolutionaries had stormed Gaddafi's weapon deposits.[28] Yet, common people too had taken part in the looting, and whereas some had submitted their guns to the new government, those who did not feel protected had kept them, so that many of my informants had a firearm at home. This was an extremely dangerous state of affairs, especially in the climate of economic crisis – and further increase in unemployment – that had followed the sudden dismantling of the *jamahiriya*. As the new government struggled to reopen schools and universities due to ongoing conflicts between rival militas, many young Tripolitans were essentially left with no school to attend and no work to do. As could be expected some of these youngsters had begun to patrol the suburbs of Tripoli, bored and armed. This was increasingly worrying the majority of my informants, who were constantly trying to stop their children from joining these gangs.[29]

In the months and years that followed my last visit to Libya the situation kept deteriorating. Militias began to offer a salary to their recruits.[30] Youth gangs started regularly to engage in extortion and robbery. Being part of an armed group quickly became the most profitable profession in the capital. Meanwhile, alternative governments proliferated. Foreign powers fuelled these divisions, and in Skype conversations and phone calls, my informants told me that they felt as if they had been robbed of their future. The revolutionary leadership had behaved like the Colonel, preaching one way and acting another. This political dissonance had thrown Tripolitans once again into a deep state of stuckness, pushing some to barricade themselves at home, and others – particularly the most vulnerable ones – to join armed bands because, as the sister of a gang member once told me, 'they have nothing else to do'. In one of these conversations – perhaps the most moving exchange I had with my Libyan interlocutors – Ibrahim, a sixty-year-old man whom I had befriended, told me that one of his sons had died. It was unclear whether the child had been killed in a firearm accident while playing with his friends or he had taken part in a fight that had escalated into an armed conflict. Either way, the boy had been murdered by the tedium and the hopelessness of his killers. These, in turn, had been the victims of a new incarnation of old contradictions.

A blessing behind every obstacle

The scenarios I have described show that both under Gaddafi and after the end of his rule revolutionary leaders projected certain expectations on Tripolitans, but then, through their incongruous actions, they prevented my informants from fulfilling such expectations. My aim has been to demonstrate that boredom was the product of this discrepancy. As I have suggested at the beginning of the chapter, this realisation pushes us to concentrate on the political nature of ennui, thus problematising the notion held by some scholars that boredom stems from an inevitable discord between experiences and grand narratives that allegedly characterises the human condition. With reference to this point, I will now present an additional consideration. In particular, I will show that whereas revolutionary discourses clashed with the everyday dimension of my informants, other grand narratives stood in accordance with it. More specifically, I will briefly elucidate how some religious discourses resonated with my friends' lives and allowed them to situate their ennui within the wider order of things.

Naturally, in proposing that these religious grand narratives matched the experiences of Tripolitans – whereas revolutionary projects did not – I am not inferring that the spiritual lives of my informants were devoid of ambiguities. Nor am I suggesting that my interlocutors were able to fulfil the demands that religion imposed on them perfectly. Rather, I argue that these grand narratives did not always entail the expectation for my informants to be perfect. On the contrary, these discourses presented imperfection as a normal feature of existence: a factor that helped my friends to cope with boredom, and, at times, overcoming it. Bearing this in mind, I should also clarify that the approach I adopt in this last part of the discussion differs from that of other anthropologists who have documented the contradictions that Muslims often experience when trying to lead a pious existence (Marsden, 2005; 2007; Schielke, 2009b; Osella and Soares, 2010: 11). In their works, these scholars have put the emphasis on the dissonance that frequently characterises the relation between the discursive and the experiential aspects of religious life. However, in the case of my informants – at least some of them – these dimensions seem not to contradict each other.[31]

First of all, it is important to explain that even though, as I have shown, Tripolitans identified the roots of their boredom in the actions of the revolutionary leadership, some contextualised this dynamic within another, broader dynamic. These informants told me that, even though the incongruous behaviour of their leaders was the most immediate cause of their unwellness, in the end it was God who had allowed these contradictions to unfold. Naturally, my friends did not articulate this notion in terms of static predestination, but rather through the idea of 'malleable fixity' that is often found in Islamic conceptualisations of destiny (Elliot, 2016b; Elliot and Menin, 2018): an understanding of God's plan that leaves space for human agency. Furthermore, unlike other ethnographic settings (Hage, 2009: 97–106), those who expressed this view did not necessarily describe their sense of stuckness as something to be heroically endured. Rather, the idea that a merciful God allowed suffering in their lives helped my interlocutors to transcend their totalising perception of ennui, and to articulate boredom as a partial component within a larger cosmological process. A process where, as stated in the Qur'an, 'after hardship comes ease', and where both the obstacles of life and the human limitations in overcoming these obstacles were part of a divine plan leading towards the highest good.

Such an attitude was verbalised in common religious sayings that were frequently used by Tripolitans in our conversations. Expressions such as *kulli taukhera fiha khera*, 'behind every obstacle there is a blessing', or *Allah ghalib*, 'Allah is victorious', with reference to the fact that, when God puts hindrances on your way – and you fail to overcome them – he has 'won'. His will has prevailed, and you have to contemplate the possibility that God might have different plans for you, or that there might be other ways to solve your problems. Within this perspective, my friends envisioned a degree of 'fixed openness': the perception that there might be other possibilities written in one's destiny, and that, though life might appear to be static, the engine of God's providence is always in motion. As in the case of Khalid, a twenty-five-year-old unemployed accountant who, at the time of our meeting, was struggling to gather the money to organise his wedding. 'It is *maktub* ('written') that my marriage will happen, *Insha 'Allah* it will', he told me, specifying that this hopeful approach helped him to face the sense of ennui that his difficult situation generated in him, and encouraged him to think about ways of overcoming his challenges.

Similar attitudes have been documented by other ethnographies of North Africa that have shed light on how the idea of a written destiny might help people 'to open themselves and tentatively precipitate what is already "there", but unknown, in specific, hopeful ways' (Elliot, 2016b: 493).[32] More importantly, at least for the purposes of this chapter, within this perspective, immobility, boredom and inaction featured as temporary elements within the equation of life – problematic elements no doubt, but something to be expected – as opposed to revolutionary narratives where, as we have seen, these feelings were merely portrayed as the *wrong* response to a calling to live the *right*, active kind of life. These principles could be detected especially in the context of Tripolitan Sufi traditions: a form of religiosity that has been harshly criticised both by Colonel Gaddafi and by militiamen, and that has often been labelled as heterodox by them. Notwithstanding the revolutionaries' opposition to Sufism, forms of Islamic mysticism have been part of Tripolitan popular devotion – and, more broadly, of Libyan social fabric – for centuries, and it is important for me to give a succinct account of the presence of Sufi groups in the capital, so as to illuminate the role that the discourses and practices of these groups played in the dynamics I am describing.

Sufi gatherings took place once or twice a week in different parts of Tripoli. In the case of the 'Issawiya – the largest Sufi fraternity in the city – these meetings entailed the recitation of the *hezb*: a litany aimed at invoking the blessing of God and of the saints over the assembly. Interestingly, the main body of the *hezb* involved a lengthy catalogue of divine attributes as well as a list of human characteristics, so that the litany constituted a weekly reminder that Allah is great, eternal, never changing and perfect, while human beings are small, mortal, mutable and imperfect. Given that these meetings were open both to self-described Sufis and to occasional attendees, I often had a chance to hear from a variety of people about the emotional effects that the recitation had on them. In some instances, my interlocutors told me that the litany had encouraged them to remember that they were mere mortals, and that, since the world of mortals is marked by imperfection, it was no wonder that their everyday life was characterised by weaknesses, failures, and obstacles.

In sharp contrast with revolutionary narratives, these discourses thus allowed my informants to perceive an adhesion between discourses and experiences, and to look at their existence with a sense of congruity. Moreover, Sufi practices seemed to help some of my friends to physically experience the possibility that their sense of immobility could be overcome: an aspect that was particularly evident in the context of Sufi ritual occurrences. As with other Sufi traditions (Pinto, 2005; 2010) Tripolitan Sufi rituals involved rhythmic bodily movements and enthusiastic proclamations of religious formulas. Even though these kinetic performances tended to happen on feast days dedicated to local Sufi saints, they attracted large gatherings of Tripolitans, including people who had no interest in Sufism.

During these rituals, some participants would be so entangled in the movements, that they fell into a trance, whirling and spinning, with an ecstatic expression on their faces. Some claimed that this was just a way of releasing stress – and that Sufi performances were ultimately a form of *ryadha*, 'sport'. Others, however, maintained that the ritual allowed them to experience God's healing presence in their spirits and in their bodies. A revitalising process that, I was told, 'produces movement and heat' in the soul: a phenomenon that – as noticed by other anthropologists who have observed Sufi performances – seemed to invest the participants with 'the possibility of experiencing more bodily forms of action and emotion'

(Marsden, 2010: 62). Either way, the attendees often clarified that after the ritual they went home energised, refreshed and better equipped to face their issues. And when I listened to such comments, I could not help but thinking that Libyan mysticism provided Tripolitans with the opportunity to taste a true and deep form of motion: a chance to experience that dynamicity that earthly powers had promised, but never delivered.[33]

The politics of inaction

Through an examination of the mechanics of ennui in post-revolutionary Libya one realises that boredom was ultimately an instrument of domination. By forcing my informants to live in a contradictory state that crystallised their condition of stasis, revolutionary leaders decreased the capacity of common Libyans to challenge their authority actively. A tragic state of affairs given that, as I have shown, the perpetrators of this process presented themselves as the champions of agency and freedom. In the end, the reason that pushed me to stress the political, rather than the existential quality of boredom, was precisely this: the need to show that, while it is true that everyday life and grand narratives often diverge in significant ways, it is also true that frequently this divergence is strategically enhanced by powerholders. And if we fix our gaze solely on the discordant fabric of human existence, we might miss this extremely worrying fact. Perhaps this might even bring us to contemplate similar processes that take place in our own context, or in settings that are closer to ours.

As a final remark, I wish to consider the broader implications of this datum. In particular, I want to reflect on how 'action' – broadly understood as the capacity to be free agents who intervene, at least to some degree, on reality – has often been understood as the basic unity of politics. This view frequently remains implicit in scholarly investigations, but it has also been expressed in explicit terms by some distinguished thinkers (Arendt, 1998). In light of the analysis I have provided, however, I wish to emphasise that 'inaction' is an equally important component of the political domain, one that, when thoroughly contextualised, allows us to read the multiple ways in which oppression occurs. So far, this component has largely dominated the lives of Libyans. But let us hope that a balance will soon be re-established, and that Libyans will eventually regain their ability to act and move. If it is true, as Libyans say, that 'behind every obstacle there is a blessing', let this be the blessing that has hidden behind their failed revolutions. Let this be a reassurance that under the thick surface of inactivity, the possibility of action always lies – latent, but existent.[34]

Notes

1. In the chapter I use the term boredom to indicate a form of depressive ennui informed by the all-encompassing perception that life is monotonous and static, 'an emotion about emotion's absence or failure' (Duncan, 2015: 176).
2. In Bateson's view, the double bind occurs when a subject is given two or more mutually contradictory injunctions, one through words and the other through non-verbal hints, both of which may generate punishment if they are not fulfilled (Bateson, 2000:207). For a different reading of this concept see Spivak, 2013.
3. Interestingly, Schielke notices that even when the experiences of Egyptians clashed with these promises, they did not necessarily discard them (Schielke, 2008; 2009b; 2015: 13). In fact, 'promises of perfection are powerful as long as they are unfulfilled. Because they are unfulfilled, things can always be better' (Schielke, 2015: 23). Schielke's approach confirms the findings of other anthropologists who have emphasised the primacy of the experiential dimension of people's lives over the narratives they use to give meaning to their lives (Csordas, 1994; Jackson, 1996).
4. See also Mittermaier, 2019: 155–78. On the relationship between boredom, global capitalism and consumption-driven society see Anderson, 2004: 741; O'Neil, 2014; 2017; and Jeffrey, 2010. On boredom as an experience related to the perception that something better is available elsewhere see Svendsen, 2005: 42.
5. Musharbash presents her argument on boredom as a way of reconciling these two approaches (2007: 315). In philosophical terms, Sartre also famously provided a perspective that mediates between the two positions. Initially a champion of the notion that ennui is intrinsically part of human existence (1992), later in his life Sartre proposed of a more contextual – and more decisively Marxist – approach that linked the experience of boredom to specific socio-historical contradictions (2004). Some have also distinguished between existential and situational boredom (Svendsen, 2005). When considering the need to identify the political roots of boredom in contexts such as Libya one should also remember that this approach helps us to discard the racist and orientalist notion that the 'Orientals' bodies are lazy' (Said, 2014: 253).
6. 'Boredom is friend and foe at once of grand schemes, a shadow that follows them anywhere' (Schielke, 2015: 46).
7. Gender segregation is extremely strict in Libya, and can be found across social classes. Given that the world of Tripolitan women was scarcely accessible to me, I will concentrate mainly on male interlocutors, though in this chapter I will also comment on the condition of female informants.
8. The text of Gaddafi's speeches was kindly made available to me by the personnel of the World Centre for the Study and Research of the Green Book in Tripoli. The text was in digital form, and unnumbered, hence the absence of page numbers in my references to the speeches. The translation from Arabic is mine.
9. For a linguistic analysis of the term, and for a survey of its use in the scholarship, see Varisco, 2007: 270.
10. For a review of the vast literature on Libyan tribalism, and for an analysis of the role that tribal networks played in Libyan society both under Gaddafi and after the collapse of the *jamahiriya* see Cherstich, 2014a.
11. The figures presented in this paragraph were reported by the World Bank, and refer to data collected in 2010 (World Bank, 2015: xii). Similar statistics are found in Otman and Karlberg, 2007: 377–9. Though one can detect a degree of anti-Gaddafi bias in these sources, the data match my field observations. These surveys also show that during the last years of the Gaddafi government, the public sector – what I refer to as 'desk jobs' – accounted for the majority of the work activity, while employment in industry (mainly the oil sector) and agriculture constituted only ten per cent of the labour force.
12. Women comprised only 34 per cent of the total employed labour force (World Bank, 2015: xii; Otman and Karlberg, 2007: 377–9). On gender inequality and on the condition of Libyan women see Davis, 1987: 271–3 and Obeidi, 2001: 168–97.
13. Heroin and morphine derivatives could be purchased in the inner areas of the old city. However, these drugs mainly belonged to the deprived world of migrants – the only inhabitants of that part of town – and the government was not concerned with heroin consumption in the migrant

ghetto as long as it did not spread to other districts of the capital. As for alcohol, one could find *bokha* (home-made grappa) in the countryside. But none of my friends partook. Having tried it, I am inclined to believe that this had to do with the fact that *bokha* tasted like gasoline. Furthermore, it was common knowledge amongst my informants that, due to the high level of ethanol in home-made grappa, regular consumption could affect eyesight, potentially causing blindness. It was also common knowledge that people close to the government could acquire good quality alcohol from Malta or Tunisia without encountering any difficulties.

14. Parallels can be found in Honwana and De Boeck, 2005; Christiansen et al., 2006; and Frederiksen, 2016.
15. An anthropological analysis of the embodied quality of boredom is provided by O'Neil (2014; 2017).
16. On how, in situations of political alienation, subjects turn from protagonists of their own lives into spectators see Debord, 1994.
17. Deleuze was inspired by Spinoza's view of the dynamics of affect. For an analysis of the similarities and the differences between the two thinkers see the literature referenced in this paragraph.
18. In relation to this point, consider Adorno's view that, under oppressive power structures, subjects lose the capacity to spend their free time in truly autonomous ways. Conversely, for Adorno 'whenever behaviour in spare time is truly autonomous, determined by free people for themselves, boredom rarely figures' (1991: 192). See also Moran, 2003: 170. A thorough study of the relation between affect and domination in Egypt is provided by Malmström (2019).
19. This contrast becomes evident if one considers that Gaddafi famously surrounded himself with female bodyguards, the so-called 'Revolutionary Nuns'. I should also add that, notwithstanding the dynamics I have identified in this paragraph, I have met Tripolitan families who did not have strong political connections, and yet they encouraged their daughters to pursue whatever profession they preferred, even when their career choices exceeded traditional notions of femininity.
20. On the relationship between monotony and work see, amongst others, Thompson, 1967 and Mollona et al., 2009.
21. On waiting see Hage, 2009; Jeffrey, 2010; Honwana, 2014; and Elliot, 2016a.
22. Whenever I refer to immobility in the text I do so with a variety of connotations, including in a geographical sense. Gaddafi had dismantled the Libyan railway network in the aftermath of his revolution, thus forcing people to travel via aeroplane or car. Both airports and roads, however, were filled with military checkpoints that forced travellers to stop regularly during their travels in order to show their identification cards. On the relation between revolution, locomotion, and freedom of movement see Arendt, 1965: 32.
23. On the challenges to achieving social adulthood in contexts of economic uncertainties and youth unemployment see, amongst others, Honwana, 2014 and Johnson, 2018.
24. Di Nunzio provides a particularly illuminating analysis of how, in contexts similar to the one I am describing, people find ways 'of living through their condition of subjugation and marginality, while reinstating the possibility of being something other than their constraints' (Di Nunzio, 2019: 11).
25. On boredom as an experience that can push one to seek change, and, therefore, as a condition with a revolutionary potential, see Vaneigem, 2012: 74 and Moran, 2003: 173. Contrast this consideration with the famous situationist slogan 'Boredom is always counter-revolutionary'.
26. For a reading of the significance of Gaddafi's death in Libyan political perceptions see Cherstich, 2014b. For a more detailed ethnographic depiction of the aftermath of the 2011 revolution see Cherstich, forthcoming.
27. On the complex vicissitudes of political Islam in Libya see Pargeter, 2005; 2013: 164–7; 2016.
28. This is how militias had built their arsenals, in addition to receiving supplies from foreign powers.
29. On the relationship between boredom, despair, political disillusionment and violence, see Abbink and Van Kessel, 2005; Pratten, 2006; Musharbash, 2007: 313–14; and Weiss, 2009: 43, 201. For a critical approach to these notions, one that highlights how violent ways to kill time can stem not so much from boredom, but from the joy that one derives from consciously acting in self-contradictory manners see Verkaaik, 2004.
30. In some cases, the regional governments that have emerged after the revolution have hired the militias and have used them as an irregular army. In other cases, the militias have blackmailed

the governments and extorted money from them in order to fund their own activities. Either way, the source of this funding is always the local population, who is subjected to some form of taxation by the governments. This results in a curious situation where the money that is collected through taxes is often used to fund rival militias. In the desperate words of one my informants 'We are funding our own civil war!'

31. These important and path-breaking works have been unfairly accused of omitting the point of view of committed Muslims (Fadil and Fernando, 2015) while in fact they simply aim at showing that living a life, Muslim or otherwise, is a complex affair (Marsden and Retsikas, 2013: 8). Even still, it is important to remember that Muslims (Eickelman and Piscatori, 1996) and non-Muslims (Varisco, 2005) define Islam differently according to different historical circumstances. In this perspective, the approach of these anthropologists should be contextualised within current epistemological trends. I am referring particularly to a postmodernist diffidence towards grand schemes that continues to characterise the anthropological debate, and that, in my view and in the view of others (Kallinikos, 1997), is ultimately informed by specifically Western historical conditions. In short, I respectfully wonder whether it is the informants who explicitly describe their relationship with Islam as contradictory, or if it is the postmodernist ethnographers who project their own interest for ambiguities and contradictions onto the informants. Similar questions have been raised by Hirschkind, 2014.
32. Sometimes it is revolutionary narratives that help subjects to develop this approach, as shown by Porter in his work on the Yemeni revolution (Porter, 2016: 65). Porter, however, does not describe this process in terms of openness, but rather as a way to 'straitjacket the future' (Porter, 2016), and achieve freedom from uncertainty.
33. On the way in which rituals can help subjects to deal with their state of immobility see Johnson, 2018. Interestingly, according to thirteenth-century Sufi master Sharafuddin Maneri 'Sufism is ceaseless motion' (Maneri, 2010: 7): a set of mystical practices aimed at enabling a spiritual transition 'from stagnation to motion' (Maneri, 2010: 47). Similarly, Deleuze argues via Spinoza that in some forms of mysticism God is conceptualised as the ultimate source of intensity and vibrancy (Deleuze, 1978). From this perspective, the idea of 'being close to God' entails a particular kind of affection, one that injects human beings with dynamic energy and increases their capacity to move. With reference to this point, one might also consider the Aristotelian view of God as the primary cause of all motions: a concept that has been deployed in various strands of Islamic theology and philosophy (Nasseem, 1992).
34. I wish to thank Hélène Neveu Kringelbach, whose bibliographic suggestions proved invaluable for the writing of this chapter.

References

Abbink, J. and Van Kessel, I. (eds). 2005. *Vanguards or Vandals: Youth politics and conflict in Africa*. Leiden: Brill.
Achilli, L. 2015. *Palestinian Refugees and National Identity: Nationalism, politics and the everyday*. London: I. B. Tauris.
Adorno, T. 1991. 'Free time', in *The Culture Industry: Selected essays on mass culture*. London: Routledge, 187–97.
Adorno, T. 2005. *Minima Moralia: Reflections on a damaged life*. London: Verso.
Al-Werfalli, M. 2011. *Political Alienation in Libya*. Reading: Ithaca Press.
Anderson, B. 2004. 'Time-stilled space-slowed: How boredom matters'. *Geoforum*, 35(6): 739–54.
Anderson, L. 2014. *The State and Social Transformation in Tunisia and Libya, 1830–1980*. Princeton: Princeton University Press.
Arendt, A. 1965. *On Revolution*. London: Penguin.
Arendt, A. 1998. *The Human Condition*. Chicago: University of Chicago Press.
Badiou, A. 2003. *Saint Paul: The foundation of universalism*. Stanford, CA: Stanford University Press.
Bateson, G. 2000. *Steps to an Ecology of Mind*. Chicago: University of Chicago Press.
Baudelaire, C. 2006. *The Flowers of Evil*. Middletown, CT: Wesleyan University Press.
Benjamin, W. 1999. *The Arcades Project*. Cambridge, MA: Belknap Press.
Brown, K. 2008. 'All they understand is force: Debating culture in Operation Iraqi Freedom'. *American Anthropologist*, 110(4): 443–53.

Cherstich, I. 2014a. 'When tribesmen do not act tribal: Libyan tribalism as ideology (not as schizophrenia)'. *Middle East Critique*, 23(4): 405–21.

Cherstich, I. 2014b. 'The body of the colonel: caricature and incarnation in the Libyan Revolution', in Werbner, P., Webb, M. and Spellman-Poots, K. (eds), *The Political Aesthetics of Global Protest: The Arab spring and beyond*. Edinburgh: Edinburgh University Press, 93–120.

Cherstich, I. Forthcoming. 'Now I want the law! Libyans seeking non-state justice in the hope of state justice', *Middle East Law and Governance*.

Christiansen, C., Shroff, C., Utas, M. and Vigh, H. (eds). 2006. *Navigating Youth, Generating Adulthood: Social becoming in an African context*. Uppsala: Nordiska Afrikaninstitutet.

Conrad, P. 1997. 'It's boring: Notes on the meaning of boredom in everyday life'. *Qualitative Sociology*, 20(4): 465–75.

Csordas, T. (ed.). 1994. *Embodiment and Experience: The existential ground of culture and self*. Cambridge: Cambridge University Press.

Davis J. 1987. *Libyan Politics: Tribe and revolution*. London: I. B. Tauris.

Debord, G. 1994. *The Society of the Spectacle*. Princeton: Zone Books.

Deleuze, G. 1978. *Continuous Variation*. Seminar at the University of Paris-Vincennes St. Denis, translated by T. S. Murphy. https://deleuze.cla.purdue.edu/sites/default/files/pdf/lectures/en/Continuous%20Variation%2001%20%281969-11-30%29.pdf. Accessed 1 December 2020.

Deleuze, G. and Guattari, F. 1986a. *Anti-Oedipus: Capitalism and schizophrenia*. Minneapolis: University of Minnesota Press.

Deleuze, G. and Guattari, F. 1986b. *Kafka: Toward a minor literature*. Minneapolis: University of Minnesota Press.

Deleuze, G. and Guattari, F. 2004. *A Thousand Plateaus*. Minneapolis: University of Minnesota Press.

Di Nunzio, M. 2019. *The Act of Living: Street life, marginality and development in urban Ethiopia*. Ithaca, NY: Cornell University Press.

Duncan, P. 2015, *The Emotional Life of Postmodern Film: Affect theory's other*. London: Routledge.

Dunn, J. 1989. *Modern Revolutions: An introduction to the analysis of a political phenomenon*. Cambridge: Cambridge University Press.

Durham, D. 2000. 'Youth and the social imagination in Africa: Introduction to parts 1 and 2'. *Anthropological Quarterly*, 73(3): 113–20.

Egan, M. and Tabar, P. 2016. 'Bourdieu in Beirut: *Wasta*, the state and social reproduction in Lebanon'. *Middle East Critique*, 25(3): 249–70.

Eickelman, D. and Piscatori, A. 1996. *Muslim Politics*. Princeton: Princeton University Press.

Elliot, A. 2016a 'Paused subjects: Waiting for migration in North Africa'. *Time and Society*, 25(1): 102–16.

Elliot, A. 2016b. 'The makeup of destiny: Predestination and the labor of hope in a Moroccan emigrant town'. *American Ethnologist*, 43(3): 488–9.

Elliot, A. and Menin, L. 2018. 'For an anthropology of destiny'. *HAU: Journal of Ethnographic Theory*, 8(1–2): 292–9.

Fadil, N. and Fernando, M. 2015. 'Rediscovering the "everyday" Muslim: Notes on an anthropological divide'. *HAU: Journal of Ethnographic Theory*, 5(2): 59–88.

Frederiksen, M. 2016. *Young Men, Time and Boredom in the Republic of Georgia*. Philadelphia: Temple University Press.

Freydberg, B. 2017. *A Dark History of Modern Philosophy*. Bloomington: Indiana University Press.

Gaddafi, M. 1982. Speech delivered to the Students Revolutionary Committee on the eighteenth of March 1982. Tripoli: World Centre for the Study and Research of the Green Book.

Gaddafi, M. 1995. Speech delivered in the Multaqa al Tasawwuf al Islami al 'Alami on the sixteenth of the month of al Fateh 1995. Tripoli: World Centre for the Study and Research of the Green Book.

Gaddafi, M. 2005. *The Green Book*. Tripoli: World Centre for the Study and Research of the Green Book.

Goodstein, E. 2005. *Experience without Qualities: Boredom and modernity*. Stanford, CA: Stanford University Press.

Graber, D. 2011. *Revolutions in Reverse: Essays on politics, violence, art and imagination*. Oakland, CA: AK Press.

Hage, G. 2009. *Waiting*. Melbourne: Melbourne University Press.

Healy, S. D. 1984. *Boredom, Self and Culture*. London: Rutherford.

Heidegger, M. 1995. *The Fundamental Concepts of Metaphysics: World, finitude, solitude.* Bloomington: Indiana University Press.

Hirschkind, C. 2014. 'Everyday Islam: Commentary by Charles Hirschkind'. *Cultural Anthropology.* https://journal.culanth.org/index.php/ca/everyday-islam-charles-hirschkind. Accessed 21 December 2020.

Holbraad, M. 2014. 'Revolución o muerte: Self-sacrifice and the ontology of Cuban Revolution'. *Ethnos*, 79(3): 365–87.

Honwana, A. 2014. 'Waithood: Youth transitions and social change', in Foeken, D., Dietz, T., De Hann, L. and Johnson, L. (eds), *Development and Equity: An interdisciplinary exploration by ten scholars from Africa, Asia and Latin America.* Leiden: Brill, 28–40.

Honwana, A. and De Boeck, F. (eds). 2005. *Makers and Breakers: Children and youth in postcolonial Africa.* Oxford: James Currey.

Jackson, M. 1996. 'Introduction: Phenomenology, radical empiricism and anthropological critique', in Jackson, M. (ed.), *Things as They Are: New directions in phenomenological anthropology.* Bloomington: Indiana University Press, 1–50.

Jeffrey, C. 2010. *Timepass: Youth, class and the politics of waiting in India.* Stanford, CA: Stanford University Press.

Johnson, J. 2018. 'Feminine futures: Female initiation and aspiration in matrilineal Malawi'. *Journal of the Royal Anthropological Institute*, 24: 786–803.

Kallinikos, J. 1997. 'Classic review: Science, knowledge and society: The postmodern condition revisited'. *Organisation*, 4(1): 114–29.

Kierkegaard, S. 1995. 'Either/or: A fragment of life', in Hong, H. V. and Hong, E. H. (eds), *The Essential Kierkegaard.* Princeton: Princeton University Press, 37–66.

Klapp, O. 1986. *Overload and Boredom: Essays on the quality of life in the information society.* New York: Greenwood.

Lackner, H. 2016. '*Wasta*: Is it such a bad thing? An anthropological perspective', in Ramedy, M. (ed.), *The Political Economy of Wasta: Use and abuse of social capital networking.* London: Springer, 33–46.

Lefebvre, H. 2011. *Introduction to Modernity.* London: Verso.

Legg, G. 2018. *Northern Ireland and the Politics of Boredom: Conflict, capital and culture.* Manchester: Manchester University Press.

Mains, D. 2012. *Hope is Cut: Youth, unemployment, and the future in urban Ethiopia.* Philadelphia: Temple University Press.

Malmström, M. F. 2019. *The Streets are Talking to Me: Affective fragments in Sisi's Egypt.* Berkeley: University of California Press.

Maneri, S. 2010. *Letters from a Sufi Teacher.* Mountain View, CA: Golden Elixir Press.

Marlovits, J. 2013. 'Give me slack: Depression, alertness and laziness in Seattle'. *Anthropology of Consciousness*, 24(2): 137–57.

Marsden, M. 2005. *Living Islam: Muslim religious experience in Pakistan's north-west frontier.* Cambridge: Cambridge University Press.

Marsden, M. 2007. 'All male sonic gatherings, Islamic reform, and masculinity in northern Pakistan'. *American Ethnologist*, 34(3): 473–90.

Marsden, M. 2010. 'A tour not so grand: Mobile Muslims in northern Pakistan', in Osella, F. and Soares, B. (eds) *Islam, Politics, Anthropology.* Malden, MA and Oxford: Wiley-Blackwell and the Royal Anthropological Institute, 54–71.

Marsden, M. and Retsikas, K. 2013. 'Introduction', in Marsden, M. and Retsikas, K. (eds), *Articulating Islam: Anthropological approaches to Muslim worlds.* London: Springer, 1–32.

Masquelier, F. A. 2013. 'Teatime: Boredom and the temporalities of young men in Niger'. *Africa*, 83: 470–91.

Massumi, B. 2004. 'Notes on the translation and acknowledgement', in Deleuze, G. and Guattari, F., *A Thousand Plateaus: Capitalism and schizophrenia.* London: Continuum, xvi–xix.

Massumi, B. 2015. *The Politics of Affect.* Hoboken, NJ: Wiley.

Mittermeier, A. 2019. *Giving to God: Islamic Charity in Revolutionary Times.* Berkeley: University of California Press.

Mollona, M., De Neve, G. and Parry, J. (eds). 2009. *Industrial Work and Life: An anthropological reader.* Oxford: Berg.

Moran, J. 2003. 'Benjamin and boredom'. *Critical Quarterly*, 45(1–2): 168–81.

Musharbash, Y. 2007. 'Boredom, time, and modernity: An example from aboriginal Australia'. *American Anthropologist*, 109(2): 307–17.
Nasseem, Z. B. 1992. 'Motion in Muslim Peripatetic school: Brief exposition and echo of Al-Ghazzali's critique'. *Islamic Studies*, 31(4): 451–61.
Negri, A. 2003. *The Savage Anomaly: The power of Spinoza's metaphysics and politics*. Minneapolis: University of Minnesota Press.
Obeidi, A. 2001. *Political Culture in Libya*. Richmond: Routledge Curzon.
O'Neil, B. 2014. 'Cast aside: Boredom, downward mobility, and homelessness in post-communist Bucharest'. *Cultural Anthropology*, 29(1): 8–31.
O'Neil, B. 2017. *The Space of Boredom: Homelessness in the slowing global order*. Durham, NC: Duke University Press.
Osella, F. and Soares, B. 2010. 'Islam, politics, anthropology', in Osella, F. and Soares, B. (eds), *Islam, Politics, Anthropology*. Malden, MA and Oxford: Wiley-Blackwell and the Royal Anthropological Institute, 1–22.
Otman, W. and Karlberg, E. 2007. *The Libyan Economy: Economic diversification and international repositioning*. New York: Springer.
Pargeter, A. 2005. 'Political Islam in Libya'. *Terrorism Monitor*, 3(6). The Jamestown Foundation. https://jamestown.org/program/political-islam-in-libya-2/. Accessed 14 December 2020.
Pargeter, A. 2013. *Libya: The rise and fall of Qaddafi*. New Haven, CT: Yale University Press.
Pargeter, A. 2016. *Return to the Shadows: The Muslim Brotherhood and An-Nahda since the Arab Spring*. London: Saqi Books.
Pinto, P. 2005. 'Bodily mediation: Self, value and experience in Syrian Sufism', in Heiss, J. (ed.), *Veränderung und Stabilität – Normen und Werte in Islamischen Gesellschaften*. Vienna: Verlag der Österreichischen Akademie der Wissenschaften, 201–24.
Pinto, P. 2010. 'The anthropologist and the initiated: Reflections on the ethnography of mystical experience amongst the Sufis of Aleppo, Syria'. *Social Compass*, 57(4): 464–78.
Porter, R. 2016. 'Tricking time, overthrowing a regime: Reining in the future in the Yemeni youth revolution'. *Cambridge Journal of Anthropology*, 34(1): 58–71.
Pratten, D. 2006. 'The politics of vigilance in south-eastern Nigeria'. *Development and Change*, 37(1): 707–34.
Ralph, M. 2008. 'Killing time'. *Social Text*, 26(4): 1–29.
Ruddick, S. 2010. 'The politics of affect: Spinoza in the work of Negri and Deleuze'. *Theory, Culture and Society*, 27(4): 21–45.
Sahlins, M. 1972. *Stone Age Economics*. Chicago: Aldine-Atherton.
Said, E. 2014. *Orientalism*. New York: Vintage Books.
Sartre, J.-P. 1992. *Being and Nothingness*. New York: Washington Square Press.
Sartre, J.-P. 2004. *Critique of the Dialectic Reason: The intelligibility of history*. London: Verso.
Schielke, S. 2008. 'Boredom and despair in rural Egypt'. *Contemporary Islam*, 28(2): 251–70.
Schielke, S. 2009a. 'Being good in Ramadan: Ambivalence, fragmentation and the moral self in the lives of young Egyptians'. *Journal of the Royal Anthropological Institute*, 15: S24–S40.
Schielke, S. 2009b. 'Ambivalent commitments: Troubles of morality, religiosity and aspiration among young Egyptians'. *Journal of Religion in Africa*, 39: 158–85.
Schielke, S. 2015. *Egypt in the Future Tense: Hope, frustration and ambivalence before and after 2011*. Indianapolis: Indiana University Press.
Schielke, S. and Debevec, L. 2012. 'Introduction', in Schielke, S. and Debevec, L. (eds), *Ordinary Lives and Grand Schemes: An anthropology of everyday religion*. New York: Berghahn, 1–16.
Spacks, P. M. 1996. *Boredom: The literary history of a state of mind*. Chicago: University of Chicago Press.
Spivak, G. 2013. *An Aesthetic Education in the Era of Globalization*. Cambridge, MA: Harvard University Press.
Svendsen, L. 2005. *A Philosophy of Boredom*. London: Reaktion Books.
Thompson, E. P. 1967. 'Time, work-discipline and industrial capitalism'. *Past and Present*, 38: 56–97.
Toohey, P. 2011. *Boredom: A lively history*. New Haven, CT: Yale University Press.
Vaneigem, R. 2012. *The Revolution of Everyday Life*. Oakland, CA: PM Press.
Varisco, D. M. 2005. *Islam Obscured: The rhetoric of anthropological representations*. New York: Palgrave Macmillan.
Varisco, D. M. 2007. *Reading Orientalism: Said and the unsaid*. Seattle: University of Washington Press.

Verkaaik, O. 2004. *Migrants and Militants: Fun and urban violence in Pakistan*. Princeton: Princeton University Press.
Weiss, B. 2009. *Street Dreams and Hip Hop Barbershops: Global fantasy in urban Tanzania*. Bloomington: Indiana University Press.
World Bank. 2015. *Labor Market Dynamics in Libya*. Washington, DC: World Bank.

4
Religious transformations after the 1979 Iranian Revolution: from Imam Husein as exemplar back to intercessor

Mary Elaine Hegland

Introduction

During the Iranian revolutionary period of 1978–9, many Iranians began placing more importance on Shiʻa Islam, as some spokespersons interpreted this religion as a model for struggling against tyranny and injustice.[1] Specifically, several religious leaders had reinterpreted the meaning of Imam Husein's martyrdom at Karbala (in present-day Iraq) in 680 CE. Typically, Shiʻa Muslims saw his sacrifice as endearing him to God to the extent that he could serve as an intermediary to help them with problems in this world and to attain redemption for the next, much as many Catholics turn to Catholic saints and shrines. The new meaning of Imam Husein's martyrdom – as providing an example to emulate of struggle against tyranny and the will to sacrifice for the sake of justice for believers – spread during the revolutionary upheaval. In my article 'Two images of Husain: Accommodation and revolution in an Iranian village' (Hegland, 1983a), I analysed the two interpretations of the Karbala paradigm and their implications for believers' religious and political approaches. In this chapter I revisit the findings of the 1983 article to investigate the direction of change in the relative commitment to these two interpretations since the 1979 Revolution as well as the attention people now confer on Shiʻa Islam in general. Fieldwork and discussion with interlocutors support the conclusion that the intercession interpretation has again gained ascendance over the exemplar meaning. People participate in rituals and make donations hoping for favour from Imam Husein and the other saints. Further, for very many Iranians, especially the younger ones, Shi'a Islam does not hold as significant a place in their lives. According to my field research up until spring 2018 and many conversations and WhatsApp calls with people in the Shiraz and Tehran areas since then, very many Iranians now feel extremely unhappy about the Islamic Republic of Iran government and society in spite of early enthusiastic support for the Revolution (see Hegland, 2022).

In 1978 I flew to Iran to conduct anthropological field research for a PhD in social-cultural anthropology. Although I had not prepared to conduct fieldwork during a revolution, I was fortuitously able to become a participant observer in the Iranian revolutionary period that culminated in the downfall of the Pahlavi government on 11 February 1979. As I had travelled to Iran in June 1978 and soon settled in Aliabad, I lived in this village for about six months before the day of Revolution, building relationships, listening to complaints about issues in the past and current conditions, and observing the build-up of revolutionary fervour among many of my friends. After the Revolution, I was able to stay in Aliabad for another ten months. In addition, seven more research trips to Aliabad and nearby Shiraz between 2003 and 2018 have allowed me to follow events, economic, social, cultural, and religious changes, and people's evolving evaluations and analyses of post-Revolution developments.

In the following paragraphs, I present information about the village of Aliabad and the sources of local people's dissatisfaction and motivations for involvement in the revolutionary movement. I provide a condensation of the 1983 article, explaining the reinterpretation of the central Shi'a Muslim event – the martyrdom of Imam Husein in 680 CE – as a main framework for the revolutionary movement and the development of a revolutionary self that was presented as the means to eliminate the causes of people's dissatisfaction. During the revolutionary period, the meaning of the 680 CE martyrdom of Shi'a Islam's central figure, Imam Husein, changed. From seeing him as a powerful intermediary to God who can assist believers with their problems and hopes for this world and the next, he became an exemplar demonstrating how believers can follow his example of self-sacrifice for the good of religion and society. According to this new meaning, believers can achieve redemption through that path as well as solve shortcomings and problems through their own actions (Hegland, 1983a; 1983b).

Providing a background, I discuss the revolutionary period and summarise major post-Revolution economic, social and cultural changes, some of them partly brought about by the Revolution and subsequent

Islamic Republic government, and some resulting from other influences. Finally, I demonstrate the return of emphasis on rituals, vows, and donations and the implications of Imam Husein's martyrdom that again turn him and other saints into powerful intercessors between believers and God.[2]

In general, other than hoping for assistance from the saints, many Iranians, in Aliabad and elsewhere, have been losing interest in Islam. Some have been giving attention to Christianity, Zoroastrianism, Sufism, and pre-Islamic Persian history.

Aliabad in 1978

When I first arrived in Aliabad, the village had about 3,000 residents. Only two or three decades earlier, most men had been sharecroppers and/or low-level itinerant traders. Because of the 1962 land reform and the burgeoning population, by 1978 agriculture as a way of life was declining. Some older men worked for the largest landowner as cultivators and vineyard tenders. Some earned money from house construction and repair. Several shopkeepers provided food supplies and other simple necessities for the local population; other men worked as itinerant traders and shopkeepers in rural areas further out. A few more provided services, such as public bath attendant, local cleric, and making low, round platforms for rolling out dough for the round, flat bread.

Women preserved, prepared, and served food; cared for animals in their courtyards and managed their products; tended children; did housework; and maintained relations with relatives and neighbours. With one exception, only women who did not have a man to support them worked outside their own homes: three worked in the kindergarten, and another cooked for the kindergarten, another acted as midwife and did other odd jobs. A widow helped some women with baking bread in return for bread and a few coins. Public education started with kindergarten and continued through fifth grade, with boys and girls studying together.

In the decade before the Revolution, villagers were increasingly finding jobs outside of Aliabad. The population was growing dramatically, and the 1962 land reform had not provided cultivators with sufficient land to earn their subsistence from agriculture. Younger men found jobs in factories, construction, service, shops and businesses in Shiraz, and in government as the police and the military.

Pre-revolution sources of dissatisfaction

Economic complaints

Work opportunities for men and high school studies for families who could afford it, took young men outside of Aliabad. They could compare the living standards of their own families with those of upper middle classes elsewhere. A road and a new bus line provided cheap transportation to and from Shiraz for Aliabad people's shopping, errands, visits to relatives, and pilgrimages to shrines in the city. More people now became dissatisfied with their relative deprivation and minimal standards of living in the village and began to want and expect more.

Political complaints

Aliabad residents had long suffered from political repression. During the time of the absentee landlords, the Qavams, sharecroppers and their families lived precarious lives under the control of the landlord's local representatives, the *kadkhodas*. With the backing of the Qavams, who owned large areas of land in southwestern Iran, they held power much like little shahs. After the overthrow of the elected prime minister, Dr Mohammad Mossadeq, in the 1953 coup engineered by Britain and the USA, the returning Shah's forces punished local Mossadeq supporters (see Abrahamian, 2015; Amirani, 2019; De Bellaigue, 2013; Katouzian, 1990; Kinzer, 2008; Rahnema, 2014). When sharecroppers staged a strike against the Qavam landlord in order to obtain a larger share of the harvest, they were brutally put down; many sharecroppers lost their rights to agricultural land.

In the early 1960s, the Qavams learned about the upcoming land reform in Iran because of their in-law relations with Mohammad Reza Shah. They secretly sold half of Aliabad land to their main supporter in Aliabad. During the Iranian land reform, agricultural land was to be divided among those already cultivating it. With the implementation of land reform in Aliabad in 1962, sharecroppers learned that half of the village land – the best, irrigable areas, had already been sold. Other corrupt practices also took place during the land reform process. About this and other corrupt practices, the sharecroppers and those who had lost agricultural rights due to the strike were furious. The ensuing violent battle between the locals and the landlord and his faction lasted a year. Finally, the landlord was able to enlist the assistance of Qavam, who arranged for government forces to quell the local uprising violently.

The landlord and his closest confederates moved into Shiraz to escape the rancour of the locals. His brother became head of the village, and his close supporters gained the other governmental village offices. Villagers learned that they could do nothing against the power and authority of the two brothers who had the backing of the nearby gendarmerie station. If villagers went to the gendarmes to complain about their treatment, such as being cheated out of pay for work, the gendarmes beat and tortured them. Helpless in the face of the local authorities, people could not protect their economic interests.[3]

Cultural and religious complaints

I do not remember hearing cultural or religious complaints early in my visit. The local *akhund* (low-ranking cleric, *mullah*) surely felt dissatisfied with inappropriate behaviour and dress and Western cultural and political influences in Iran, but others did not talk about these issues until they became involved with the revolutionary movement through leaflets, tapes, mosque sermons, and religious gatherings and protests in Shiraz.

The new Shi'a Muslim framework and the revolutionary movement

As other forms of political organisation were prevented, a religious framework remained as the only means of channelling growing resentment. At the same time, Shi'a Muslim clerical networks had been organising and undertaking outreach work in reaction to the Pahlavi regime's actions, which had been aimed at cutting back on the clerics' power and wealth and modernising and westernising Iranian society.

Fliers, tapes, graffiti, talks by clerics in the mosques, and conversations among friends, relatives, and colleagues spread the resistant stance of Ayatollah Khomeini from his exile in France. Many other clerics nevertheless remained quiet, and some continued to support the Pahlavi regime. The activist stance of lay theologian, Ali Shariati, spread through tapes and discussions. One of my neighbours in Aliabad, a young *seyyid*[4] kindergarten teacher, excitedly played his tape, *Fatimeh Fatimeh Ast* ('Fatimeh is Fatimeh'), about the daughter of the Prophet Mohammad and mother of the two *imams*,[5] Hassan and Hossein, and their sister, Zeinab. Ali Shariati had studied at the Sorbonne. He combined philosophies he encountered there with Shi'a Muslim theologies and historical myths to develop a new interpretation of the meaning of the main

Shi'a event, presented by him as the original and real interpretation (Abrahamian, 1982).

This call to action emerging from urban religious elites implied a new, activist expectation for Shi'a Muslim believers' personhood, character, and place in the world. From the traditional meaning of Imam Husein's martyrdom as intercessor between God and believers, and for believers to depend for help on him and the other saints, Shi'a Muslims now turned Imam Husein into an exemplar; through his example, they could gain a sense of self-reliance, personal power and worth, capability and personal efficacy; they could learn to pursue goals actively and directly; and to cooperate with others to resist unjust authority and to make a better world (see 1983a).[6]

This combination of Shi'ism and western philosophies to develop a new perspective on Shi'a Islam's central myth – the martyrdom of Imam Husein – appealed to a wide spectrum of Iranians: the networks of clerics at various levels; the religious bazaar merchants and traders; and regular believers long accustomed to commemorating the martyrdom of Imam Husein as a means of courting his favour to request his help in this world and the next. It appealed to the many educated professionals, high school and university students, teachers and professors, that is, the more modernised, westernised middle classes. They could interpret the story of the martyrdom of Imam Husein and his supporters and the enslavement of his sister Zeinab and the other womenfolk after the battle of Karbala in 680 CE as a struggle for religion and justice. Of course, as I observed in Aliabad, people could entertain multiple motivations for active involvement in the movement, such as social contacts, desires to enjoy outings, the excitement and euphoria of demonstrations, and self-interest (see Hegland 1983a; 1983b; 1987a; 1987b; 1990; 1991; 2014.).

The symbolic complex of Karbala became the umbrella under which large sectors of the Iranian population could unite, under the leadership of the Shi'a clerics, to oppose Mohammad Reza Shah's government successfully. Pious women were called to action through the examples of Zeinab and Fatemeh. Many educated, professional women and students joined because of the progressive promise of independence, self-assertion, and freedom in the umbrella ideology of resistance to the Shah's government. Whether wishing for more social justice and participatory politics, hoping their commemorative involvement would bring the favour of Imam Husein for intermediation, and/or wanting to follow his example of standing up for justice, millions of Iranians could all come together under this encompassing framework.

During the revolutionary period, people developed a sense of community. Helping others in the movement became mainstream behaviour and was especially apparent during the many marches against the Shah's government which was viewed by protestors as illegitimate, corrupt and unjust.

The sense of euphoric self-empowerment, confidence, determination and unity was apparent when I interviewed participants about their experiences in revolutionary marches and demonstrations. The Revolution brought millions out on the streets to protest – including many Aliabad people, both men and women, who went into Shiraz for marches and then formed nightly protest marches in Aliabad. The commemorative processions in honour of Imam Husein in December 1978 transformed from mourning into protest and marked the turning point of the Revolution. The dramatic, audacious activities throughout the country led to the downfall of the Shah's government on 11 February 1979.

What happens to a new, outspoken, self-reliant, empowered, determined, confident, cooperative sense of selfhood, highly appropriate during a revolutionary movement against a powerful armed government that is backed by an even more powerful armed government, when the government is overthrown and the backing government expelled from the country? Immediately after the 11 February 1979 Revolution, a main fear of the revolutionary population was that the US would replicate the coup against Prime Minister Mossadeq in 1953. Continuing marches and demonstrations expressed a resolve and determination to oppose such a possibility. The referendum for the Islamic Republic government and the new constitution might be seen as a continuation of resistance against the Shah's government and its US backers. Then Iraq attacked Iran, and for the eight-year war, Iraq – supported by the US – became the main enemy of the Revolution and the Islamic Republic.

With the US and Israeli pressure against Iran's development of atomic power, the right to do so became a focus of protest marches in Iran. Israel's threats, US sanctions, the Trump administration's withdrawal from the nuclear agreement, and, most recently, the coronavirus pandemic (Schwartz and Gölz, 2020) all provided the government occasions to encourage demonstrations of resistance and proclamations of self-reliance and confidence.

With the exception of the Iraq–Iran War (1980–8), however, calls for determined resistance and confident, unified, cooperative activism against these diverse, scattered foci were never as immediate, unifying, and emotionally involving as resistance against the Pahlavi Shah's government. What were now needed were acquiescent, loyal, obedient, pious followers rather than self-empowered, self-reliant, self-confident, outspoken individuals cooperating with others to overthrow an unjust system.

After the Islamic Republic's victory at the polls, it soon embarked on a brutal crackdown of its opponents through imprisonment, torture and execution. This divided the population into those who accepted these actions due to loyalty, religiosity, and/or self-interest; those who wisely thought it best to stay away from politics as much as possible; and those believing the Islamic government personnel to be as bad or much worse than the Shah's repressive personnel had been. Even worse than the Shah's *SAVAK*, the new secret police, the Revolutionary Guards, and the morality guards, the *Basij* (the paramilitary group with both men's and women's sections) stood ready to punish even minor infractions and disobedience of rules of dress and behaviour severely. They even invaded family and personal space to force compliance with 'Islamic' rules. With some ups and downs, regulations controlling individuals became more restrictive in practically all areas of life. Many more people were imprisoned and executed than had been during the Shah's regime.

Forty years after the event: changes in Aliabad after the revolution

Unfortunately, I was not able to return to Aliabad for 23 years following my departure in mid-December 1979 and was unable to communicate much with friends there. In September 2003, I was able to visit for two weeks. By then, the former village of Aliabad and its residents had seen tremendous change and transformation. It was no longer a small, quiet rural village of some 3,000 people mainly living behind a high village wall, with four towers on each corner and narrow alleyways between the mud brick walls of courtyards.

Aliabad evolved into an urban-like suburb and became formally incorporated into the city of Shiraz several years ago. The population is now at least 15,000, increased by an influx of many Afghans and people from distant areas who had taken advantage of the jobs available before the economic downturn that started about a decade ago. Aliabad had become a busy town, boasting all types of shops and business. On the approach towards Aliabad from Shiraz, businesses line the highway on both sides on what used to be agricultural land. People live in urban-type homes of fired brick with tiled courtyards and have modern kitchens, shower rooms and computers. Some people built homes of several storeys, and some investors constructed multistorey apartment buildings. By 2016, iPhones were ubiquitous and young and middle-aged people were tied to a screen when not otherwise occupied. The village walls disappeared decades ago. The settlement has increased tremendously in size, taking up much of the former agricultural land. Agriculture has almost entirely disappeared, and men are working in services, shops and businesses.

In the last decade, the formerly lucrative real estate businesses, shops other than grocery stores, construction, and factory work have all declined with the economic downturn. Unemployment is rife, and people complain that young men do not have the finances or jobs to enable them to get married (see Hashemi, 2020; Hegland, 2021; Khosrovi, 2017). The sanctions, corruption and government mismanagement have brought about financial hardships for nearly everybody, whether they live in Aliabad or in Shiraz, as they have for people all over Iran – all the more since US President Trump pulled out of the nuclear agreement and imposed even more sanctions (see Moaveni and Tahmasebi, 2021; Osanloo, 2020; and Shahrokni, 2020). All of these great economic, political and socio-cultural changes have had an impact on local religious life as well, and these are the focus of this chapter.

Greater amounts of time, attention, and funds for religious spaces, rituals, and donations

Pilgrimages, shrine visitations, donations and other shows of attention and devotion to the Karbala martyrs and their descendants have, however, permeated social life far more than the upheavals of national and international politics. During the revolutionary period, people continued to honour the Shi'a saints while the calls to follow Imam Husein's example of fighting against injustice secured much more public attention. At present, while the Islamic government's elicitations of support receive attention, a turn to Imam Husein and the other saints for intercession and help in need is far more pervasive in people's lives. The agents of the Islamic Republic encourage this tendency by providing sizeable funds for rebuilding and expanding shrines and by sponsoring pilgrimages, Shi'a rituals, and religious activities. The people themselves I observed during my seven research trips to Aliabad and Shiraz in the twenty-first century seemed glad to take advantage of opportunities to honour the saints and had many reasons to seek their sympathy and intermediation.

Aliabad religious rituals in 1978–9

Religious rituals for men included mosque attendance, mourning for the deceased in homes, and *Moharram* processions in the alleyways.[7] In the 1970s, Friday services were held at the mosque. To bury the dead, men marched out to the cemeteries behind the coffin for the graveside ritual. For *Moharram* processions men generally convened at the mosque before marching in the alleyways around the village, shouting commemorative couplets while self-flagellating.

Women were not allowed to attend burials at the cemetery. They could mourn only in a home space separate from mourning men. Women did not go to the mosque and had no *Moharram* rituals. On Thursday afternoons, they went to the cemeteries to remember the dead and pray for their souls. They might serve fruit or sweets to others, in the hope that they also would pray for their departed relatives. Several women hosted weekly women's gatherings led by a local male reciter of *Moharram* stories in their homes. In 1978, two women from the Zahra School in Shiraz had begun to come to the home of a *seyyid* woman once a week to teach about religion.

A few wealthy men in the village held religious rituals in their homes during *Moharram* and provided evening meals in their homes to break the *Ramazan* fast.[8] Several people hosted meals for men at noon following the processions commemorating the third day after the martyrdom of Imam Husein and his followers.

More religious ritual venues

Since 1979, more venues for religious activities have been developed. A *Huseiniyyeh* – a structure for mourning ceremonies for Imam Husein and his followers – was built by one of the wealthy Aliabad traders in the name of his son, who had been killed in the 1980–8 Iran–Iraq War. This large building with a spacious basement is also used for other religious activities – prayers, Friday religious services, women's Quran classes, meals donated during the month of fasting, and mourning ceremonies for the deceased. During large gatherings, women use the basement and men the upper floor. Three other shrines have been built or rebuilt, and another large building has been constructed for religious activities.

The family of the richest man in Aliabad – brother to Qavam's main ally – who had all moved to Shiraz or elsewhere, built a large structure on the site of their previous home in the village for rituals and gatherings.

Funeral services for residents or Aliabad people who have moved to Shiraz are frequently held there. The main mosque has been rebuilt at least twice since the Revolution and is now a large (although incomplete) structure with a spacious basement and courtyard. Both graveyards have been further developed. One has a high wall around it and many trees have been planted, turning it into a pleasant shady green area. Buildings for washing bodies are located close to each of the two main graveyards. A seminary has been established, although as far as I know, only men from outlying areas attend classes there. Women are not allowed inside the seminary, I was told.

Throughout Iran, the government has been building larger, more extravagant shrines to replace older shrines and has enlarged the important shrines throughout the country, such as the shrine of Imam Reza in Mashhad and Shah Cheraq in Shiraz. In some cases, rooms are provided for overnight stays of families, or for women who want to remain at the shrine overnight to give greater attention to the saint. Older people have become more involved in visiting shrines in Aliabad, Shiraz, other cities in Iran – Mashhad and Qom especially – and travel to Shi'a shrines in Iraq – Karbala and Najaf – and Syria, and to Mecca and Medina in far greater numbers and more often than before the Revolution.

Proliferating rituals

Shrines and religious rituals in Iran are flourishing. Many more rituals are held in Aliabad than before the Revolution, with much greater expenditure and much greater numbers of participants. Part of the reason for the greater numbers of participants is the huge population growth that had begun even in the 1960s and 1970s, but with the push for more births during the 1980–8 Iran–Iraq War, the numbers grew even greater.

Aliabad's expanded population, both those who live in the settlement and those who have moved into Shiraz or elsewhere, attend mourning ceremonies in large numbers. Irrespective of attitudes about religion and politics, people view coming to the communal ceremonies to mourn and pray for the souls of the dead as an obligation and sign of community membership. (I do not know what will happen after the anti-regime uprising that began in fall of 2022.)

Government personnel and organisations, such as the local *akhund*s, the local offices of government propaganda, the village council members, the *Basij* and the Revolutionary Guards – the *Pasdaran* – and other local government employees hold many rituals in public religious buildings, organise trips to shrines, and help advertise the great number of women's rituals, such as Quran classes, readings and mourning rituals for the Karbala saints. The migration of people from more outlying areas has also caused the Aliabad population to grow tremendously. In general, these newcomers have less global attitudes and do not have the middle-class advantages enjoyed by many long-time Aliabad families. Many of these people attend Aliabad Shi'a Muslim religious rituals, such as *Moharram* mourning rituals and evening dinners to break the fast during *Ramazan*, along with some older Aliabad people. The number of religious rituals in Aliabad has increased to such an extent that especially during the months of mourning for the Karbala martyrs, women can choose to attend some five rituals a day, some held in public places and others in private homes open to all who want to attend.

Before the Revolution, high school students took classes in Arabic language and Islam. Now Shi'a rituals have been added to the curriculum. Boys practise self-flagellation while chanting mourning couplets. During *Moharram*, ideally the entire country becomes a site of mourning and honouring of the Karbala martyrs.

Women's rituals

Another dramatic change in religious practice has been the proliferating participation of Aliabad women in religious activities and religious rituals. Before the Revolution, they did not have many religious opportunities. Even mosque attendance was not possible; only a very few elderly, extremely pious women attended evening prayers and Friday noon prayer. Younger women knew that people would judge them as parading in front of men even if they were going to the mosque. During *Moharram* processions, only a few younger girls and even fewer women sat on the flat roofs, well covered and back from the edges to maintain modesty, or they might cling to house walls to watch the chanting, self-flagellating men pass by.

Now every religious space includes areas for women, either on a different floor, different rooms, or behind curtains. Usually even more women attend gatherings in public spaces than men. Women more recently came into such opportunities and also are not occupied by work outside of the home as are men. In addition, women hold their own numerous home-based rituals for family, relatives, friends, and neighbours and for all who wish to come. Men do not have comparable home rituals.

Most women who have been Aliabad residents from long ago do not take part in rituals in public spaces. They sometimes say that the newcomers participate in those rituals for the sake of the provided food.

Rather, middle-aged women hold their own rituals in their own homes. When I go to public rituals, I see very few Aliabad women I know, except for a few elderly men and women and of course religious and political leaders and office holders.

Extravagant religious rituals

Yet another great change in religious practices has been the relative extravagance, the spending of much greater amounts of money for rituals, including for food provided for mourning services in mosques. Dinners and sometimes breakfasts are served at the mosques and shrines during *Moharram* and *Ramazan*. For the greater number of mourning gatherings now held, a packaged drink and a packaged cake are handed out in addition to tea. Even at women's home-based rituals, in addition to tea, fruit, packaged drinks, and sweets are served. The materialism, conspicuous consumption, and competition visible during wedding ceremonies, and in dress, make-up, hair styles, homes and cars that have developed in Aliabad since the revolutionary period are also apparent during religious rituals and gatherings.

Many people donate resources for meals and hospitality at rituals, both in public places and in homes. People comment that during important religious months, no poor people have to go hungry. One can always eat at the public religious sites, and, in Shiraz, get good meals during important days on the religious calendar – which are many. Sadly, during the last few years since US President Trump withdrew from the nuclear agreement and imposed even greater sanctions on Iran, followed by the recent economic problems arising from the coronavirus pandemic, such donations from individuals – so helpful in the face of increasing food insecurity – have been diminishing.

Aliabad people have donated in other ways for religious purposes as well. Wealthy people fund the renovation of shrines. A person may buy chains for self-flagellation, drums, lights, and placards to carry in religious processions or pay for hired horses and camels and pay the actors for *Moharram* processions. People may buy hangings, photos, paintings, banners, and other paraphernalia to decorate mosques and shrines during *Moharram* before being carried out with the processions. People spend a great deal of money for pilgrimages, go on the *hajj* to Mecca, and may even join the walking march of thousands to Karbala commemorating *Arbaʿeen* – the 40th day after Imam Husein's martyrdom (Rahimi, 2019; Szanto, 2020; forthcoming).[9]

Imam Husein: from exemplar back to intercessor

During the revolutionary period forty years ago, clerics and revolutionary activists taught a different interpretation of Imam Husein's martyrdom. Rather than seeing his sacrifice as making him God's beloved so that his pleas on the part of believers would be efficacious (Betteridge, 1985; 2001), people were encouraged to see his sacrifice as an example for others to follow. Rather than redemption and the granting of wishes through the intermediation of the powerful figure of Imam Husein, people were encouraged to follow his example by being self-sufficient and becoming active, confident, and selfless in the pursuit of justice (Hegland, 1983a).

In recent years, however, the overwhelming attention paid to donations for religious purposes has become most noticeable in Aliabad. All of these buildings, meals, and other donations are given by people, usually of the older generation, who hope for assistance from the saints or to thank them for assistance given. Imam Husein and the other martyrs of Karbala as well as the descendants of the Imams have again taken positions as powerful intercessors for beseeching believers. Reading the Quran, calculating the number of times one says a religious phrase on a finger counter, the performance of flagellation by men, the visiting of shrines, and the holding of religious gatherings are all provided upon fulfilment of votive promises (*nazr*) or petitions and requests. A mother, rather than accruing the religious credit for herself, may donate her own entire *hajj* experience to request that her son obtain a good wife, or a mother may visit shrines and pledge money for her daughter's acceptance by a good university, or for a child to pass a test, or for her son to find a good place to stay while attending university. A family may provide lemonade to flagellants and marchers if *Moharram* falls in summer or hot sweetened milk if it falls in winter, in the hope for family members to maintain good health. Donations and actions may be larger or smaller. One woman may host an entire ritual and provide the related hospitality in her home. Another may bring a candle to light at the ritual to request that a wish be granted. Although they may not practise other required Muslim rituals, even some young people – especially females – may make attempts to obtain spiritual help for this-worldly problems, possibly in part because they lack many other options. A young divorced woman may compulsively recite a religious phrase over and over again throughout the day in the hope of finding another, better husband. A number of young women may join together and vow to read sections of the Quran, hoping that their joint efforts may prove efficacious for success in school or for attracting good suitors.

Wealthy men pay for a meal to be served to the huge crowds at the new, large mosque or the large *Huseiniyyeh* during *Moharram* or *Ramazan*. The meals are often handed out in take-away packets that may be brought home. One man paid for the renovation of an old, decrepit shrine outside Aliabad, turning it into a building with a shining interior covered with mirror work. A woman may prepare several glasses of *sharbat* (fruit syrup mixed into water) to put on a tray and hand out to people who pass her courtyard.

The most poignant requests I heard about were those of the parents of a little two-year-old girl – a delightful, lively and much-loved child. Pardis had come down with a fever. They were extremely devoted and loving parents and took her to a hospital in Shiraz. At the change of shifts, the in-coming nurse wanted to give her a tranquilising shot. They said no as another nurse had just done so before her shift ended. She asked them whether they or she were the medical expert, and gave the daughter the shot. Pardis went into a coma and clearly suffered terrible brain damage. The parents did everything they could think of, reading the Quran over her, calling on religious experts to write a verse from the Quran, putting the piece of paper in water and giving it to her to drink. They cooked a large pot of stew and distributed it among neighbours and relatives with the hope that the saints would heal her. Finally, some years later, the father went to Karbala, in Iraq, to the shrine of Imam Husein. He said 'I will cry and cry at his tomb, until he is forced to raise up my daughter'.

I saw Pardis several years after the terrible event. She was lying down and would smile when relatives tickled her. The last time I was a guest at her grandmother's home along with all her children and their families in spring 2018, Pardis was lying down in an adjoining room. I couldn't make myself go in to see her. I didn't feel able to face this tragedy.

These days one does not hear much about following the example of Imam Husein and fighting against injustice. Rather the emphasis seems to be mainly again on Imam Husein, as the Beloved of God who, because of his sacrifice, can be an effective intercessor. By making promises of donations and honouring saints with visits and gifts of money, people hope for help with all of the many problems of life these days from the beloved figures in Shi'a history in the face of an increasing inability to find concrete courses of action. The main emphases in religion have once again become outward behaviours, religious rituals, and donations to the saints of Karbala and their descendants in return for assistance and favours.

Politically efficacious religious donations

A great difference between donations to the saints for requests or thanks before the Revolution and the present is that gifts for the saints, shrines, and religious rituals are appreciated by government officials and clerics and can be helpful in practical ways to bring individuals rewards in this temporal world. As before, donations for shrines, mosques, and rituals bring appreciation and status from relatives, neighbours and the community as well as from holy figures, but can also bring better connections and consideration from governmental organisations and authority figures. Personal spiritual and temporal advantages are hoped for in the practices of today's Shi'a Islam.

Trends towards declining adherence to Islam

In many ways Iranians' lives have become similar to the lives of Europeans. In contrast to the bazaari middle and upper middle classes, with their religiosity and close contacts with the clerical establishment, many of these modern groups came to see religion as a private issue and did not follow required rituals such as the Shi'a three prayer times a day, fasting during the holy month of *Ramazan*, or making the pilgrimage to Mecca that is required for those who can afford it. Many did not commemorate the Karbala martyrs and survivors during *Moharram* either.

With the revolutionary movement, religious activities, gatherings, slogans, myths, appreciation of religious leaders and particularly 'Imam' Khomeini, became ubiquitous. People read fliers from religious leaders, listened to tapes, attended mosque sermons, painted religious slogans on walls, put up photographs and placards of Ayatollah Khomeini and other religious figures. They bought and read writings and listened to the tapes of the lay theologian Ali Shariati.

Through the men working and studying in Shiraz and the *seyyid* traders and shopkeepers who went into the city to purchase goods and sell rural produce, this religious framework spread to Aliabad. Men, and a few more women than previously, crowded into the local mosque to listen to sermons. Many men, especially *seyyid* traders, younger men and some women went into the city to participate in the anti-government marches largely organised and led by clerics. *Seyyid* women and a few other pious women initiated anti-government and pro-uprising and pro-Khomeini marches in the village (Hegland, 1983c; 1990; 1991).

Before, during, and after the Revolution, many of the upper-class beneficiaries of the Pahlavi regime's development programmes left the country. Some others were executed. Many of the Iranians I have worked among in California's Bay Area, especially the older ones, had liked their opportunities and lifestyles during the Pahlavi period. They were forced to leave, several told me, in order to retain the lives they had been accustomed to during the Pahlavi period.

After the Revolution and the eight-year war with Iraq, Islamic Republic leaders turned more attention to rural and lower classes and to development in rural areas (Harris, 2017). Access to better education, technology, and white-collar jobs, to urban areas and travel outside Iran made modern standards of living and global worldviews available to a much larger proportion of the population (Hegland, 2011; 2014; 2021).

Middle and upper-middle class aspirations for individuation and comfortable lifestyles along with the IRI's corruption, ineptitude, and insistence on conformity in religion, and severe punishment for disobedience and dissent have resulted in declining interest in Shi'a Islam. This trend can be observed even in the formerly poor, subsistence-level village of sharecroppers and low-level itinerant traders of Aliabad, especially among the young who are now part of a mainly middle-class suburb of Shiraz.

The great majority of young, unmarried Aliabad women, especially high school and university students do not participate in rituals, not even in women's home-based rituals, and do not attend religious gatherings in public spaces. Young women are present to help with hospitality at a ritual only if a close relative is hosting it.

Not that many younger men take part in religious rituals either. Even for the most significant rituals of the year, the processions and rituals to mourn for Imam Husein and his companions, few Aliabad young men take part. Many sit on roofs to watch the processions. Some do take part in the self-flagellating rituals as pretty much their only religious involvement during the year, much as many US Christians may only go to church for Christmas or Easter. In Aliabad these central *Moharram* rituals have become somewhat like a cultural festival, an aspect of people's identity and something to watch and enjoy, rather than an expression of religious feelings and meanings. People take photographs, bring video cameras, and use their iPhones to capture the activities and the crowds. One may see young men with chic haircuts and young women with make-up, colourful clothes, and headscarves barely covering dyed, fashionable hairstyles. Religious leaders warn people about dressing appropriately to avoid attracting attention when they mourn for Imam Husein. In Shiraz people told me that young people take advantage of *Moharram* rituals by using them as an excuse to get out of the house and meet up with friends of the opposite sex (see also Afary and Anderson, 2005) or even hold post-mourning parties that include alcohol.

People have developed an array of different attitudes about Imam Husein, Shi'a Islam, Islam itself, and religions in general. Even older, pious, practising Shi'a Muslims are generally against coerced religion. They are against forcing women to practise *hejab*, the wearing of a cover over the hair and a loose cloak over the body. Some younger people say all religions are to help people become better human beings. Islam is no better or worse than any religion. Some people say religion is a personal, internal thing, and not what one shows to others. Others say they have their own religion, the government has its religion, and they do not have anything to do with each other.

A severely troubled economy

The main causes of dissatisfaction before the 1979 Revolution in Aliabad were the low standard of living – in spite of Iran's oil wealth – and economic inequity. The Revolution and the Islamic Republic were to solve these problems. In Aliabad, after the end of the Iran–Iraq War, the standards of living improved a great deal through new jobs, government loans, smuggling activities, shops and trades as well as land sales and a booming real estate business. However, with the worsening of the economy during the last decade, many people feel deprived and hopeless now that their raised expectations have not been met. The coronavirus pandemic in Iran – the worst in the Middle East (Wintcur, 2020) and the economic suffering accompanying it – seems to have been the last straw (*New York Times*, 2021). It is hard for people to scale down their lifestyles.

Returning repression and the lack of freedom

For Aliabad residents, repression and the power of the two wealthiest brothers, the gendarmes, and central government forces over them constituted the major sources of dissatisfaction in the period before the Revolution. During revolutionary demonstrations and marches, Iranians – and Aliabad people – shouted '*Istiqlal, azadi, jumhuri-ye islami*' (independence, freedom, Islamic republic). Many dissidents expected social and economic justice from the Islamic Republic. However, repression, injustice, and corruption have increased.

By the time I returned to Aliabad in 2003, communities were run by local councils. Several of the young men who had come back from Shiraz to lead the revolutionary faction in Aliabad and organise the seizure of a large area of the richest man's land had become members of the village council. The council took charge of gathering funds to pave the alleyways and make other improvements. People appreciated this but also pointed out that several council members had built themselves the best homes in town.

Early in the twenty-first century, the large area of land seized from the wealthiest brother shortly after the Revolution was finally divided among the men of Aliabad. Each married man was to receive enough land for a house and courtyard. The village council members took charge of the distribution, and people accused them of playing favourites with themselves and their own family members. The less favoured could do nothing. Several council members gained ownership of valuable sections of land next to the highway, thereby managing to become very wealthy.

Corruption has become a way of life. Those who have the funds to 'buy' authorities and cultivate useful relations can do what they want. Land ownership has become obscured, Aliabad people comment; by bribing land office officials, land has gone from one hand to another so many times that there is no telling to whom it should belong. As during the Qavam period until 1962 and the post-land reform period until 1979, a lack of political power these days results in a lack of ability to protect one's economic resources.

People complain about the clerics who send money to foreign banks just as the powerful members of the Shah's family and government did. The government seized a large area of former agricultural land in Aliabad to develop a suburb for administrative employees working in Shiraz.

Again, Aliabad residents complain, the powerful mistreat the powerless, the powerful support each other, and those holding power can do what they want and get away with it. There is no justice.

The Revolution and the Islamic Republic of Iran were supposed to bring justice, to end the arbitrary, violent misuse of power against common people, and instead to cooperate in making a better, fairer society. However, the majority of Aliabad people deny that this has happened and instead feel that political conditions are worse, that the corrupt government is inept, that it curtails freedom and treats people in ways abhorrent to Islam.[10]

Attitudes towards culture and religion

Rather than harbouring negative attitudes about foreign cultures, the majority, especially young people, seemed to enjoy global culture and wish to live more like foreigners do. They also shared critical comments about the religion and the personnel of the Islamic Republic. Some said the government was doing things that are not Islamic, such as killing people, taking money, fostering corruption, squandering funds abroad, or supporting the Palestinians while Iran's own needs remain unmet. Commenting that Islam teaches us to take care of our own house before we give to others, people complained about the government paying for a gold door to the shrine of Imam Husein in Karbala. They complained about ayatollahs who send money to their foreign bank accounts and send their children to the best foreign universities while ordinary people are left with substandard education in Iran. Young people especially complained about the education available in Shiraz – the teachers do not come to class, do not hold office hours, arrive unprepared, and do not care about their students. The education they receive is worthless.

Interest in other religions – Zoroastrianism, Christianity, Sufi orders – is growing. People are becoming interested in the pre-Islamic history of Iran. Several Aliabad people have gone to the gatherings at the tomb of Cyrus the Great near Persepolis to celebrate his rule (about 590–529 BCE), even though the regime has pronounced this celebration to be illegal.

Some people speak out against Islam because, they say, it was a foreign religion that was forced on them. Critics do not like Arab (Muslim) names and say there was a reason God sent Islam to the Arabs: 'they were so backward, but it hasn't done them any good – they are still backward'. They ask: 'Why mourn for someone who died so long ago? Other people have done much more important things – why don't we honour them instead? In any case, Imam Husein was just fighting to get power, to serve his own interests.'

In Aliabad, most young people do not show much interest in religion. This generation has grown up in and lived in a different world from their elders. They are busy with other interests and also worried, along with their parents, about their futures. Pious Muslims often blame the Islamic Republic government for turning the young away from religion. For some years I have heard the comment that Ayatollah Khomeini and his supporters have secularised Iranian society far more effectively than the Shah ever could. However, despite the criticism, I have not heard anybody from Aliabad say that they did not believe in God, though perhaps by now a few might do so.

For some people of Aliabad as well as for many Iranians elsewhere, religion is either personal, a source of help from the saints and/or the authorities, or a bankrupted belief framework used for advancement of one's own interests. One middle-aged *seyyid* woman, a toddler at the time of the Revolution, said to her father, 'We are *nasl-e sukhteh* (the burnt generation) – just because you had to go out and shout "Death to the Shah, hail Khomeini".' (see also Amir-Ebrahimi, 2021). These days many people see a distinction between Iranian Shi'i Muslims who use outward religious piety to identify themselves with the government and gain the resulting benefits, and those who adhere to the true, traditional Shi'a Islam.

Concluding comments

The perception and practices of Shiʻa Islam have changed since the revolutionary movement of 1978–9. Then, Shiʻa Islam was interpreted as a call to struggle against the Shah's tyranny. The faithful were exhorted to follow the example of Imam Husein to stand up selflessly and fight for social justice and make a better world for all. One could attain redemption by joining Imam Husein in his struggle for justice.

Since then, the perceptions and practices of Shiʻa Islam have largely reverted to the idea of Imam Husein as intercessor. Because he is 'beloved of God' due to his martyrdom, he can help petitioners solve problems in this life and attain redemption for the next world when they honour him with donations or *nazr* (votive promises).[11]

Religiosity and donations to religious organisations, figures, and sites have also become the means to curry political favours. Some younger people have confided to me that they feel forced to participate in government-organised religious groups and practices in order to keep their jobs or improve their standing in their professions, such as university teaching. Outward behaviour and performances of acquiescence have become more significant than inward faith and beliefs. A few people in Aliabad who found jobs in the government propaganda organisations explained that their outward government support is part of their job, that it is for the sake of employment. Many people, especially younger ones, consider Islam to be a religion like any other; it should help people to become better human beings. Especially among younger people, interest in Shiʻa Islam is declining.[12] Most young people I have talked with are unhappy with the government, and, along with many older people, feel that religion should not be forced. Some young people are extremely bitter and cynical and would like to leave the country. In light of the poor economic situation, the inflation, the devaluation of the Iranian monetary unit the *rial*, and the lack of jobs and opportunities, they feel hopeless about the future.

At the same time, some people in Aliabad continue with their quiet belief in God and their Shi'a Muslim practices of prayer three times a day, fasting during daylight hours of the month of *Ramazan*, and honouring Imam Husein during *Moharram*. A few people who had been devout before the Revolution remain loyal to the 'Islamic' government, but many older, pious people blame the government's wrongdoing for turning young people away from religion, declaring, 'If this is Islam, we don't want it.' From a revolutionary theology during the uprising of 1978 and 1979, Shi'a Islam, as many Iranians see it, has been turned into the organising, self-serving ideology of an ineffective government whose leaders and personnel fail to live up to the teachings of Islam and therefore alienate faithful Muslims.

Notes

1. For funding research and writing, I acknowledge the assistance of the Social Science Research Council and American Council of Learned Societies, Anthropology Department of the State University of New York, Binghamton, the American Association of University Women, Santa Clara University, the American Institute of Iranian Studies, the Fulbright Scholar Program, IREX, and the National Humanities Center. Many thanks to Erika Friedl, Janet Afary, Ashraf Zahedi, Shahla Haeri, and Bridget Blomfield for helpful comments. Most of all, I am grateful to my dear friends and research partners of Aliabad. This article was originally presented at the 15–17 May 2019 international conference 'After the Event: Prospects and Retrospects of Revolution' held at the UCL Anthropology department in London. Since then I have been told that conditions in Iran have deteriorated a great deal more due to government ineptitude, corruption and sanctions. According to my many conversations with Iranians by telephone and WhatsApp, more and more people are increasingly cynical and dissatisfied. Since the anti-regime uprising beginning in the autumn of 2022, with *Woman, Life, Freedom* as its motto, many more people are horrified at the brutal attempts to stop dissent, the many arrests, the violence against protestors on streets and in universities and schools, and the high numbers of murders – even of children. Because the regime uses a window-dressing of Islam, distaste for that religion – or how the regime defines it – is surely increasing even more, especially among the young.
2. In Catholic Christianity, holy figures hold positions in some ways similar to holy figures in Shi'a Islam, in that both can serve as intercessors between God and believers who turn to them for assistance and compassion. By taking the shorthand of using the word 'saint' here for the 12 *imams*, descendants of *imams* and other holy figures in Shi'a Islam, such as Zeinab and Fatimeh, I evoke their intercessory similarities with Catholic saints. See Bill and Williams, 2002.
3. For more information about the economic and political dissatisfactions of Aliabad villagers before the 1979 revolution, see Hegland, 2014.
4. A title meaning a descendant of the Prophet Mohammad through his daughter Fatimeh, carrying a connotation of greater religiosity and closeness to God and holy figures.
5. The 12 *imams* have served as the heads of Shi'a Islam throughout its history.
6. Edith Szanto has rightly criticised the binary view of the 'Karbala paradigm' (see also Bell, 2009). Szanto points to the great variety of meanings and interpretations different people have found in the 680 CE Karbala event, the martyrdom of Imam Husein and his followers. She presents examples of the many interpretations in different contexts and time periods of the role of Holy Zaynab, sister of Imam Husein, who survived the Karbala battle. According to Shi'a legend, she went on to spread the story and initiate mourning rituals (Szanto, 2013a).

   Since the 1978–9 research for my article on 'Two Images of Husain' (1983a), many scholars have conducted fieldwork about the meanings and practices related to Shi'i Muslim myths, so the comment about multiple rather than binary understandings about Imam Husein's martyrdom would be difficult to dispute. See, as examples, Aghaie, 2004; 2005; Blomfield, 2015; Deeb, 2006; Deeb and Harb, 2014; D'Souza, 2014; Fischer, 1982; Fischer and Abdi, 2002; Flaskerud, 2010; Hegland, 1997; 2003; Kamalkhani, 1998; Korom, 2003; Pinault, 1993; 2001; Ruffle, 2014; Schubel, 1993; Szanto, 2013a; 2013b; 2019a; 2019b; forthcoming; and Torab, 2006. During the 1978–9 revolutionary period in Iran, the two interpretations of Intercessor versus Exemplar became most prominent and the focus of debate. At the same time, of course, a multitude of less publicly contested understandings were held by Iranian Shiʻi Muslims.

In common with adherents to other religions, Shiʻa Muslims can find many different understandings of their religion and its myths. In his brilliant book, *Islam in Practice: Religious beliefs in a Persian village* (1988), Reinhold Loeffler documents the startlingly diverse belief systems of 21 mainly illiterate Shiʻa Muslim men. For another brilliant book on Islam as actually lived by people in an Iranian Luri settlement, see Friedl, 2020.

7. During the Islamic month of *Moharram*, and sometimes also during the following two months, Shiʻa Muslims traditionally commemorate the martyrdom of Imam Husein and his supporters on the plains of Karbala in present-day Iraq, on the tenth day.
8. During the Islamic month of *Ramazan* (Ramadan), Muslims are required to abstain from food, drink, smoking and sex during daylight hours.
9. Again, such spending by individuals has been declining in the last few years.
10. Unfortunately, I was not able to have open, satisfactory conversations with those whom Aliabad people considered to be pro-government figures in reality. The difficulty of doing so means that the publications of those anthropologists and sociologists who do manage research with pro-regime people are all the more valuable. See, for example, Bajoghli, 2019; Harris, 2017; Lob, 2020; Osanloo, 2009; 2020; Tawasil, 2015; 2019; and Wellman, 2017a; 2017b; 2021.
11. Requests to saints, promising a donation if the wish is fulfilled, or a donation in the hope of the fulfilment of a request or thanks for one.
12. With the prevention of other means of expressing dissent, the networking and organising work of clerical figures and their supporters in the bazaars and elsewhere, and the fashioning of the new Shiʻa Muslim revolutionary symbolic complex that could appeal to a wide spectrum of the population, people turned to Islam during the revolutionary period in search of economic and political justice. Based mainly on research in 1970–1 and 1976, Reinhold Loeffler argued that most likely, '… religious beliefs will tend to be dismissed … this final solution must be expected to become more prevalent in the future' (1988: 283). In spite of the dramatic increase of interest in Islam during the revolutionary period, this prediction seems to be turning into reality. The revived interest in religion apparent during the revolutionary period has been declining dramatically. A recent large study conducted from the Netherlands shows that while 90 per cent of Iranian respondents said they came from religious families, only 40 per cent of them self-identified as Muslim! Forty-seven per cent of those polled reported losing their faith during the course of their lives, and 72 per cent opposed laws requiring *hejab* (women's coverings) (Maleki and Tamimi Arab, 2020). Of course, the survey likely failed to reach various sectors of the population.

References

Abrahamian, Ervand. 1982. 'Ali Shariati: Ideologue of the Iranian Revolution'. *MERIP Reports*, 102: 24–8.
Abrahamian, Ervand. 2015. *The Coup: 1953, the CIA, and the Roots of Modern U.S.–Iranian Relations*. New York: New Press.
Afary, Janet and Anderson, Kevin. 2005. *Foucault and the Iranian Revolution: Gender and the seductions of Islamism*. Chicago: University of Chicago Press.
Aghaie, Kamran. 2004. *The Martyrs of Karbala: Shi'i symbols and rituals in modern Iran*. Seattle: University of Washington Press.
Aghaie, Kamran (ed.). 2005. *The Women of Karbala: Ritual performance and symbolic discourses in modern shi'i Islam*. Austin: University of Texas Press.
Amirani, Taghi (director). 2019. *Coup 53* (film), London: Amirani Media.

Amir-Ebrahimi, Masserat. 2021. 'The emergence of independent women in Iran: A generational perspective', in Afary, J. and Faust, J. (eds), *Iranian Romance in the Digital Age: From arranged marriage to white marriage*. London: I. B. Tauris, 11–31.

Bajoghli, Narges. 2019. *Iran Reframed: Anxieties of power in the Islamic republic*. Stanford, CA: Stanford University Press.

Bell, Catherine. 2009. *Ritual Theory, Ritual Practice*. Oxford: Oxford University Press.

Betteridge, Anne. 1985. Ziarat: Pilgrimage to the shrines of Shiraz. PhD thesis University of Chicago.

Betteridge, Anne. 2001. 'The controversial vows of urban Muslim women in Iran', in Falk, N. and Gross, R. (eds), *Unspoken Worlds: Women's religious lives in non-Western cultures*. Belmont, CA: Wadsworth, 157–67.

Bill, James and Williams John. 2002. *Roman Catholics and Shi'i Muslims: Prayer, passion, and politics*. Chapel Hill: University of North Carolina Press.

Blomfield, Bridget. 2015. *The Language of Tears: My journey into the world of Shi'i Muslim women*. Ashland, OR: White Cloud Press.

Deeb, Lara. 2006. *An Enchanted Modern: Gender and public piety in Shi'i Lebanon*. Princeton: Princeton University Press.

Deeb, Lara and Harb, Mona. 2014. *Leisurely Islam: Negotiating geography and morality in Shi'ite south Beirut*. Princeton: Princeton University Press.

D'Souza, Diane. 2014. *Partners of Zaynab: A gendered perspective of Shia Muslim faith*. Columbia: University of South Carolina Press.

Fischer, Michael. 1982. *Iran: From religious dispute to revolution*. Cambridge, MA: Harvard University Press.

Fischer, Michael and Abdi, Mehdi. 2002. *Debating Muslims: Cultural dialogues in postmodernity and tradition*. Madison: University of Wisconsin Press.

Flaskerud, Ingvild. 2010. *Visualizing Belief and Piety in Iranian Shiism*. New York: Continuum.

Friedl, Erika. 2020. *Religion and Daily Life in the Mountains of Iran: Theology, saints, people*. London: I. B. Tauris.

Harris, Kevan. 2017. *A Social Revolution: Politics and the welfare state in Iran*. Berkeley: University of California Press.

Hashemi, Manata. 2020. *Coming of Age in Iran: Poverty and the struggle for dignity*. New York: New York University Press.

Hegland, Mary Elaine. 1983a. 'Two images of Husain: Accommodation and revolution in an Iranian village', in Keddie, N. R. (ed.), *Religion and Politics in Iran: Shi'ism from quietism to revolution*. New Haven, CT: Yale University Press, 218–36.

Hegland, Mary Elaine. 1983b. 'Ritual and revolution in Iran', in Aronoff, M. (ed.), *Political Anthropology, Volume II: Culture and political change*. New Brunswick, NJ: Transaction Books, 75–100.

Hegland, Mary Elaine. 1983c. 'Aliabad women: Revolution as religious activity', in Nashat, G. (ed.), *Women and Revolution in Iran*. Boulder, CO: Westview Press, 171–94.

Hegland, Mary Elaine. 1987a. 'Islamic revival or political and cultural revolution? An Islamic case study', in Antoun, R. and Hegland, M. E. (eds), *The Islamic Resurgence in Comparative Perspective*. Syracuse, NY: Syracuse University Press, 194–219.

Hegland, Mary Elaine. 1987b. 'Conclusion: Religious resurgence in today's world – refuge from dislocation and anomie or enablement for change?', in Antoun, R. and Hegland, M. E. (eds), *The Islamic Resurgence in Comparative Perspective*. Syracuse, NY: Syracuse University Press, 233–56.

Hegland, Mary Elaine. 1990. 'Women and the Iranian Revolution: A village case study'. *Dialectical Anthropology*, 15(2–3): 183–92.

Hegland, Mary Elaine. 1991. 'Political roles of Aliabad women: The public/private dichotomy transcended', in Keddie, N. and Baron, B. (eds), *Shifting Boundaries: Gender roles in the Middle East, past and present*. New Haven, CT: Yale University Press, 215–30.

Hegland, Mary Elaine. 1997. 'A mixed blessing: The *majles* – Shi'a women's rituals of mourning in north-west Pakistan', in Brink, J. and Mencher, J. (eds), *Mixed Blessings: Gender and religious fundamentalism cross-culturally*. New York: Routledge, 179–96.

Hegland, Mary Elaine. 2003. 'Shi'a women's rituals in northwest Pakistan: The shortcomings and significance of resistance'. *Anthropological Quarterly*, 76(3): 411–42.

Hegland, Mary Elaine. 2011. 'Aliabad of Shiraz: Transformation from village to suburban town'. *Anthropology of the Middle East*, 6(2): 21–37.

Hegland, Mary Elaine. 2014. *Days of Revolution: Political unrest in an Iranian village*. Stanford, CA: Stanford University Press.

Hegland, Mary Elaine. 2021. 'Changing perceptions and practices of marriage among people of Aliabad from 1978 to 2015: New problems and challenges', in Afary, J. and Faust, J. (eds), *Iranian Romance in the Digital Age: From arranged marriage to white marriage*. London: I. B. Tauris, 174–96.

Hegland, Mary Elaine. 2022. 'Challenges facing Iranian youth: To migrate or not to migrate?'. Paper presented at the panel on 'Challenges facing middle eastern youth' at the IUAES Middle East Commission Conference, Istanbul, 7–9 September.

Kamalkhani, Zahra. 1998. *Women's Islam: Religious practice among women in today's Iran*. London: Kegan Paul International.

Katouzian, Homa. 1990. *Musaddiq and the Struggle for Power in Iran*. London: I. B. Tauris.

Kinzer, Stephen. 2008. *All the Shah's Men: An American coup and the roots of Middle East terror*. San Francisco: Wiley.

Korom, Frank. 2003. *Hosay Trinidad: Muharram performances in an Indo-Caribbean diaspora*. Philadelphia: University of Pennsylvania Press.

Lob, Eric. 2020. *Iran's Reconstruction Jihad: Rural development and regime consolidation after 1979*. Cambridge: Cambridge University Press.

Loeffler, Reinhold. 1988. *Islam in Practice: Religious beliefs in a Persian village*. Albany: State University of New York Press.

Maleki, Ammar and Tamimi Arab, Pooyan. 2020. 'Iranians' attitudes toward religion: A 2020 survey report'. Tilburg University GAMAAN project. https://bit.ly/3Ua17Ny. Accessed 23 May 2021.

Moaveni, Azadeh and Tahmasebi, Sussan. 2021. 'The middle-class women of Iran are disappearing: And the United States is partly to blame'. *New York Times*, 27 May https://nyti.ms/3DF0PqW.

New York Times. 2021. '"Maximum pressure" on Iran has failed: A return to the nuclear deal is the first step out of the morass'. Editorial. 10 April. https://nyti.ms/3zO7duV.

Osanloo, Arzoo. 2009. *The Politics of Women's Rights in Iran*. Princeton: Princeton University Press.

Osanloo, Arzoo. 2020a. *Forgiveness Work: Mercy, law, and victims' rights in Iran*. Princeton: Princeton University Press.

Osanloo, Arzoo. 2020b. 'Entanglements: Lives lived under sanctions', SAIS Initiative for Research on Contemporary Iran. Washington, DC: Johns Hopkins University. https://bit.ly/3fDV1Ww.

Pinault, David. 1993. *The Shiites*. New York: Palgrave.

Pinault, David. 2001. *Horse of Karbala: Muslim devotional life in India*. New York: Palgrave.

Rahimi, Mahboobeh. 2019. 'Reframing *Arbaeen* pilgrimage in Western media through a cultural translation: A framing analysis'. *Society and Culture in the Muslim World*, 1(1): 65–87.

Rahnema, Ali. 2014. *Behind the 1953 Coup in Iran: Thugs, turncoats, soldiers, and spooks*. Cambridge: Cambridge University Press.

Ruffle, Karen. 2014. *Gender, Sainthood, and Everyday Practice in South Asian Shi'ism*. Chapel Hill: University of North Carolina Press.

Schubel, Vernon. 1993. *Religious Performance in Contemporary Islam: Shi'i devotional rituals in South Asia*. Columbia: University of South Carolina Press.

Schwartz, Kevin L. and Gölz, Olmo. 2020. 'Going to war with the coronavirus and maintaining the state of resistance in Iran'. *Middle East Report Online*, 9 January. http://bit.ly/3i3Udey.

Shahrokni, Nazanin. 2020. 'Bursting at the seams: Economic sanctions and transformation of the domestic sphere in Iran', SAIS Initiative for Research on Contemporary Iran. Washington, DC: Johns Hopkins University. https://bit.ly/3NKyQLa. Accessed 28 November 2022.

Szanto, Edith. 2013a. 'Beyond the Karbala paradigm: Rethinking revolution and redemption in twelver Shi'a mourning rituals'. *Journal of Shi'a Islamic Studies*, 6(1): 75–91.

Szanto, Edith. 2013b. 'Contesting fragile saintly traditions: Miraculous healing among twelver shi'is in contemporary Syria', in Bandak, A. and Bille, M. (eds), *Politics of Worship in the Contemporary Middle East: Sainthood in fragile states*. Leiden: Brill, 33–52.

Szanto, Edith. 2019a. 'The 'Alimahs of Sayyida Zaynab: Female shi'i authority in a Syrian sanctuary', in Künkler, M. and Steward, D. (eds), *Female Religious Authority in Shi'i Islam: A comparative history*. Edinburgh: Edinburgh University Press, 307–22.

Szanto, Edith. 2019b. 'Economies of piety at the Syrian shrine of Sayyida Zaynab', in Rahimi, B. and Eshagh, P. (eds), *Muslim Pilgrimage*. Chapel Hill: University of North Carolina Press, 172–82.

Szanto, Edith. 2020. 'The largest contemporary Muslim pilgrimage isn't the hajj to Mecca, it's the Shiite pilgrimage to Karbala in Iraq'. *The Conversation*, 9 September. https://bit.ly/3zNQ6JE. Accessed 15 May 2021.

Szanto, Edith. Forthcoming. 'On the trail of tears: Hospitality, community, and sacred space in contemporary Iraqi *Aarba'in* practices', in Funke, C. (ed.), *Lamenting Karbala: Commemoration, mourning, and memory*. Leiden: Brill.

Tawasil, Amina. 2015. 'Towards the ideal revolutionary shi'i woman: The *howzevi* (seminarian), the requisites of marriage and Islamic education in Iran'. *Hawwa*, 13(1): 99–126.

Tawasil, Amina. 2019. 'Reading as practice: The *howzevi* (seminarian) women in Iran and Clair de Lune'. *Anthropology and Education Quarterly*, 50(1): 66–83.

Torab, Azam. 2006. *Performing Islam: Gender and ritual in Iran*. Leiden: Brill.

Wellman, Rose. 2017a. 'Sacralizing kinship, naturalizing the nation: Blood and food in post-revolutionary Iran'. *American Ethnologist*, 44(3): 503–15

Wellman, Rose. 2017b. 'Substance, spirit, and sociality among shi'i Muslims in Iran', in Thomas, T., Malik, A. and Wellman, R. (eds), *New Directions in Spiritual Kinship: Sacred ties across the Abrahamic religions*. New York: Palgrave Macmillan, 171–94.

Wellman, Rose. 2021. *Feeding Iran: Shi'i families and the making of the Islamic Republic*. Berkeley: University of California Press.

Wintour, Patrick. 2020. 'Iran at breaking point as it fights third wave of coronavirus'. *The Guardian*, 14 October. https://bit.ly/3hfJm0L.

Part Two:
Rethinking revolutionary afterlives: anthropology and beyond

5
The 'revolution before the revolution': radical organising across the *longue durée* in twentieth-century Peru

David Nugent

Introduction

In the closing decades of the twentieth century, the Communist Party of Peru-Shining Path (PCP-SL) attempted to seize control of the Peruvian government through force of arms. The ensuing civil war, which lasted well over a decade, claimed perhaps 70,000 lives. While much has been written about the Shining Path (DeGregori, 1990; Gorritti, 1999), the armed struggle that it launched is rarely connected in any systematic way to prior forms of revolutionary activity.[1] Instead, the tendency has been to orientalise this radical Maoist-inspired movement – to treat it as an extraordinary episode, an aberration from what had come before.

In this chapter I argue that the revolution precipitated by the Shining Path is best seen not as an event but rather as part of the 'aftermath' of previous revolutionary initiatives. That is, the PCP-SL is usefully understood as having emerged from an extended period of widespread radical endeavour that stretched across much of the twentieth century. I illustrate this argument by exploring the 'revolution before the revolution' – by analysing radical initiatives from earlier in the twentieth century and showing their connections to the PCP-SL. I focus on the forms of subjectivity, organisation and discipline that emerged across the *longue durée* of revolutionary activity in twentieth-century Peru. In so doing, I seek to raise new questions about the temporality of revolutionary politics, the ambiguity of revolutionary legacies and the scale of the everyday in revolutionary transformation.

We may usefully date the beginning of the *long durée* of revolutionary activity to the late nineteenth century, when foreign capital from the North Atlantic began pouring into Peru in unprecedented quantities. The flood of foreign capital stimulated two interrelated processes. The first of these was widespread dislocation, pauperisation, instability and the spread of violence, as existing socio-political relations were undermined, and groups from across the social spectrum struggled to control the new opportunities of the era.

The second process that was stimulated by the flood of foreign capital was rapid – even explosive – export-oriented economic growth. Peru's economic boom lasted for three decades, and made it possible for elements of the country's geographically dispersed and internally fragmented elite groups to come together in a shared if fraught project of rule. The key elements of this alliance were the owners of coastal plantations, highland mines and 'feudal' landed estates in the Andes (Burga and Flores-Galindo, 1987).[2]

The expansion of the capitalist export sector produced a displaced, precarious, wage-labouring population of unprecedented proportions. By 1930, labouring groups had organised themselves into a range of radical and populist political parties that burst onto the political scene, presenting a major challenge to the country's export-oriented elite (Sulmont, 1985). In this context, the unity formerly enjoyed by Peru's three main elite factions disintegrated, with the coastal plantation elite displacing the other two groups (Klarén, 2000).

While Peru's radical political parties were unable to overthrow the elite power structure, neither could elite groups dismantle the era's movements from below. Instead, Peru's dominant elite faction – the coastal plantation oligarchy – joined together with the armed forces in an attempt to maintain control over national affairs. The four decades after 1930 were characterised by long periods of military rule punctuated by brief interludes of quasi-democratic control. During the latter, a member of Peru's coastal oligarchy would generally serve as president. Repression of radical alternatives was fierce throughout this entire period.

It was in this tense, repressive climate that underground political organising took shape in the twentieth century. While a range of political parties came into being, by far the most influential was APRA, the Popular American Revolutionary Alliance, which was founded in 1924 (Klarén, 1973; García-Bryce, 2018). In its original incarnation, APRA was committed to nationalising land and industry, establishing workers' cooperatives in all branches of the economy, and establishing a broad, participatory democracy in which women and other minorities would exercise a direct voice. APRA was able to establish a very strong following in a very short period of time. It was especially strong among the working classes of the enclaves of the export economy. But the party was also very influential throughout the Peruvian highlands.

This chapter examines the processes that led to the consolidation of APRA in Chachapoyas, an agrarian region in the highlands of northern Peru, which had long been dominated by a 'feudal', landed elite. As was the case in much of Peru, challenges to the elite-led power structure in Chachapoyas coalesced in the 1920s, in the context of the widespread disruptions of national life resulting from the influx of foreign capital and the growth of the export economy. Opposition to the status quo in Chachapoyas was led by youth from marginalised poor and middle sectors, who had few avenues of upward mobility and were denied opportunities for social recognition. At great risk to themselves, in the mid-1920s these disaffected youth organised an underground communist cell in Chachapoyas. In secret, night-time meetings that continued throughout the 1920s, they read and discussed a range of radical literature that had to be smuggled into the region over seldom-used mule trails to avoid detection by the police.

By 1929 these youth had turned away from communism and towards APRA. The former, while a powerful and important set of ideas, seemed to Chachapoyas's young radicals as too European. They regarded APRA, on the other hand, as promoting a form of socialism based on the peculiarities of Latin America. Particularly important in this regard was their belief that collective forms of land tenure had been common in the indigenous polities (especially the Inca) that had controlled the region prior to the devastation caused by Spanish colonialism. In the early months of 1930, the radical youth of Chachapoyas smuggled a message out of the region to APRA's Central Committee in Lima asking for more information about the Party of the People (as APRA called itself).

In response to their call, later that year the party leadership in Lima sent Manuel Chávez Várgas – a skilled organiser – to Chachapoyas to provide in-depth training to the region's youth. This training, which extended over a period of years, introduced the young Apristas to essential new disciplines of the body and mind, which were intended to transform them into new kinds of subjects. The training was also intended to change the social structure of which the Apristas were a part – by providing the novices with the practical, organisational skills they needed to recruit the general population to the Aprista cause and to challenge the 'feudal' power structure.

Chávez Várgas steeped his followers in party doctrine. He emphasised in particular the crucial importance of nationalising land and industry, creating workers' cooperatives and forming an inclusive, participatory democracy – one that was based on the generalised participation of the entire populace in the key, everyday activities upon which social life was based. But he also stressed the importance of other factors that he believed were at least as important as these 'structural' issues. According to Chávez Várgas, among the most damaging legacies of feudal, aristocratic rule was that the population had been deeply affected by a cultural politics of *difference*. This oppressive set of arrangements had done more than force people to accept lives of poverty, humiliation and abuse. So scarred had the populace been by the physical and symbolic violence of elite domination, Chávez Várgas instructed, that the invidious racial distinctions of the aristocratic order had lodged themselves deep in people's emotions and psyches. In the process, the aristocratic order had distorted people's entire system of values and life aspirations.

Not only had *Indios* and *mestizos* come to believe in their own inferiority, they also strove to be like the rich – pampered, indulgent and abusive. While structural change was essential, Chávez Várgas taught, it would be insufficient unless people were first led through a series of profound personal and cultural transformations. In other words, only the most sweeping and systematic of assaults on the entire aristocratic order – with its focus on hierarchy and racial difference – could lay the groundwork necessary for democratic transformation.

APRA saw it as the party's special task to seek out and destroy any and all manifestations of hierarchy, no matter where they were found. The party approached this problem with nothing short of missionary zeal, treating virtually any expression of difference as a form of depravity or moral outrage that simply *had* to be effaced from the earth. To take but one example, which invoked the equality APRA attributed to the Inca empire:[3]

> The Inca Empire was based on *equality*. A single call from a *cacique* [a local elite] would bring out all the people to work together to build terraces, redirect rivers, harvest the fields. This was the period of *democracia salvaje* [savage democracy] … We were united at this time, and we were equal, so we were democratic, but we relied on systems of violence. Brutal punishments were used then, especially for the lazy person, the one who thought he was better than others,

who refused to work like the rest. The *caciques* would grab people like this and march them to the top of a fortress, lie them down on the wall of the fortress and, pa! smash their heads in with a large rock. This was how they carried out justice. This was how they protected their democracy.

Such was the movement's vision of a world made equal and democratic, in which all would work as one for the collective good.

Considering what was at stake – the creation of a new world order based on equality and justice – APRA believed that its assault on difference and hierarchy could not be undertaken by just anyone. Rather, it could be entrusted only to the most worthy and committed of individuals. Only people who had demonstrated beyond any doubt that they were prepared to make the enormous sacrifices required of them could be trusted to lead APRA's assault on inequality. Only those who had been specially trained could be allowed to wage the war for democracy.

The training provided by Chávez Várgas was intended to prepare just such a vanguard. The first step in this process was to free the novice Apristas from the cultural weight of aristocratic rule. The new disciplines he taught his followers were meant to rid the novice Apristas of their fear and awe of the elite, of their desire to live pampered, indulgent, privileged lives. One of the central goals of APRA's indoctrination process was to do away with such ambitions by producing highly disciplined subjects who would be wholly committed to the principles of democracy, equality and freedom for which the party stood. Indeed, the novices in training were meant to exemplify political principles that are usefully thought of as 'sacropolitical' – as based on group sacrifice in the present to bring about a new future (Nugent, 2019).

The training of this elite vanguard of Apristas was both broad and rigorous. To learn new disciplines of the mind, Chávez Várgas had the novices read, discuss and critique major works of political and economic theory that had bearing on the problems of Latin America. Chávez Várgas was careful to place special emphasis on his trainees' ability to explain the strengths and weaknesses of different doctrines to simple, untutored folk, and constantly tested and assessed the abilities of his charges to do so.

To assist his apprentices in developing new disciplines of the body, Chávez Várgas taught his novices to avoid the excesses considered typical of youth – sex and alcohol in particular. The Aprista leader encouraged good hygiene and regular sleeping habits. He taught his young followers to do calisthenics daily, upon waking. He also helped them organise soccer and volleyball teams, and insisted that they practise and compete on a regular basis. This helped everyone learn to work together and cooperate as equals.

Chávez Várgas also carefully monitored the conduct of his charges in these areas, and had them monitor one another's conduct as well. As APRA's representative in Chachapoyas, Chávez Várgas even established an underground court system, where party members who were not able to abide by APRA's disciplinary precepts were subjected to trial and judgement by their peers. In this way Chávez Várgas introduced into the education of his leaders-in-training a distinctive structure of surveillance – one in which all of the young Apristas would hold all of the others in intersecting horizontal gazes of evaluation and assessment based on the party's disciplinary precepts.

Chávez Várgas also sought to make his novices as 'cultured' (as he put it) as possible. There were two dimensions to this process of inculcating a distinctly Aprista culture in his followers. First, aspiring party leaders had to acquire the knowledge and master the skills needed to defend themselves from physical assault. For example, they had to master self-defence techniques, become proficient in the use of firearms and explosives and learn how to evade the police. They also, however, had to acquire the skills needed to fend off verbal assault – to develop a thorough grasp of the works of Marx, Proudhon, Gonzalez Prada and Gandhi, and be able to explain them succinctly and spontaneously to the various hostile and ignorant audiences they would encounter in the course of organising.

Second, the future APRA leaders had to develop courage and integrity – by drawing upon their newly developed knowledge and skills to face the dangers involved in challenging injustice. To help them do so, Chávez Várgas involved his apprentices in *misiones* (missions) that required them to perform important tasks for the party. These took a variety of forms: from delivering secret messages to Apristas in other towns to spreading party propaganda in the dead of night (see below), from gathering intelligence from the police and other government functionaries to organising among the peasantry.

The missions that Chávez Várgas assigned to his followers even included having them make extended visits to rural villages, where they were to do what was necessary to organise new party cells, and to attract new followers to the cause. The missions were graded by level of difficulty, and Chávez Várgas was careful to expose his fledgling party leaders to progressively more risk. In this way he was able to gauge the degree to which the novices developed the courage necessary to assume positions of party leadership. As these two elements of becoming cultured imply, APRA understood 'culture' to refer to the ability to translate knowledge and skills into action, especially in dangerous circumstances, in order to challenge injustice and inequality.

The arts of deception

Chávez Várgas took great care to inculcate new habits of thought and action, new forms of awareness in his followers, which would help them negotiate the grave risks involved in being underground political organisers. It would be difficult to exaggerate these risks. The central government and also conservative social forces regarded APRA as a dangerous evil. Those who joined the party thus placed themselves in real and constant danger – of assault, arrest, torture, deportation and (in extreme cases) even death. It was therefore essential that party members be equipped with skills and understandings that would help minimise the risks they faced. Chávez Várgas devoted much of his training efforts to ensuring that his followers would be prepared to overcome the dangers in question.

An indispensable part of the education that Chávez Várgas provided to his students was focused on this problem, and consisted of instructing them in the 'arts of deception'.[4] That is, Chávez Várgas gave his followers detailed instruction in how to evade and deceive the Guardia Civil (the police), who, as the representatives of the central government, had been assigned the task of eradicating (or at the very least controlling) the party. The leaders-in-training ran the constant risk that they would be apprehended by the Guardia Civil, in large part because the apprentices attended party meetings and carried out missions on an ongoing basis – not uncommonly, several times a week. If they were arrested during the course of carrying out these activities, it was very likely that they would be detained, and physically mistreated, which put both the individual who was arrested and the party as a whole in danger.

In light of the risks that were associated with arrest and abuse, and the constancy with which the novice Apristas were confronted with these risks, Chávez Várgas taught his students skills that would help ensure that they remained invisible to police scrutiny. For example, Chávez Várgas made the young leaders-in-training study and memorise the patterns by which the police patrolled the streets of Chachapoyas: how many Guardias there were in each of the city's four barrios, what progression of streets they followed in making their rounds, and when they changed shifts. By knowing when the police were likely to be patrolling which streets, Chávez Várgas told his followers, they would be far less likely to have a chance encounter with these representatives of the forces of order.

It was the element of *chance* that Chávez Várgas was intent upon eliminating, to whatever extent possible. In other words, the Aprista leader was determined to replace unpredictable occurrences with order, control and predictability. With the same goal in mind, Chávez Várgas explained to his followers the importance of changing the time and location of party meetings on a regular basis. Were they always to meet at the same time and place, he told his apprentices, they would be likely to arouse the suspicions of the police – who would notice that the same individuals were congregating day after day at the same locale. Chávez Várgas also gave his apprentices the responsibility for planning these changes in the time and place of party gatherings – for ensuring that there were no patterns in the movements of the Apristas that could come to the attention of the Guardia. In this way, Chávez Várgas taught his followers to mimic the lack of order or regularity that he attributed to ordinary, everyday life.

Chávez Várgas also explained to his students that, to avoid making the police suspicious, they should not arrive for meetings at the same time, nor come in groups, nor follow the same route. Rather, they should come from different directions, alone, and at different times. At the conclusion of every meeting, he would ensure that each cell member understood what route that person would follow in coming to the next meeting, and at what time he would arrive. Here as well, the Aprista leader showed his novices how to mimic innocent patterns of behaviour, to avoid doing anything that would make them visible or transparent to the forces of order.

In other words, Chávez Várgas taught his followers that they should always assume that they were under *surveillance*, and not only by the authorities, but by everyone who was associated with the status quo. He taught his students that they could not afford the luxury of acting without careful planning and forethought. Indeed, the novice Apristas were told that their very survival, and the survival of their fellows, would depend on everyone's ability to anticipate problems with the authorities *before* they occurred. These problems could be avoided by means of dissimulation – by identifying and acting out patterns of behaviour that would be regarded as wholly innocuous. In order to do so, Chávez Várgas told his followers, they would have to learn to view themselves from the perspective of the authorities. That is, they would have to learn to identify and then eliminate any and all behaviours that would draw the attention of the police. Otherwise, it would be impossible for them to remain invisible to the scrutiny of the state and its representatives.

Chávez Várgas did more, however, than simply encourage his followers to reflect upon this problem. He also trained them in how to do so. He helped them identify which forms of behaviour were most likely to put them at risk, and then shared with them the task of doing the day-to-day planning necessary to eliminate that risk, and to keep the party safe. In this way, Chávez Várgas sought to ensure that the movements of the Apristas did not betray any patterns that would draw the attention of the authorities.

By involving his followers in the planning process that was necessary to keep APRA invisible to police scrutiny, Chávez Várgas did more than simply provide his students with extensive practice in the arts of deception. He also *habituated* them to thinking and acting as if they were under official scrutiny. Under Chávez Várgas's tutelage, the young Apristas came to accept surveillance as an inevitable, ongoing part of the environment to which they had to adapt. They also came to accept the necessity of changing their behaviour accordingly, and of doing so on a round-the-clock basis. Only to the extent that they remembered that they were constantly being watched, Chávez Várgas conveyed to his students, could they avoid actually being seen. Only in this way could they be sure that they did not act 'thoughtlessly' (in the words of party members) – that they would not act in ways that would put them and their party at grave risk.

Chávez Várgas knew, however, that no matter how disciplined his apprentices became, no matter how careful they were to mould their behaviour in order to avoid arousing the suspicions of the authorities, it was inevitable that some of his students would eventually have an unanticipated encounter with the police, and in circumstances that the latter would consider suspicious. In situations such as these, the apprentices' degree of 'culture' would be sorely tested. In order to prepare his leaders-in-training for this eventuality, Chávez Várgas gave them explicit instructions.

If the police did try to apprehend them as they were making their way to or from a party meeting, they should attempt to flee. As they did so, Chávez Várgas told them, they could not allow their emotions to overwhelm them and flee in panic. Rather, they had to conquer their fears and act in a disciplined manner. They should never run in the direction of the locale where the party meeting was held, as the police might stumble upon the meeting place in the course of their pursuit. Nor should they flee in the direction of their homes, as the police might assume that they would seek the safety of their families, and might decide to search the residences that were located along their escape route. Rather, if they decided to flee, Chávez Várgas told his followers, they had to resist the temptation of seeking the immediate sanctuary of home or party, as this is precisely what the police would expect them to do. Instead, they had to conquer their fear, and had to follow a disciplined, reasoned strategy for avoiding capture – one that would anticipate the responses of the Guardias as fully as possible.

In addition to insisting that they take the steps necessary to lead the police away from their comrades, and away from their families, Chávez Várgas went into considerable detail about the disciplined strategy he wanted his students to follow. He told his apprentices that there were techniques they could employ in the very act of fleeing that would help minimise the risk of capture. Primary among them was the following: they should always try to run towards the forested areas that surrounded Chachapoyas, as the police would generally not pursue them beyond the limits of the city. The Aprista could then spend the night in the woods, and enter the town in the morning, when many other people would be doing the same. In this way the apprentice Apristas would become indistinguishable from everyone around them.

If they could not reach the woods, Chávez Várgas told them, as they fled through the streets of Chachapoyas they should not run in a straight line, but should zigzag, and should turn corners and reverse direction whenever possible. This was important, Chávez Várgas told his leaders-in-training, so as not to offer a fixed target to the police – who would at times shoot their weapons at fleeing Apristas (after having first fired a warning shot into the air). The moment they were out of sight of their pursuers, he told them, they should leap over the wall that separated the street from adjacent houses. Having done so, they should conceal themselves in the back garden of the nearest house, where they should hide, making no noise whatsoever, until the police passed by. Once they were well concealed, Chávez Várgas counselled his followers, they should sit patiently and wait. After an hour or so, they could make their way carefully from one back yard to the next, and only when they were as far away as possible from the point at which they had disappeared should they return to the street. Using extreme caution, they could then make their way home, always being sure to follow a roundabout route.

Chávez Várgas recognised, however, that it would not always be possible for his apprentices to flee. In order to help them escape arrest and possible physical abuse when they could not avoid being apprehended, Chávez Várgas told them that they were to prepare themselves so that they could maintain the illusion of innocence that their party was at such pains to maintain. In other words, they were to make up stories *in advance* to explain their presence in the street after hours – stories that the police would find credible. They were also to be ready to tell these stories in a convincing manner, at a moment's notice. Chávez Várgas told them that taking this precaution would help them avoid being caught unprepared – something that they should never allow to happen.

Chávez Várgas wanted to be sure that his leaders-in-training had followed his instructions – that they had thought up credible excuses that could explain their presence in the street after hours. He also wanted to be sure that his students could deliver these stories effectively, at a moment's notice, if they were apprehended by the police. In order to satisfy himself that his charges were truly prepared, he began testing them in this area during party meetings:[5]

> All of a sudden, with no warning, Chávez Várgas would say to one of us, 'Suppose it is 2.00 a.m., and you have just left one of our meetings. As you turn a corner, you encounter a pair of Guardias. Suppose that I am one of them.' And then, pretending to be a Guardia, Chávez Várgas would grab one of us by the shirt, and, looking very angry, he would demand information. He would shout into this person's face, 'WHO ARE YOU? WHAT ARE YOU DOING OUT SO LATE?' Chávez Várgas was an intimidating man, and all of us were a bit afraid of him to begin with. When he began shouting at us, it was frightening. He had told us [earlier] to have stories that we could tell the police, but few of us were ready when he first surprised us in this way. Several *compañeros* were caught completely unprepared, and were humiliated. Chávez Várgas was furious with us. After that, no one ever made the same mistake again.

After this experience, all members of the cell were careful to come to meetings fully prepared. Chávez Várgas continued trying to surprise them, and this gave them the opportunity to develop the discipline and foresight required to make it impossible to do so. Indeed, because the Aprista leader refused to relent about this issue, the young Apristas had the opportunity to continue practising the delivery of excuses on a regular basis. Whenever they did so, Chávez Várgas and the other members of the cell would critique the excuse itself, and also its delivery. Repeated practice in delivering their lines to a hypothetical audience of suspicious police allowed the Apristas to develop confidence in their ability to be convincing, to become practised in the arts of deception.

Although it was very important for the apprentices to develop the confidence necessary to deceive the police, this exercise did considerably more than simply act as a confidence booster. Much to his dismay, in acting out the role of a Guardia demanding information after hours, Chávez Várgas succeeded in *surprising* (and humiliating) his students – in catching them unawares. The implication was clear. Thus far, his students had not done what was necessary to anticipate the behaviour of the police. Nor had they readied themselves accordingly, so that they could mimic the innocence that party members were told to cultivate in order to protect themselves and their party.

That is, it was clear that the apprentices were not taking their responsibilities as apprentices as seriously as they should, and were not preparing themselves with the care that their positions as underground organisers required. Chávez Várgas's success in surprising his students sent another message to them as well. Were the police (rather than Chávez Várgas) to catch them unprepared, the consequences would be far more serious than mere humiliation. Experiences such as these made the leaders-in-training realise that, if they were to protect one another or their party, they would have to learn to be more disciplined: they would have to maintain themselves in a constant state of vigilance.[6] They could not ever afford the luxury of letting their guard down, of being caught unprepared.

Chávez Várgas's efforts to train his students in the arts of deception turned out to be well worth the effort. In the course of making their nightly rounds about Chachapoyas, the police would intermittently stumble upon a party member in what they considered suspicious circumstances. While many of these Apristas managed to deceive the Guardias, some were less effective than others in delivering their lines. Those who failed to convince the police of their innocence were generally taken to jail, where they were interrogated. A number were beaten or tortured. Events such as these drove home to the Apristas the very real nature of the dangers they faced, and the importance of developing the mental and emotional discipline necessary to remain invisible to the forces of order.

Instruction in the arts of deception did more than just serve the pragmatic needs of the party and its members – did more than simply help protect the Apristas, and allow them to continue with party activities. Instruction in the arts of deception also did more than inculcate in the apprentice Apristas new forms of mental, affective and behavioural discipline – forms of discipline that were shared by the group as a whole. By teaching his students that deceiving the authorities was a strategy that they should adopt as a matter of course in going about their everyday lives, and by habituating them to this strategy through continual repetition, Chávez Várgas helped form (or reinforce) a definite attitude towards state rule. He taught his followers that the government was never to be regarded as a source of moral authority. The authorities were neither to be honoured, revered, respected nor obeyed. Rather, they were to be deceived, ridiculed, outwitted and outmanoeuvred. Furthermore, the forces of order were to be outwitted by adopting the very behaviours the authorities regarded as innocent and innocuous. State rule, Chávez Várgas conveyed to his students, was a fundamentally immoral domain. APRA was the only valid source of moral authority – because of its commitment to equality, justice and social transformation.

An Aprista mission

Government narratives attributed the poverty that plagued Peru to such causes as 'feudal backwardness', the racial inferiority of the country's indigenous people and a lack of foreign capital and know-how that would enable development. According to Chávez Várgas, it was imperative for the party to present its own counter-narrative. One of the most effective ways of doing so, he said, was to print up propaganda sheets that explained the party's objectives and goals, and to distribute these sheets as widely as possible throughout the town.

Because of the government's determination to define the parameters of what could and could not be said in public, APRA's attempts to disseminate propaganda sheets put party members at grave risk. There were three small printing presses in Chachapoyas in the 1930s, but even approaching these presses about printing 'subversive' literature was foolhardy. As a result, the Apristas were forced to do their own printing work, with the use of a *planógrafo* – a primitive printing apparatus. Producing and circulating propaganda sheets was one of the missions that Chávez Várgas entrusted to his charges on a regular basis.

In order to carry out these missions, the Apristas typically printed several hundred sheets and distributed them about town. Chávez Várgas told his apprentices that, in order to complete this mission successfully, they had to slide one propaganda sheet under the door of as many homes as possible. He also told them to attach a sheet to the main door of all government offices – including the Prefecture and Police Headquarters, where there were usually armed guards on duty around the clock.

Missions of this nature were very dangerous. In order to minimise the risk involved, Chávez Várgas insisted that the most detailed of plans be made, and that the strictest of rules be followed. The *misiones* involving the distribution of APRA propaganda sheets were always carried out by teams of four to five Apristas, in the dead of night. As with all *misiones*, Chávez Várgas would appoint one person the *jefe de equipo*, the head of the team. This person was responsible for drawing up a detailed plan for how the mission was to be carried out. The plan had to explain the progression of streets that the team would follow in distributing the propaganda sheets. The plan also had to take into account the movements of the police, who worked in pairs, and followed a regular pattern as they made their rounds through Chachapoyas.

Once Chávez Várgas (and the cell as a whole) had approved the plan, the *jefe de equipo* chose three to four Apristas from among the members of his cell who would assist him in the mission. Of these individuals, two would actually slide the propaganda sheets under doors. As they did so, the *jefe* and the other team member(s) would wait at either end of the block where the propaganda sheets were being distributed. The function of these additional members of the group was to provide security for the team – to act as lookouts, in case the police deviated from their normal routine. Should the lookouts see the police approaching, they were to give a low whistle to warn the other team members, so that all could flee.

The *jefe de equipo* also had a second function. In addition to helping provide security for the team, he was to evaluate the behaviour of the other team members – especially those who were sliding propaganda sheets under the doors of homes, and were attaching these sheets to the doors of government offices. The *jefe* was to assess whether or not these people were sufficiently brave, daring and efficient in carrying out their duties. When the team had finished with its work, the *jefe de equipo* was the person who reported to Chávez Várgas on the success or failure of the endeavour. As was the case with the other *misiones*, he would say, 'mission accomplished', or 'mission not accomplished', according to the outcome of the team's work. In the next cell meeting, the team and Chávez Várgas would review the details of the *misión*, so that the cell as a whole could learn from what transpired.[7]

Despite their precautions, however, it was inevitable that these teams of propagandists would eventually have a run-in with the authorities. If the police stumbled upon a team of Apristas in the course of distributing party literature, there would be no opportunity for them to attempt to explain away what they were doing. If discovered, their only alternative would be to flee. Chávez Várgas told his students that, if the authorities did stumble upon them in the course of such a *misión*, each member of the team should run in a different direction. The police patrolled the streets in pairs, and by running in different directions the Apristas would force the police to split up in order to pursue them. They would also ensure that the constabulary could pursue only two members of the team.

It would be easier for those being pursued by the police to elude one Guardia, Chávez Várgas told his apprentices, than two. Chávez Várgas also recommended that, if they were pursued, they should follow the strategy of flight that he had recommended to them in order to evade the police when they left party meetings (see above). They should never run towards their homes or their party comrades. Rather, they should always try to run towards the forested areas that surrounded Chachapoyas, where they could easily hide from their pursuers. If they were forced to stay within the confines of the town, Chávez Várgas said, they should conceal themselves by vaulting into the garden of a nearby house, where they were to wait patiently until danger had passed.

The above-mentioned activities, while difficult and dangerous, afforded the novices-in-training with the opportunity to put their training to good effect. In other words, it gave them the chance to show Chávez Várgas that they had developed the degree of Aprista culture that the party leader had explained to them they would need to demonstrate if they were to be entrusted with the all-important task of waging war on injustice and inequality. It was this task that was APRA's central preoccupation.

New forms of embodiment

The training that Chávez Várgas provided to his followers did not end there. The Aprista leader devoted much time and energy to helping his charges develop the skills required to recruit the general population to the party cause. An important part of the training they received consisted of developing what are usefully regarded as 'communication skills'.

As noted above, one of the missions that Chávez Várgas assigned to his followers was to travel to the countryside, stay in peasant villages, and take whatever steps were necessary to organise party cells and bring the rural population into the party fold. Chávez Várgas told his apprentices repeatedly that their ability to succeed in this task would depend in large part on their ability to communicate effectively with people of humble backgrounds. The goal, he told his students, was to impress people, so they would say, 'oh, how well he speaks'.[8]

As the education of the novices progressed, he explained that the impact they would have on people would depend in part on the content of what they spoke about – on their ability to help poor people solve the problems that were most pressing in their everyday lives. Their impact would also depend on the language that they employed – on their ability to use terms and concepts that were direct and concrete. Equally important to their ability to bring rural cultivators into the party, Chávez Várgas told his students, was the manner in which they presented themselves to their audience. As their training continued, Chávez Várgas advised his students about the problem of presentation – emphasising how they could use their physical presence in order to contribute to the effectiveness of their oratory.

In initiating this aspect of their education, Chávez Várgas sought to make his students conscious of a problem that few had previously considered – how other people would regard and evaluate them as they engaged in the act of public speaking. Chávez Várgas assured his apprentices that, by viewing themselves through the eyes and ears of their listeners, they would be able to anticipate the reactions of their audience. This in turn would allow them to adjust their style of oratory accordingly, and to the best possible effect.

In order to develop this new form of self-awareness in his students, Chávez Várgas gave them instructions that caused them to view their bodies in a new way – as objects of performance, as objects that could be placed at the command of their consciousness and will so as to be manipulated, posed and postured, and in order to achieve specific, communicative ends. In order to help them achieve maximum effect, Chávez Várgas encouraged them to disaggregate or 'dismember' their bodies, and to re-aggregate them in a new form. That is, Chávez Várgas helped his followers reflect on how their listeners would view each of the various parts of their bodies that could be most effectively employed towards holding the attention of an audience.

For example, Chávez Várgas showed his followers how to hold their heads when they spoke – to hold their heads high, with their chins slightly elevated. He told them to stand as straight as possible, and to hold their torsos erect, with their shoulders squared, and with their chests forward. He stressed to his apprentices the importance of gesturing with their arms in order to emphasise particular points – to raise their arms, bent at the elbow, with the palms of their hands facing upward. He told them to be sure to make eye contact with the people in the audience – to engage one person after another, in order to draw everyone into the presentation, and to hold their attention thereafter. Chávez Várgas showed them when they should stand in order to give emphasis to a particular point, when they should pause, how to raise and lower their voices to achieve dramatic effect, and how they should sit in order to bring their performance to a conclusion. He told his followers to speak with force, with conviction, and always to move as they spoke, so that people did not become bored or start 'counting the roof beams'.⁹

Chávez Várgas also explained to his students that, as they spoke, the people in the audience would view them from different spatial perspectives. Some would see them from head on, others would view them in profile, and still others in semi-profile. Chávez Várgas showed his apprentice orators that any particular way of holding their heads and bodies, any particular way of gesturing, would make a different impression on people, depending on where they were in the audience, and whether they viewed the speaker head on, in profile, etc. Chávez Várgas also showed his students which ways of presenting themselves were most effective according to the perspective from which they were viewed. He told them that, as they spoke, they should try to keep in mind the multiple perspectives from which people would regard them.

Chávez Várgas did more than just explain these points to his students. He also trained them in the use of these skills. The cells that Chávez Várgas formed in Chachapoyas were the setting in which the young Apristas practised the art of public speaking. When he decided that they were ready, Chávez Várgas began insisting that his students practise the public speaking techniques he had taught them, and that they do so in the context of group meetings. In order to give them practice in this area, Chávez Várgas began presenting them with a new kind of hypothetical problem. Entirely without warning, for example, he would tell one apprentice that this person was to suppose that he was in the hut of a peasant family, talking to a group of rural cultivators about the advantages of forming rotating credit associations.

After distributing the other members of the cell in various places about the room – in order to simulate the various positions from which the speaker would be viewed – Chávez Várgas would insist that the speaker put into practice the techniques of oratory that they had learned. As each person took turns making their presentation, the other members of the cell were told to evaluate and critique the performance. After they had done so, Chávez Várgas would assess the presentation itself, and also its evaluation by the other cell members.

Through repeated trial and error, and continual coaching from Chávez Várgas, the young Apristas were slowly prepared in the art of communicating with the masses. They also learned to speak in terms that were clear, direct and easily accessible, and in a manner that was carefully staged and choreographed. And because the leaders-in-training worked together to refine these skills, in the process of doing so they formed a common awareness of the challenges involved in the art of public speaking. They also arrived at shared understandings of the most effective ways of using public oratory.

Chávez Várgas's instructions to his students to view themselves from the perspective of their listeners resulted in the emergence of a specific kind of evaluative gaze within the context of the cell. And although he attributed this evaluative gaze to a hypothetical audience of 'ordinary people', the standards according to which Chávez Várgas told his followers to evaluate themselves, and in which he schooled them to evaluate one another, had little to do with the perceptions of the Apristas' intended audience. Rather, these standards were actually those of Chávez Várgas himself, and the party he represented.

By raising his apprentices' self-consciousness about this issue, however – by subjecting them to a common evaluative gaze, and by involving them in the process of subjecting one another to that gaze – Chávez Várgas ensured that all of his apprentices would collude in the process of moulding the subjectivity of each cell member along similar lines. That is, Chávez Várgas helped his followers develop an embodied understanding of how they should present themselves in public that was shared by all members of the group. Once they began making trips to the countryside, and took on the responsibility of organising the rural population, these were the techniques that the leaders-in-training used in an effort to recruit followers from among the peasantry.

As the Aprista vanguard deepened their training, and participated in the kinds of activities described above, Chávez Várgas carefully evaluated his novices' progress, paying special attention to each person's strengths and weaknesses. He did so to see who would be best suited to lead each of the various ministries, or secretariats (culture, discipline, propaganda, peasant affairs, etc.) of which the party was composed. After training these apprentices for over half a decade, and observing their behaviour in increasingly trying circumstances, Chávez Várgas concluded that they had become sufficiently 'cultured' to be able to assume direct control over the party apparatus. It was at this point – when their education was complete – that these individuals began to refer to themselves as '*sacerdotes de la democracia*' (priests of democracy). This was a term of deep respect, that only the most committed Apristas used with one another.

The young Apristas thus came to see themselves as the vanguard of a transnational movement of equality, justice and social transformation. They came to regard themselves as highly trained combatants whose task it was to do away with the region's corrupt, aristocratic socio-cultural order, and to replace it with a new social structure based on equality and participatory democracy. It is these party priests who were entrusted with the difficult task of preparing the masses for democratic transformation.

Compromise, disaffection and radicalisation

APRA had considerable success in recruiting the population to its cause in the decades after 1930. The party's organising efforts across the Peruvian highlands were made easier by the significantly weakened state of the highland estate-owning class. As time passed this group found itself in deep disarray. This was in large part because the coastal plantation oligarchy had displaced highland estate owners from any significant role in the national power structure.

As highland estate owners found themselves excluded from the national power structure, they also lost control of much of the political apparatus in the sierra. As a result, they were less and less able to maintain their traditional powers and privileges. As a result, they found it increasingly difficult to resist the efforts of the peasantry to recover their lost lands. 'Land invasions' became widespread. Demands mounted for agrarian reform. It was only because the Peruvian military kept a careful eye on dissent – and often chose to rule the country directly – that radical alternatives to the status quo did not become more pronounced.

Ironically, one of the reasons that the coastal oligarchy and the armed forces were able to keep a lid on things was that they reached a kind of truce with APRA. By the 1950s, decades of government repression had generated a split in the movement. The party leadership, which had become increasingly conservative, entered into an agreement with Manuel Prado, a member of the coastal oligarchy who assumed the presidency (for the second time) in 1956, after eight years of military dictatorship. This arrangement is referred to as the '*convivencia*' (mutual coexistence). Party leaders agreed to provide Prado with the broad electoral support he needed to win. They could do so because of APRA's enormous popularity, which meant that the party faithful would turn out to vote as instructed. In return, Prado promised that he would legalise APRA (although it would be severely limited in the activities it could undertake), thus allowing it to come out of the shadows of illegality.

Many Apristas remained loyal to the party leadership despite the *convivencia*. A significant number of others, however – especially the movement's more radical elements – regarded the agreement with Prado as a betrayal, and left the party. In the years to follow they sought out membership in any one of a number of different parties that they felt remained true to APRA's original revolutionary vision. For party members like the original core group of Apristas in Chachapoyas, this made a great deal of sense. As noted earlier, they had begun their political life in the 1920s as communists.

Disaffected members of the Party of the People had much to choose from as they sought out new affiliations after the desertions caused by the *convivencia*. For APRA was not the only political party to splinter at this time. A series of developments combined during the late 1950s and early 1960s to divide the Left as a whole into a range of new revolutionary groupings, which espoused a variety of ideologies. In the aftermath of the Sino–Soviet split of 1960, the Peruvian Communist Party (the PCP) separated into two groups. Younger members abandoned the existing (Soviet-linked) PCP and established the PCP *Bandera Roja* (Red Flag), which drew inspiration from Maoist China. *Bandera Roja* then split, with the majority of its members forming the PCP *Patria Roja* (Red Nation). Those who remained loyal to the original *Bandera Roja* group espoused ties with the communists of Albania. A third group established the PCP *Sendero Luminoso* (Shining Path), which was committed to a fundamentalist version of Maoism (Fumerton, 2003; Alexander, 1999).

Complicating the scene of radical activity further were additional defections from APRA. Some of the party's more left-leaning members who had stuck with the Party of the People after the *convivencia* broke away in 1960, under inspiration from the Cuban Revolution, to form the MIR, or *Movimiento de la Izquierda Revolucionaria* (Revolutionary Left Movement). In the mid-1960s they joined forces with other radical groups to promote a rural guerrilla movement based on Che Guevara's *foco* theory of insurrection in the southern sierra, near Cuzco (Manrique, 1995: 305).

This breakdown and reconstitution of the organised Left was accompanied by a concomitant shift in how many radicals viewed revolution unfolding in time. In the 1930s and 1940s, a distinct temporality had informed the Apristas' understanding of revolution – one that reflected great 'patience' about the pace of change. The Apristas saw revolution as a long-term process. It wasn't an event but a mission or vocation, to which one devoted one's entire life. It had a beginning but no clear end point. APRA initially estimated that it would take at least 50 years, and probably more, to bring about the revolution. Activists were vague about and unconcerned with the subject.

This all changed by the 1950s. The longer the revolution was stalled, and the more profound its betrayal (the *convivencia*), the more extreme the reaction by the APRA vanguard – who fell back upon the discipline, secrecy and order that had helped their movement to begin with. What had been a naïve optimism about the eventual inevitability of transformation gave way to disillusion about the long-term approach.

In the process, the temporal horizon of revolution was compressed, and the radicals resorted to more desperate acts in order to spur immediate change. Revolution came to be seen as an event. Well before the emergence of Shining Path, a kind of 'revolutionary impatience' had developed, in which more extreme forms of behaviour were intended to bring about immediate transformation.[10]

In other words, the developments of the 1950s led large numbers of Apristas (and communists) to abandon their party in successive waves, and to search for alternative groups with which to affiliate. This meant that APRA (and also the Communist Party) infused the new radical movements of the 1960s with cadres of committed, disciplined and experienced militants. It also meant that there was direct continuity between the original Apristas and the communists, on the one hand, and the radical parties that followed. PCP-Shining Path was one of these parties.

The utility of viewing radical activity in Peru across the *longue durée* of the twentieth century is reflected in the following: groups originally formed in the early to mid-twentieth century as either Aprista or communist. Later, they joined one of the communist splinter groups that emerged during the 1960s, among which was the Shining Path. A number of these groups were damaged and/or forced underground in the context of Peru's decades-long civil war between PCP-SL and the Peruvian government – and the violence and the repression associated with it. The social forces that have generated sympathy with radical causes, however, remain. Indeed, there are widespread indications that unresolved tensions from the past remain just below the surface, and could erupt at any time.[11]

Conclusion

Is Peru a 'post-conflict society' (Rojas-Pérez, 2008)? Much of the literature on *Sendero Luminoso* (the Shining Path), and on Peru more generally, implicitly asserts such a temporality of revolution. This is in large part because Sendero has been dealt with as an *aberration* from rather than a continuation of what came before. Indeed, there is an extensive literature that focuses on the Sendero 'episode' as a distinct, separate period, and on the movement as a distinct, separate phenomenon that must be understood *sui generis*. There have been few attempts to understand the interconnections between the PCP-SL and what preceded it. Nor have there been attempts to make sense of Sendero as one specific variation of a broader pattern of revolutionary activity that pre-dated it and also continued alongside it. In other words, there has been little interest in understanding the Shining Path as a symptom of conditions that are typical rather than exceptional – as an outgrowth of Peru's *longue durée* of radical, twentieth-century political activity.

As I have suggested in the pages above, the Shining Path is anything but an inexplicable aberration. Rather, PCP-SL is usefully understood as having emerged out of an extended period of widespread radical endeavour that stretched across much of the twentieth century. I have illustrated this argument by exploring what I have called the 'revolution before the revolution' – by analysing radical initiatives from earlier in the twentieth century, and showing their connections to PCP-SL. My special focus has been on the day-to-day organising activities of the Popular American Revolutionary Alliance (APRA), and its efforts to form a revolutionary cadre among disaffected youth in Chachapoyas beginning in the 1930s. In the process, I have focused on the novel forms of subjectivity, organisation and discipline that emerged amongst the Apristas as they went about building their underground movement. In so doing, I have sought to raise new questions about the temporality of revolutionary politics and the scale of the everyday in revolutionary transformation.

I have also attempted to draw attention to the ambiguity of revolutionary legacies, by focusing on the splintering of the Peruvian Left during the 1950s and 1960s. At this time the Aprista leadership entered into a pact with Peru's conservative power structure, and took much of the party membership along with it. The compromises of the 1950s and 1960s, however, did not only serve to reinforce the status quo. They also resulted in large numbers of Apristas deserting the Party of the People. Those who stayed with the party became increasingly conservative, as did APRA itself. Those who left, however, went on to seek out affiliations with new parties, which they believed remained true to their vision of revolutionary change. In the process of seeking out these new affiliations, the former Apristas infused the new radical movements of the 1960s with cadres of committed, disciplined and experienced militants. This meant that there was direct continuity between the original Apristas, on the one hand, and the radical parties that followed. PCP-Shining Path was one of these parties.

Notes

1. Starn (1991) has called anthropologists to task for being blind to the forces in Peruvian society that generated Sendero Luminoso. My focus is related but different. I am concerned with the connections between the Shining Path and previous radical organising activities that took shape across Peru's long twentieth century.
2. See Fallaw and Nugent (2020) for a more detailed discussion of the relations that obtained between the different factions of the elite.

3. Interview with Sr Nicolás Muñoz Valenzuela, 19 August 1985. Sr. Muñoz was a member of one of the underground Apristas cells that formed in Chachapoyas in the 1930s. He was one of the party leaders in training who apprenticed with Manuel Chávez Várgas.
4. I have adapted this term from Scott, 1990.
5. Interview with Sr Nicolás Tuesta Valenzuela, 23 July 1985.
6. In this regard, it is revealing that elderly party members still remember these events from their youth.
7. See Nugent (n.d.) for a more detailed discussion of APRA's use of military language.
8. Interview with Sr Victor Santillan Gutierrez, 22 January 2001. Sr. Santillan was also a member of one of the underground Apristas cells that formed in Chachapoyas in the 1930s, and one of the party leaders in training who apprenticed with Manuel Chávez Várgas.
9. Interview with Sr Victor Santillan Gutierrez, 22 January 2001.
10. I have adapted the notion of revolutionary impatience from Mario Feit's fascinating discussion of democratic impatience (see Feit, 2017).
11. The controversies surrounding the election of 'leftist' Pedro Castillo to the Peruvian presidency in 2021, and the fears unleashed by the death of Abimael Guzmán (leader of the Shining Path) in that same year, show that these fears are very much alive.

References

Alexander, Robert Jackson. 1999. *International Maoism in the Developing World*. Westport, CT: Praeger.
Burga, Manuel and Flores-Galindo, Alberto. 1987. *Apogeo y crisis de la República Aristocrática*. Lima: Ediciones Rikchay Peru.
DeGregori, Carlos Ivan. 1990. *El surgimiento de Sendero Luminoso: Ayacucho 1969–1979*. Lima: Instituto der Estudios Peruanos.
Fallaw, Ben and Nugent, David. 2020. 'Comparative studies in nation building, *ca.* 1900–1950', in Fallaw, B. and Nugent, D. (eds), *State Formation in the Libera Era: Capitalisms and claims of citizenship in Mexico and Peru*. Tucson: University of Arizona Press, 127–54.
Feit, Mario. 2017. 'Democratic impatience: Martin Luther King, Jr. on democratic temporality'. *Contemporary Political Theory*, 16: 363–86.
Fumerton, Mario. 2003. *From Victims to Heroes: Peasant counter-rebellion and civil war in Ayacucho, Peru, 1980–2000*. Amsterdam: Rozenberg.
García-Bryce, Iñigo. 2018. *Haya de la Torre and the Pursuit of Power in Twentieth-Century Peru and Latin America*. Chapel Hill: University of North Carolina Press.
Gorriti, Gustavo. 1999. *The Shining Path: A history of the millenarian war in Peru*. Translated by Robin Kirk. Chapel Hill: University of North Carolina Press.
Klarén, Peter F. 1973. *Modernization, Dislocation, and Aprismo: Origins of the Peruvian Aprista party, 1870–1932*. Austin: University of Texas Press.
Klarén, Peter F. 2000. *Peru: Society and nationhood in the Andes*. Oxford: Oxford University Press.
Manrique, Nelson. 1995. *Historia de la República*. Lima: Fondo Editorial de COFIDE.
Nugent, David. 2019. *The Encrypted State: Delusion and displacement in the northern Peruvian Andes*. Stanford, CA: Stanford University Press.
Nugent, David. n.d. 'The Longue Durée of Revolution: Secrecy, security and sacrifice in 20th Century Peru'. (Unpublished manuscript.)
Rojas-Pérez, Isaias. 2008. 'Writing the aftermath: Anthropology and "post-conflict"', in Poole, D. (ed.), *A Companion to Latin American Anthropology*. Malden, MA: Wiley-Blackwell, 254–75.
Scott, James C. 1990. *Domination and the Arts of Resistance: Hidden transcripts*. New Haven, CT: Yale University Press.
Starn, Orin. 1991. 'Missing the revolution: Anthropologists and the war in Peru'. *Cultural Anthropology*, 6(1): 63–91.
Sulmont, Denis. 1985. *El movimiento obrero peruano, 1890–1980*. Lima: Tarea.

6
Cosmogony and second nature in revolutionary Cuba
Martin Holbraad

Introduction

Revolutions are habitually considered as dramatic, one-off political events whose aim is to bring about wholesale political and societal change. This is most obviously evident in the imagery that revolution often conjures – the storming of the Bastille, of the Winter Palace, the occupation of Tahrir Square, masses flooding the streets in effervescent uprising – as well as the standard tendency to date revolutions as singular historical upheavals (July 1789, October 1917, May 1968, January 2011 ...). As conceptual historian Reinhart Koselleck has suggested (2005), such a conception of revolutions as event-like ruptures in and with time is constitutive to the very idea of time in post-Enlightenment modernity. If, as Lévi-Strauss has suggested, the French Revolution is the origin myth of modernity (1966: 254), then, for Koselleck, one of the ways in which it has been transformative is in recasting time itself as a matter of development, with the present as a hiatus between a past that is gone and a future that is unknown. Revolution, as Koselleck writes, 'assumes a transcendental significance; it becomes a regulative principle of knowledge, as well as of the actions of all those drawn into revolution' (2005: 46–7).

The conception of revolutions as singular, world-changing events, however, presents a profound problem for revolutions that are successful in toppling *ancien regimes* and putting in their place new orders. There is a fundamental tension between, on the one hand, the idea that revolutions are about radical change and, on the other, that their very raison d'être is to precipitate transformations that themselves aspire to be permanent and, to boot, typically do this by means of state structures that are themselves also permanent, or at least more permanent than the revolutionary currents that seek, perforce, to change and repurpose them. Indeed, of prime concern also for the protagonists of revolution themselves, this tension shoots through the social and political theory of revolution. For example, the seemingly oxymoronic notion of 'permanent revolution' (broadly, the problem of how to ensure that revolutionary projects for radical change are carried through in the face of a host of stultifying and regressive conditions), has been a standard concern among Marxist theorists and leaders alike (e.g., Marx and Engels, 1969; Trotsky, 1969; Schram, 1971), as has the possibility that the state apparatus ought ultimately to 'wither away' (Lenin, 2011). Conversely, the question of how to rein in the sweeping forces of revolutionary upheaval, as they are often imagined, once they have been successful in taking hold of the state apparatus is also standard fare in the history of revolutions. A particularly vivid account is provided by Susan Buck-Morss (2002), for example, in her captivating study of the tussle between avant-garde artists and the Bolshevik vanguard in the early years of Soviet Russia. Initially co-opted by the political leadership as a conduit of revolutionary transformation, avant-garde artists' effervescent experimentations with possible futures – 'the future is our only goal!' (Rodchenko and Stepanova, 1991) – was gradually hemmed in, first by Lenin and then by Stalin's teleology of unilinear Party-controlled progress, which found its ultimate expression in socialist realism as the only art appropriate to the revolutionary emancipation of the proletariat.

This essay explores the inner dynamic of this tension between change and permanence – rupture and perdurance – in revolutionary politics with reference to the experience of revolution in Cuba. Its central contention is that the tension is constitutive to the process of revolution, at the heart of its inner logic. The apparent paradox that revolutions, such as the Cuban, are liable to produce orders that are as inimical to change as the orders they originally replaced is neither an accident of history, nor merely proof that, notwithstanding their own rhetoric, successful revolutions tend to fizzle out (though this is no doubt true, also in Cuba, as we shall see), nor even an indication that previous orders are harder to wipe away than revolutions may hope or claim (which is also surely true). Rather, the sense of permanence, perdurance, and even stasis that revolutions evince when they proceed actually to build the (putatively) new and better world that they initially set out to prove was possible is a function of the logic of transformation that their initial rupture-like character sets in motion. Permanent orders are not where revolutions go to die. They are what revolutions are bound to become, because that is what the form they give to change achieved must look like by its very nature – its form, in fact, as 'second nature', as we shall see. In the terms laid out in the introduction of this volume, the condition of permanence is not the death of successful revolution but rather its afterlife – as much part of its inner logic as the impulse and desire for radical change.

An attempt logically to conjoin change and permanency in the study of revolution rejects the tendency in political science and theory to adopt the common narrow definition of revolution as a matter of radical change and rupture alone, and then assume by fiat that when revolutions transfigure themselves into permanent orders of various kinds they must, by that token, become something else. While I have contributed elsewhere to criticising the normativity of such approaches (Cherstich et al., 2020: 5–10), here we may note as an illustrative case Max Weber's famous account of the so-called 'routinisation' of charismatic leadership (2019). Written in the aftermath of the October revolution in Russia, as well as the revolution in Germany itself at the end of the Great War, the parts of *Economy and Society* in which Weber's discussion of charisma appears are littered with anxious references to the actions of revolutionary socialists at the time. Lurking across the text's exposition of the power of charismatic authority to displace the legitimacy of established political orders is a concern with the populist attractions of revolution and how to bring them to heel. Tellingly, however, for Weber, the revolutionary power that is inherent in charismatic leadership is also what is most at risk when it is channelled into institutional forms of its own. If charisma must be 'routinised' when its bearers come to occupy the machinery of government, Weber argues, it must thereby also dissipate and risk losing the ground of its original appeal. Underpinning Weber's analysis, in other words, is the standard normative premise about revolution (and its charisma) as an act of rupture: the hallmark of revolution has to be radical change and upheaval, so that, when its transformational powers are tempered and routinised institutionally, it must by definition lose its credentials as a genuine revolution and become something else.

While similar assumptions are as pervasive in public discourse about revolution as they are in political science and theory, in this essay I want to sketch out how an anthropological vantage on revolution can provide a more capacious analysis, one that treats the question of revolutionary change and permanence symmetrically, as part of a single, unifying analytical scheme. Shifting the analysis of revolution squarely onto anthropological terrain, my first major claim will be that revolution can fruitfully be considered as an act of political cosmogony, that is, a deliberate and self-conscious effort to orchestrate transformations that are so all-embracing that they can be both claimed and experienced as radical attempts to change the constituents of the world people inhabit. While this is a point I have sought to make elsewhere for revolutions at large (Cherstich et al., 2020), as well as for revolution in Cuba in particular (Holbraad, 2014; 2018; see also Cumbrera Mesa et al., 2020), the point is worth remaking here because bringing world-making into the fray in this way sets up my second main contention, namely that the transformations that revolutions precipitate can be analysed in terms of the well-developed anthropological discussion about the relationship between nature and culture. Drawing on Roy Wagner's sophisticated work on this theme (1981; 1986), I want to show that the relationship between change and permanence in revolution can be parsed out analytically in terms of the relationship of mutual implication between nature and culture, which renders change and permanence in revolution logical functions of each other, too. In a nutshell, my suggestion will be that if revolution can be seen as the political apogee of modernity, that is because its action can be viewed in Wagner's terms as a transformation of innate nature into the artifice of culture. Rendering this transformation as a function of radical, 'progressive' change, however, means that when revolutions slow themselves down in efforts of political consolidation and institutionalisation, the changes they institute as 'culture' come to regress back into a state of innateness, experienced as a once-again permanent order that is inimical to change. Understood as cosmogony, then, revolution entails its own afterlife as 'second nature', where this classic philosophical concept is repurposed in a distinctively anthropological, not to say specifically Wagnerian, tenor.

I have referred to this chapter as an essay because it operates very much like a sketch. For example, rather than building up the argument from my long-term ethnography of the experience of revolution in Cuba, I use mainly two snippets of ethnography (I call them 'scenes'), merely to set up in a vivid way the argument about change and permanence, which I then go on to develop with reference also to the history and discourse of revolution in Cuba. Rather than a tight intervention in the (near saturated) literature on revolution in Cuba, therefore, the essay is offered more as a think piece about how anthropological ways of thinking about cosmogony, nature and culture can provide a fresh vantage for thinking about revolution, using Cuban materials to show how that might work, and what new aspects of revolution it might reveal.

Still, the essay's meta-argument about the analytical value of an anthropological approach to revolution is motivated in typical anthropological fashion by two admittedly broad, but nevertheless significant ethnographic observations that stem from my exposure to the experience of revolution in Cuba since the late 1990s. Taken together, I suggest, the two observations provide an ethnographic warrant for the essay's anti-normative insistence on revolutionary permanence, and all that entails for the reconceptualisation of the problem in anthropological terms.

The first stems from the fact that, as it turns out, in Cuba, the term revolution itself – *la revolución* – refers more to permanence than to rupture. Contrary to the idea that revolution is change by definition, in Cuban common as well as political discourse a clear distinction is made between the sequence of events that brought Fidel Castro to power in 1959, which even critics refer to formulaically as *el triunfo de la revolución* ('the triumph of the revolution'), and the total project of social, economic, political, and indeed moral transformation that these events set in train, which is what people refer to as 'the Revolution' – *la revolución Cubana*. Taken as a proper noun, then, in Cuba the term 'revolution' denotes permanence, deeply and abidingly. It is the project the country embarked upon all those years ago (*el proyecto nacional*, as official discourse often has it), and which is still ongoing, albeit severely ailing in all sorts of ways, and confronting all sorts of obstacles, difficulties and compromises, as we shall see. Thus imagined, the revolution is ever unfolding, 'firmly' moving forward towards victory, following that initial burst of energy that brought it to power, 'until always' – *hasta siempre* – as the sloganised address associated with the death of Che Guevara vividly conveys (a standard form of farewell that might be translated as 'so long', repurposed as a political locution that speaks to the peculiar temporality of the project – not to say the projection – of revolution).

The second preliminary observation is that, taken as an ethnographic object rather than a political form defined a priori, revolutionary politics very much *includes* the question of what a revolution might even be, and not least whether and how it might be understood as either a rupture or a permanent condition, or somehow both. As the two vignettes with which I shall seek to bring this dilemma to life illustrate, asking questions about what counts as revolution, whether, to what degree and in what sense the revolution one is meant to be part of is genuine, how and how far a project of revolution might shift in character, and so on, are all proper parts of what it is to experience a revolution. Certainly, daily life in Cuba today and throughout the revolutionary period can be perceived in significant ways as a contrapuntal dialogue with the official discourse of the revolutionary government, in which the very meaning as well as the value, purpose and direction (or lack thereof) of the revolution are the topic. Treated ethnographically, one might say in a very general way, revolutions are inherently reflexive – they ask questions about themselves. Therefore, starting with an a priori definition of revolution (e.g. as rupture) is not only counter-anthropological, but also, at least in the Cuban case, ethnographically blinkered. The two ethnographic scenes with which I set the argument on change and permanence on its tracks also serve to make this point.

Rupture and permanence: two scenes

Both scenes are from a five-month stint of fieldwork conducted in (still) state-socialist Cuba in 2015. The first is of an elderly lady sitting at a bench of Parque Central, in downtown Havana, within earshot of where I was standing waiting for a bus, on a relentlessly sunny afternoon in August 2015. Even though the bench was in the shade, the woman was sweating desperately, and so was I and everyone else in the bus queue. Mechanically wiping her brow and chest with her handkerchief, in that way Cubans have of performing their summer heat, the lady vocalised her desperation, speaking in a 'grumpy old woman' style to herself or the world at large – it was not quite clear which. But what came out was not the standard comment on the heat one expects to hear in Cuba on hot days like that – '¡qué calór!' people will typically exclaim, as if to remonstrate with the airless atmosphere. Rather, the lady's tirade turned out to be political:

> 'When these guys (*esa gente*) got rid of Batista I was with them – everything then was change (*todo era cambio*). But holy mother of mine (*madre mía*), who'd have known we'd still have them nailed there fifty years later (*ahí clavados*). No one can stand this! (*¡Esto no hay quien lo aguante!*)'

Uttered in a different context or by a different kind of person, these words would be, to use another Cuban heat metaphor, ¡*candela!*, which is to say 'too hot to handle' – incendiary. Saying things like that about the government in public is risky – you can get arrested for it, and have your card marked with the security services. Of interest here, however, is not the outspoken character of the old lady's words, but their profound ambiguity. This is owing in large part to the odd match between the political content of the monologue and the meteorological connotations of the manner and context in which it was delivered. Indeed, if the woman felt she could say such a thing in public at all, that may be because the context of the heat, and the pragmatics of her performance of it, effectively merged the two levels, rendering them homologous. It is not just that the 'this' of her statement – 'no one can stand this' – rendered the heat an alibi for her complaint about the government. It is more that the homology between the content and the context of the statement rendered the two as versions of each other. While the heat itself can be personified as an oppressive condition, political oppression – a government that brought about revolutionary change only to then ensconce itself in power for nearly 60 years – can in turn be experienced as an objective condition that, like the Caribbean heat, can only be endured: something one must 'stand', even if, as with the summer sun, no one really can. Politics, then, as weather.

The second scene is from a conversation that took place in that same summer, though now in the fan-assisted cool of my shared office at the Institute of Philosophy of the Cuban Academy of Sciences, the elite government-sponsored research centre where I was a visiting scholar during my fieldwork at the time. This was the time when the left-leaning government of Alexis Tsipras had called a referendum on the terms of the European bail-out in Greece, where part of my family is from. I had come into work full of thoughts about this, and vented my own political frustrations, a little like the lady at the bus stop, out loud, to myself and anyone who cared to listen. My behaviour was certainly indiscreet since the Institute of Philosophy is very much at the heart of the Cuban government's continuing ideological project and, consequently, colleagues there were favourable to Tsipras and his government by default, as was the state media at the time. Still, as it turns out, my outburst produced one of the most vivid explanations of what it means to be revolutionary in Cuba. Having heard my heated commentary, one of the senior and most charismatic researchers at the Institute came to my desk and illustrated my error by picking up my stapler:

> 'Listen, my Greek friend. You think politics is like this:' He took the stapler and, play-acting with it like a child might do with a toy car, dragged it slowly from the edge of the desk and in towards the centre, on a steady trajectory of movement. 'But revolutions are not like that. Revolutions are like *this*:' Having rested the stapler at the edge of the desk, he picked it up with an abrupt gesture and in one fell swoop moved it to the centre of the desk and let it drop there, willy-nilly. 'Revolutionary action is an impulse, a push. You can't

know in advance where it will lead you. But you do it to change things. Everything changes! Once you're there [pointing to the stapler at the centre of desk], then you find out what needs to be done. Sometimes that's what's needed – a push, a change, *action*. That's what your friend Tsipras is doing. We know about that here.'

My two scenes – with the old lady and the stapler – are of course just anecdotes. Taken together, however, they illustrate the aforementioned duality of permanence and rupture, which runs deep in understanding not just how revolutionary politics operates, but also how it is experienced. And hence my central puzzle in this essay: if revolutions are par excellence understood as transformative eruptions – 'everything changes', as the philosopher at the Institute said, and 'everything then was change', in the old lady's words – then how are we to conceive of them when they become permanent conditions, as the lady's hot lament would have it?

Revolution as cosmogony: change, meta-change and stagnation

In response, as mentioned, the first step is to note the cosmological proportions of the changes that revolutions characteristically seek – and, when successful, purport – to bring about. This stems from the totalising – or 'total' in Mauss's sense (1992) – character of revolutionary transformations, which, as historian Martin Malia has argued (2008), has tended to intensify in the course of revolutions' historical development as a characteristically modern political form (e.g. consider the increasingly encompassing scope of revolutionary transformation, from the 'bourgeois' French Revolution, through the proletarian revolution in Russia, and then to the successive waves of so-called 'permanent' revolution in Maoist China). Seen in the light of Marshall Berman's now classic argument in *All that is Solid Melts into Air* (1983), the modernity of revolution is most evident in its deliberately and self-consciously radical programme for change, setting out to bring about a total socio-political transformation, changing the entire framework in which people's lives are lived. The goal of revolution, one might say, is not just to make changes in the world, but to bring about a new one. Certainly, the cosmological tenor of revolutionary discourse about 'making a new and better world', in Cuba as elsewhere, is so standard as to appear banal, and is powerfully borne out by the overtly spatio-temporal referents of the transformative projects that revolutions pursue. We have already seen how, according to Susan Buck-Morss (2002), the nature of time (open futures versus linear telos) was most deeply at stake in the tussles between artists and political leaders in the early Soviet Union. Buck-Morss bolsters her argument by showing how the question of time gains cosmological proportions in the work of many of the artists who saw revolution as an experiment with it. The fact that images of the planet were adopted as emblems of the Soviet project of global communism, worn as brooches by successive Secretarys General and other officials, is just one in a long trajectory of indices of revolutions' cosmic projections. Perhaps the most striking example is the practice, which has become standard since the French Revolution, of revolutions literally inaugurating a new time by instituting their own calendar. To take the Cuban example, in official documents, including the daily press, each year since the revolution of 1959 has been dated according to its distance from that initial time-inaugurating event. So, for example, at the time of writing, according to the legend of *Granma*, the official newspaper of the Cuban Communist Party (equivalent in Cuba to what *Pravda* was in the USSR), we are traversing 'the 62nd year of the revolution'.

As I have argued elsewhere (2014; 2018), perhaps the most explicit, as well as emblematic, statement not just of the character of revolution as a cosmogonic process, but also of the particular properties of the new world it sets out to create, can be found in Fidel Castro's notorious 'words to the intellectuals' speech, which was delivered in the National Library in the summer of 1961, to a meeting of artists and writers assembled there to discuss with the revolutionary leadership their concerns about political restrictions on their creative liberty (a tussle that is in some ways comparable to the aforementioned account given of the Soviet case by Buck-Morss). Firmly setting the coordinates of the relationship between artistic production and the still young and, as he also put it on that occasion, 'improvised' revolution, the most quoted part of Fidel's speech reads as nothing short of a statement of political ontology (see Holbraad, 2014), enunciating the very *shape* of revolution as a political form:

> [Even artists and writers who are not revolutionary] should have the opportunity and freedom to express their creative spirit within the revolution. In other words: within the revolution everything; against the revolution, nothing. Against the revolution, nothing, because the revolution also has its rights, and the first right of the revolution is the right to exist, and no one can oppose the revolution's right to exist. Inasmuch as the revolution embodies the interests of the people, inasmuch as the revolution symbolizes

the interests of the whole nation, no one can justly claim a right to oppose it. This is not some special law or guideline for artists and writers. It is a general principle for all citizens. It is a fundamental principle of the revolution ... the revolution has one right: the right to exist, the right to develop, and the right to be victorious. (Castro Ruz, cited in García Luis, 2008: 116–17)

Two features are of particular interest in relation to the present argument about revolutionary cosmogony. First, the revolution here is presented as a *container*, as something that has an 'inside' that, in a certain sense, is all-encompassing (elsewhere Che Guevara said as much: 'there is no life outside [the revolution]' – Guevara and Castro, 2009: 25). It is a totality, an all-containing 'everything', *against* which nothing can exist. So, in its strictly formal properties at least, the revolution is indeed to be conceived as generating a universe of sorts. Secondly, this all-containing 'universe in the making' takes the form of a motion – it is a vector of, as Fidel says, 'development'. This may not be particularly original, of course, since the notion of forward-moving thrust has long been recognised as a central element of revolution understood as a peculiarly modern political form (Koselleck, 2005). Still, Fidel's rendering of this idea is interesting for the way in which it links a sense of 'development' to the normative idea of revolution as a container of everything. Forward motion, here, is not just the shape revolution marks over time, but a *right* that the revolution has, as *against* the putative rights of people, and particularly the counter-revolutionaries that this forward motion of development is meant to nullify. Effectively, we have here an image of revolution that realises its *telos* as a totality, or completes itself, through its own movement: a container of everything that takes the form of a *totalising current*, we might say, mixing the metaphor.

'Everything is change', then, as the old lady and the philosopher both said. Indeed, while it is beyond the scope of this essay to provide a detailed history of the ways in which this world-making project of transformation unfolded in Cuba in the first years of the revolution, one would draw attention in this regard to the rapid reforms of the early 1960s that made headlines around the world at the time, such as the famously successful literacy campaign of 1961, the quick succession of measures to nationalise industry, the agrarian and urban reform laws that passed control of all land, housing and infrastructure to the state, the institution of centralised structures of popular participation in – as well as surveillance and control by – the nascent revolutionary project (such as the Committees for the Defence of the Revolution, the Cuban Women's

Federation, and other such neighbourhood-level organisations), as well, of course, as the rapid development of universal education and health-care rights, and their impressive implementation across the island.

Accounts of this period, tend to emphasise the drastically expanded role given to the state in this process of revolutionary transformation. In the more sympathetic accounts (e.g. Diaz Castañón, 2001), the expansion of the state is viewed as a structure of economic redistribution and socio-political emancipation of the people, while more critical ones (e.g. Guerra, 2012) emphasise its capacities for oppression. In the light of the 'everything then was change' dictum of my two scenes above, however, here we may note the way state expansion operated as an agent of change, and this in an importantly dual sense. On one level, the state acts as the vehicle for suitably drastic changes that tend to envelop the whole territory in one fell swoop (e.g., that intense year of 1961 spent sending youths from the urban centres to the remotest parts of the island to teach peasants how to read, all-sweeping legal decrees that radically alter property regimes across the national territory, etc.). The state, then, as that which brings about change.

By the same token, however, though at a deeper level, both the muscle the state can bring to bear upon such changes, and its capacity in principle to implement them not only across the territory but also deep into people's lives, mean that revolutions which, like the Cuban, are able to take charge of the levers of the state have the power to expand drastically the domain of what is amenable to change in the first place. An *ancien régime* that presents itself as inimical to change and part of the natural order of things (e.g. unequal distribution of land and property, the exploitative relations this involves, brute peasants destined to die illiterate like serfs, racial hierarchies based on pseudo-scientific ideas about natural propensities, similarly naturalised ideas about gender roles, and so on) – all this is suddenly dramatised as the object of concerted transformation by the emancipatory forces of the unfolding revolution. The deeper secret of the state, then, is that it not only changes things, but also, in so doing, redraws the very distinction between what can be changed and what cannot. To the extent that revolutions blow this inherent capacity of the state-form to cosmogonic proportions, their effect for those who participate in them is often a dizzying sense of possibility. The Cuban revolutionary slogan, 'to fight against the impossible and win' (see Figure 6.1), captures this beautifully. And, once again, so does the recollection of those days by the old lady at the bus stop: 'everything then was change'. Indeed, were we to take Fidel Castro's political ontology seriously, according to which in a certain sense the revolution *is* an

Figure 6.1 'To fight against the impossible and win'. State-sponsored political billboard, photographed in Cuba in 2008 (Source: Wikimedia Commons, https://upload.wikimedia.org/wikipedia/commons/2/23/Castro_sign.jpg).

'everything', we could draw the ethnographic conclusion that the revolution itself *is*, therefore, change, and this in both senses: changing things, and thereby shifting the limits of what things can be changed at all – what we might call 'meta-change'.

How then, we may ask, are these dizzying heights of change and meta-change related to that sense of suffocating stagnation that same lady was expressing at the bus stop? One, basically correct, answer to the question would extend the story about the role of the state in the Cuban revolution, tracing the marked shifts in its relationship to the capacity for change in the years that followed the demiurgic effervescence of the 1960s. Again, historical narratives tend to present this as a shift from heady idealism to a bumpy landing in the realities of state administration in the 1970s and 1980s[1] (Kirk et al., 2018) – a period referred to officially as one of 'revolutionary consolidation', but commonly remembered as the 'grey' years, characterised by a Cold War embrace of the USSR, the wooden language of a sloganised Marxism-Leninism, and pervasive censorship and bureaucracy leading to the consolidation, if anything, of the privileges of a ruling class more interested in the perks of power than in the emancipation of the people. And no sooner had Fidel begun to try to 'rectify' some of these 'errors', with concerted efforts in 1985 to pull back some of the more ossifying effects of state bureaucracy, than the Soviet bloc's end threw the revolution in Cuba into its most traumatic period, officially branded as 'Special' in 1991, during which change became, if anything, something that happened to the island, rather than something it created for itself. Serial adjustments to dire economic need, openings to tourism and foreign investment, flirtations with Chinese and Vietnamese models of socialism with growing private enterprise under Raúl Castro, thawing relations with the US under President Obama (subsequently rescinded by the Trump presidency and the ascent to Cuban presidency of Miguel Díaz-Canel in 2019), and so on: reactions all to the vagaries of international circumstances, rather than a nation taking the reins of its own capacities for transformation. This, one might say, is roughly how by 2015 the revolution became 'them', personified as the Castro brothers, 'nailed there fifty years later', in the old lady's words.

Still, clues of a deeper relationship between the initial years of change and the subsequent condition of stagnation become apparent when one places these historical developments in the context of the more cosmologically-minded framing of revolution adumbrated above. In this connection, the snippet of political cosmology implicit in the old lady's statement is of interest, since it links back directly to the cosmogonic image of revolution as all-embracing change we found in Castro's 'words to the intellectuals', in two ways in particular. The first concerns the demonstrative pronoun on which the ambiguity of her statement turns, namely the 'this' that formed the target of her desperation: *esto no hay quien lo aguante* – 'no one can stand this'. As most people in Cuba would readily point out, 'this' – *esto* – is not just any word when uttered in such a way. Indeed, if the demonstrative pronoun operates as a transistor of ambiguity between a comment on the weather and on the government, that is because its latter sense is one that is entirely recognisable by Cubans. In the elaborate, and elaborately unstated, code for talking politics that has developed over the many decades that the lady was lamenting – a code that operates as much with gestures as with words[2] – *esto* is a signifier heavily freighted with political meaning: deploying the floating grammatical quality of the pronoun, it is coextensive in its form with the revolution itself, with the country, with society, with the state, indeed with 'the state we're in'. '*Esto*', people will say, or sometimes '*la cosa*' ('the thing'), at times gesturing with the hand towards the whole horizon of space around them, and mean by it all that, taken together: the political condition at large, to which the project of revolution most explicitly sought first to give birth and then establish and solidify as an all-embracing transformation. In the light of the earlier discussion of Castro's famous speech, then, the lady's '*esto*' is simply what his 'everything' – that is, the all-containing revolution – looks like when it is experienced from its *inside*. Something by which one is so thoroughly contained as to feel suffocated by it – inside it, yes, but not necessarily part of it, though always already conditioned by it, exactly as Castro had warned the intellectuals assembled in the National Library back in 1961.

The second and more overtly cosmological feature of the lady's pronouncement has to do with its performative elision of politics and the weather. What is most significant here is not so much whether the elision was intentional, or the fact that it was critical of the government, but rather the homology it assumes between *esto* and weather as conditions one can only endure. It is indeed noteworthy how symmetrically this inverts the image of revolution presented by the philosopher with the stapler. If for him the totalising change of everything that revolutions bring about is a project of concerted – indeed courageous – human action (what Cubans know how to do, and Alexis Tsipras in Greece was merely trying out), for her it is just the opposite: total and all-embracing like the weather, indeed, but, like the weather too, constitutively out of her (human) control. An everything that is everywhere, ineluctable and relentless, just like the revolutionary imagery of eternal progress would have it, only, instead of being produced, it is 'the thing' that can only be endured. Furthermore, the inverse symmetry with the philosopher's statement pertains to the question of change also. If in the early revolution everything was change, the complaint about the surrounding *esto* now is partly that it is so stuck, with the Castro brothers 'nailed there fifty years later'. *Esto*, then, is unbearable not only because it is what the 'everything' of revolution feels like when you are caught inside it, but also because it is what that everything becomes when its inner momentum as a current of change has long since dissipated into stagnation.

To be sure, once again, a straightforward commentary on this contrast between active change and passive stagnation would quite rightly contend that it corresponds simply to the opposing roles of those who are in charge of the revolutionary process, whether in practice (the Castros, the state machinery) or in theory (the philosopher defending it conceptually), and those who over more than half a century have found themselves on the receiving end of its institutionalisation (the old lady, and just about everyone, one may assume, who was in the bus queue listening, knowing exactly what she was talking about). The revolution looks like an action if you are doing it and like a condition if you are having it done to you. Still, as with Weber's mutual exclusion of charisma and its routinisation, the problem with this level-headed approach is that it parses change as permanence apart, distributing them in this case to different constituents of the revolutionary process, rather than understanding them as functions of one another within the coordinates of a single analytical framework.

Change: permanence: nature into culture: culture into (second) nature

This essay's second move in addressing the conundrum regarding the relationship between revolution as unfolding change and revolution as permanent condition is to see it in the light of the arch-anthropological concern with the varied ways in which the distinction between nature and culture can be conceived in different ethnographic settings. Such a move follows directly from the first one, of seeing revolution as an act of political cosmogony. To see the link, one may note that if the notion of 'political cosmogony' is interesting at all, that is because it draws an analogy across the nature/culture distinction as it is habitually made. In its modern secular understanding, the cosmos is deemed to be 'natural' in the most encompassing sense – the universe out there, in a tiny part of which we humans make our lives, and out of tiny parts of which we build our cultures. What we call 'nature' is certainly part of the cosmos at large, and may even be coterminous with it (depending on whether one would be inclined to deem a supernova, say, as 'natural'). Politics, on the other hand, is but an aspect of those cultures that human beings make in the face of the surrounding nature, which they also contain (human nature, natural instincts and drives, etc.): it is an activity, we assume, that we pursue in our attempt to carve out a collective existence, and it is one for which we hold each other responsible. Politics, thus understood, is one aspect of the cultural orders that human beings construct in order to organise their lives. To suggest that revolutions can be conceived as cosmogonic acts, then, is to plug the way we think about them into the way we think about the relationship between nature and culture. Moreover, if drawing an analogy between revolution and cosmogony cuts against the habitually sharp ways in which the respective domains of nature and culture are distinguished – the 'modern constitution' that seeks perpetually to 'purify' them, in Bruno Latour's memorable image (1993) – then, by the same token, such an analogy has the potential to destabilise just those distinctions.

In this way, the study of revolution can draw on the longstanding anthropological critique of the distinction between nature and culture (e.g. Lévi-Strauss, 1990; Strathern, 1980; Viveiros de Castro, 2012), with reference to the marked variation in the ways in which its two terms are related in different ethnographic contexts. Of particular relevance here is Roy Wagner's powerful idea that this variation can itself be tracked conceptually with reference to the way people in different settings distinguish between aspects of their lives that are taken as given, which he calls 'innate', and aspects which they deem themselves responsible for making, which he calls 'artificial' (Wagner, 1981; 1986). Briefly put: for Wagner, one particular way of conceiving the distinction between nature and culture, which anthropologists have long taken for granted as part of the human condition at large, has been to take the former, nature, as innate and the latter, culture, as artificial. To show that anthropologists have been wrong to take this for granted, however, Wagner counterposes ethnographic examples from Melanesia to show that for people there the kinds of things anthropologists take as cultural are taken as innate – as part of the given order of things – while the things we take as natural are treated as artificial – things that it is our responsibility to strive to achieve. So, for example, the anthropologist takes social structures, norms and rules as human-made culture, while things like the weather or indeed our own drives as an animal species are the innate natural conditions these cultural conventions seek to bring under control. By contrast, Melanesians take social structures, norms and rules for granted as innate conditions beyond human control, while the field we call nature is for them animated by entities and forces with which humans can engage in relationships and influence through ritual actions, including witchcraft and sorcery.

In terms of this matrix, then, the relatively uncontroversial starting-point would be to parse the idea of revolution as concerted human action – a momentous push that changes everything – as an example of what we would already assume, namely an exemplary human project of changing the social order, which is the proper domain of human artifice, against the background of innate natural conditions (see Figure 6.2, first and second lines). If anything distinguishes revolutionary action, as we have seen, it is the radical manner in which it is able to change the very *scope* of human action. To reiterate the philosopher's illustration with the stapler, what makes revolutions different from the liberal forms of politics against which it is pitted is the speed and ferocity with which its project of social transformation and control is pursued, such that 'everything changes' and 'everything is change'. But what makes revolutions so radical in this respect, as we saw, is that they deliberately disturb the balance between what can legitimately be treated as artificial ('culture') and what must be taken as innate ('nature'). While the statement 'everything is change' may not be meant as a literal claim about each and every constituent of the universe, to be sure, it nevertheless draws attention to the possibility of a radical shift in that direction. Where the *ancien régime* presents itself as the natural order of things, the radical and indeed critical role of the revolution is to unmask it as a human-made imposition, and thus render it open to drastic and radical change. So, in the more abstract terms in which Wagner's distinction operates, the field of the artificial (which we call 'culture') expands, while that of the innate (which we deem to be 'natural') contracts, such that things previously taken as given are now taken on as projects of human endeavour. Everything that is solid melts into air, and revolution takes its place at the apex of modernity, very much along the lines of Berman's arresting analysis of modernity.

But then the question arises: might this destabilisation of the distinction between the innate and the artificial also work the other way, to account for what looks like the diametrically opposed idea, articulated by the old lady, namely of the revolution becoming as 'natural' as the weather, suffocating in its all-embracing totality? Certainly, in terms of Wagner's matrix, the old lady's lament seems to invert the redistribution of the innate and the artificial, such that a revolution that presents itself as an artificial project of human action ends up getting treated as an unbudgeably innate condition – marking a regression, so to speak, from 'culture' back to 'nature'. As per the title of this essay, it seems appropriate in this context to coin anthropologically the common and philosophical phrase 'second nature', to describe the tendency, exemplified by the old lady, to treat as innate what was previously brought into being by human artifice. Second nature, one might say, as the product of what anthropologists would habitually call processes of 'naturalisation', though here the lady's spontaneously embodied analogy between revolution and weather vividly literalises both concepts.

Such a move to the concept of second nature is powerful, here, because it renders the condition of permanence of the revolution a mirror of its initial impulse of rupture and change. It is because, as we saw, the cosmogonic character of revolution renders its project of change *total* – a matter of precipitating change that is radical enough to bring forth a new 'everything' – that its subsequent naturalisation into 'this' as a permanent condition cannot but be experienced as totalising, all-embracing and, therefore, suffocating. And the logical transistor from one form of totality to another is the driving role given to change itself, doubling up

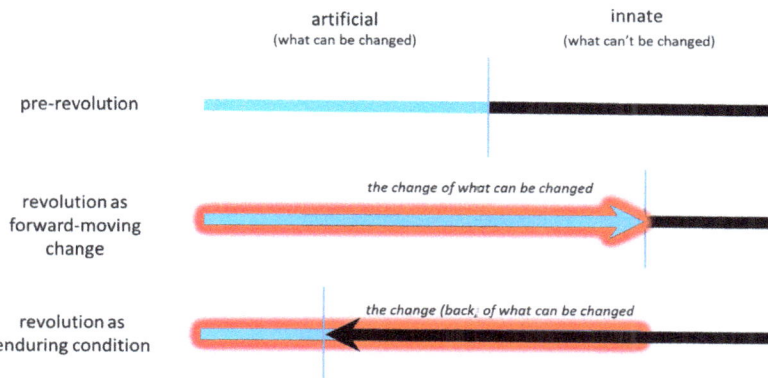

Figure 6.2 Change and endurance in revolutionary transformations as related to Roy Wagner's distinction between the innate and the artificial (Source: author, drawing on Wagner, 1981).

on itself as a deliberate and self-conscious project of meta-change. As we saw in relation to Castro's quasi-metaphysical account of revolution in his *Words to Intellectuals*, revolution constitutes a vector, changing the innate into the artificial in the wake of its forward-moving thrust. It is, so to speak, culture in motion. The transition of that into second nature, then, is a logical function of that meta-transformational energy dissipating. If and when that happens – the emblematic turning point in Cuba may have been 1971 (Fornet, 2014) – the inimical quality of the innate is able to reassert itself, only now operating on that very order that sought to dissolve it in the first place. The motion of culture relents and in so doing regresses into a new (second) natural order of things. All ('everything') that was air turns back into solid (see Figure 6.2, third line).

Conclusion

I have suggested that part of the attraction of this anthropological analysis is that it integrates change and permanence in revolution as logical functions of each other: a sense of encroaching permanence experienced as innateness, then, becomes part of the inner dynamic of revolution, rather than an external reaction against it. It is worth pointing out the stark consequence of such an argument. To the extent that revolutions marry up cosmogony (i.e. seek to precipitate transformations that are totalising) and modernity (i.e. envision their transformational projects as forward-moving vectors of progress), then they *cannot but* give rise to the kind of all-encroaching stasis the lady at the Havana bus stop was giving voice to. Unless, that is, they are able to realise the standing fantasy of 'permanent revolution', which self-designated revolutionary regimes across the world habitually invoke in one way or another, but never, it seems, deliver (and how could they?). Such a conclusion is well reflected in the pattern of so many revolutions since the French, with a host of standing regimes across the world originating in an initial revolutionary rupture which then transmogrifies in a new – and characteristically oppressive – form of immutability. Revolutionary life as rupture, then, and its afterlife as permanence. Perhaps the most consummate historical ethnography of what such an (after)life can look like is Alexei Yurchak's masterful account of 'late socialism' (2005), enacted performatively by the 'last Soviet generation' as a condition in which 'everything was forever', as the book's title has it.

To be sure, a properly anthropological analysis would be prepared to open up to ethnographic variation the logical link between rupture and permanence in revolution. Neither the cosmogonic character nor the modernity of revolution, after all, can be taken for granted as universal (see Cherstich et al., 2020). In this regard we might go as far as to suggest that, by virtue of its openings to variability, an anthropological vantage on revolution and its afterlives might be peculiarly well equipped to chart out alternatives to what is, after all, the rather dismal conclusion that revolutions must by their very (second) nature turn into their own opposite, namely, new orders that are as stifling as they are stagnant, much as the ones they originally set out to replace and improve upon were. If, as we have seen, this bleakness is premised on the conjunction of cosmogony and modernity, as illustrated by our Cuban case, then the question arises of whether a differently premised revolutionary project might entail a different, perhaps better, afterlife. Were one to speculate along these lines, one might opt for retaining the cosmogonic aspirations of revolution – the promise of bringing about a new and better world capturing its most positive impulse – and seek to provide alternatives to the linear conception of time and progress with which it has been coupled since the Enlightenment. Might one imagine the shape of revolutions' unfolding as something different than a linear vector of progress? Might there be a way of retaining their world-making potentials without thereby buying into that very metahistorical status with which Koselleck so perceptively endows revolution, based on his analysis of the iconic case of eighteenth-century France? Anthropologists receptive to *alterative* conceptions of time, space and the cosmos are most adept at keeping questions such as these open.

Notes

1. The emblematic event that shifted the revolution from effervescence to greyness is commonly taken to be the fiasco of the 10,000-ton harvest of sugarcane in 1970, which Castro's government had set up explicitly as proof of the capacities of Cuba's putative New Men in action (Mesa-Lago, 1978). According to this common view, Castro's own admission on 26 July 1970 of the failure of the revolution to meet its self-imposed challenge, and the subsequent period of 'revolutionary consolidation' in the 1970s and early 1980s, during which the revolution was substantially institutionalised, adopting Soviet-style models of bureaucratised governance, is proof positive of the unworkable idealism of Guevara's project of state–people fusion. However, it should be noted Guevara's ideas have indeed remained a leitmotif throughout the course of the Revolution since, having been reaffirmed in the process of revolutionary 'rectification' in which Castro engaged in the mid-1980s, to correct some of the excesses of the bureaucratisation of the 1970s, as well as more recently, in the 2000s, with initiatives directed at the ideological renewal of the Revolution in the face of the post-Soviet 'moral crisis' (see Kapcia, 2005).
2. For example, a subtle lift of the hand to indicate either the chin-area where a beard would grow, or the shoulder where military insignia would be displayed, would for decades be the way to refer to Fidel himself.

References

Berman, Marshall. 1983. *All That is Solid Melts into Air: The experience of modernity*. London and New York: Verso.
Buck-Morss, Susan. 2002. *Dreamworld and Catastrophe: The passing of mass utopia in East and West*. Cambridge, MA: MIT Press.
Cherstich, Igor, Holbraad, Martin and Tassi, Nico. 2020. *Anthropologies of Revolution: Forging time, people, and worlds*. Berkeley: California University Press.
Cumbrera, Osmara Mesa, Carrazana Fuentes, L. Y., Rodríguez Hernández, D., Holbraad, M., Reyes Mora, I. and Cano Orúe, M. R. 2020. 'State and life in Cuba: Calibrating ideals and realities in a state-socialist system for food provision'. *Social Anthropology/Anthropologie sociale*, 28(4): 803–26.
Diaz Castañón, Maria del Pilar. 2001. *Ideologia y revolución· Cuba, 1959–1962*. Havana: Editorial de Ciencias Sociales.
Fornet, Jorge. 2014. *El 1971: Anatomia de una crisis*. Havana: Editorial Letras Cubanas.
García Luis, Julio (ed.). 2008. *Cuban Revolution Reader: A documentary history of Fidel Castro's revolution*. Melbourne: Ocean Press.
Guerra, Lillian. 2012. *Visions of Power in Cuba: Revolution, redemption and resistance, 1959–1971*. Chapel Hill: University of North Carolina Press.
Guevara, Ernesto and Castro, Fidel. 2009. *Socialism and Man in Cuba*. New York: Pathfinder Press.
Holbraad, Martin. 2014. '*Revolución o muerte*: Self-sacrifice and the ontology of Cuban revolution'. *Ethnos*, 79(3): 365–87.
Holbraad, Martin. 2018. '"I have been formed in this revolution": Revolution as infrastructure, and the people it creates in Cuba'. *Journal of Latin American and Caribbean Anthropology*, 23(3): 478–95.
Kapcia, Antoni. 2005. 'Educational revolution and revolutionary morality in Cuba: The "New Man", youth and the new "Battle of Ideas"'. *Journal of Moral Education*, 34(4): 399–412.
Kirk, Emily J., Clayfield, Anna and Story, Isabel (eds). 2018. *Cuba's Forgotten Decade: How the 1970s shaped the revolution*. Lanham, MD: Lexington Books.
Koselleck, Reinhart. 2005. *Futures Past: On the semantics of historical time*. Translated by Keith Tribe. New York: Columbia University Press.
Latour, Bruno. 1993. *We Have Never Been Modern*. Translated by Catherine Porter. London: Prentice-Hall.
Lenin, V. I. 2011 [1917]. *State and Revolution*. Mansfield Center, CT: Martino Publishing.
Lévi-Strauss, Claude. 1966. *The Savage Mind*. Oxford: Oxford University Press.

Lévi-Strauss, Claude. 1990. *The Naked Man*. Chicago: University of Chicago Press.
Malia, Martin. 2008. *History's Locomotives: Revolutions and the making of the modern world*. New Haven, CT: Yale University Press.
Marx, Karl and Engels, Friedrich. 1969. 'Address of the central committee to the Communist League', in *Selected Works, Volume 1*. Moscow: Progress Publishers, 175–85.
Mauss, Marcel. 1992 [1924–5]. 'A sociological assessment of Bolshevism', in Gane, Mike (ed.), *The Radical Sociology of Durkheim and Mauss*. London: Routledge, 165–212.
Mesa-Lago, Carmelo.1978. *Cuba in the 1970s: Pragmatism and institutionalization*. Albuquerque: University of New Mexico Press.
Rodchenko, Aleksandr M. and Stepanova, Varvara F. 1991. *The Future is Our Only Goal*. Edited by Peter Noever. New York: Prestel.
Schram, Stewart R. 1971. 'Mao Tse-tung and the theory of the permanent revolution, 1958–69'. *China Quarterly*, 46: 221–44.
Strathern, Marilyn. 1980. 'No nature, no culture: The Hagen case', in MacCormack, C. and Strathern, M. (eds), *Nature, Culture and Gender*. Cambridge: Cambridge University Press, 174–222.
Trotsky, Leon. 1969. *The Permanent Revolution and Results and Prospects*. New York: Merit Publishers.
Viveiros de Castro, Eduardo. 2012. *Cosmological Perspectivism in Amazonia and Elsewhere*. Masterclass Series 1. Manchester: HAU Network of Ethnographic Theory.
Wagner, Roy. 1981. *The Invention of Culture*. Revised edition. Chicago: University of Chicago Press.
Wagner, Roy. 1986. *Symbols That Stand for Themselves*. Chicago: University of Chicago Press.
Weber, Max. 2019. *Economy and Society: An outline of interpretive sociology*. Berkeley: University of California Press.
Yurchak, Alexei. 2005. *Everything Was Forever, Until It Was No More: The last Soviet generation*. Princeton: Princeton University Press.

7
On the question of optimism in troubled times: revolution, tragedy and possibility in Caribbean history

Brian Meeks

The long Caribbean seventies

This is a peculiarly Anglophone Caribbean conversation, but as with all such debates emanating from this historical crossroads of modernity, there are inevitable global resonances. The British began to withdraw from the West Indies in 1962 with independence granted to Jamaica and Trinidad and Tobago in the same month. However, the great expectations of independence were never met and within the first decade, much of the region – both independent and still colonised – was in open rebellion against the painful and sordid British colonial legacies that the new leaders inherited and failed to eliminate. The particular confluence of tributaries that contributed to an insurrectionary flood included the closure of the safety valve of migration to the UK, after the labour shortages of the immediate post-Second World War years had been filled; the evident failure of the 'Operation Bootstrap' style economic policies of the newly independent states to solve growing unemployment (see Jefferson, 1971 and Carrington, 1971), and the subsequent growth of extreme poverty, particularly in the cities; the continuing oppressive racial and colour hierarchies of colonialism, which excluded black people, especially the newly educated, from access to prestigious jobs and advancement in the social order; and out of this, the emergence of new movements and accompanying philosophical frameworks for radical social change – Black Power from the United States and Rastafari in Jamaica – that seemed to provide both a theoretical and practical pathway for rebellion (see Bogues, 2014) and perhaps even revolution against the postcolonial order.

The history and arc of the Black Power movement in the Caribbean has been extensively documented and debated. In a compact sense, it began with Dr Walter Rodney's exclusion from Jamaica in October 1968, precipitating a famous one-day urban riot,[1] after protesting students were tear-gassed and beaten by the police. It gathered significant steam with the 1970 Black Power demonstrations in Trinidad and Tobago, with tens of thousands of people marching in the streets daily under black power slogans (Ryan et al., 1995; Samaroo, 2014). The Trinidad '1970 Revolution' as it has come to be known, ended after Prime Minister Eric Williams declared a state of emergency, which was immediately followed by an army mutiny of disgruntled junior officers who refused to enforce it. The mutineers, however, before reaching the capital city Port of Spain, backed down and returned to their barracks (Meeks, 1996a); loyal troops upheld the state of emergency and despite subsequent armed clashes with militants that persisted for more than two years, the Trinidad moment of popular uprising soon subsided. Further north in Jamaica, the traditional, centrist People's National Party (PNP) – under the leadership of Michael Manley and in the popular upsurge precipitated by the Rodney riots – came to power in 1972, and over the course of that decade, in the face of daunting external and internal opposition, moved steadily to the left (see Huber-Stephens and Stephens, 1986; Kaufman, 1985; and Polanyi-Levitt, 1984). Manley's regime implemented simple but long-delayed social reforms, advocated a new international economic order and crucially, established warm relationships with the neighbouring regime of revolutionary Cuba. Manley's government lost power in 1980 in a bitter and bloody election and the island resumed its post-independence policy of fealty to Washington and dependence on the international financial institutions. The final venue of this broad movement of radical insurgency occurred on the tiny southern Caribbean island of Grenada, where in 1979, the New Jewel Movement, the leading party in the parliamentary opposition coalition, overthrew the government of Prime Minister Eric Gairy. Over the following four and a half years, the People's Revolutionary Government (PRG) under the leadership of Maurice Bishop, sought to implement radical social and political policies, including, in the international sphere, establishing close relationships with Cuba and the Soviet Union (see Lewis et al., 2015; Grenade, 2015; Puri, 2014; Scott, 2014; and Meeks, 1993). The PRG, however, in an infamously tragic sequence of events, imploded in October 1983. Maurice Bishop was placed by his own party under house arrest, then shortly after, released by a huge crowd of his supporters. After marching to and occupying the island's major military base, the army sought to retake it; there was a confrontation, soldiers and civilians were killed, then Bishop and close supporters were captured and shot by members of their own People's Revolutionary Army (PRA). A week later, the United States, supported by a number of, but not all, Caribbean states, invaded Grenada. Following intense resistance from units of the PRA, the remaining leaders of the revolution, were captured, arrested and remained for more than two decades in prison under a deeply flawed trial for murder, then convicted with the threat of execution and finally released from prison in 2009. This traumatic defeat, preceded by Bishop's killing, generated deep and lasting divisions not only in Grenada, but across the Caribbean and, capped as it was by a US invasion that was welcomed by many, slammed the door shut on the 'long seventies' of radical Caribbean insurgency.

The invasion of Grenada also signalled the start of the era of neoliberal dominance that has lasted for more than three decades and, despite the 2008 global economic crisis, which at first seemed to indicate its demise, continues to dominate policy, with no immediate end in sight. The social and political features of this period in the Caribbean are similar to other international, post-radical and postcolonial sequences. To use Jamaica as an instance, traditional parliamentary politics, driven by IMF-inspired structural adjustment policies has dominated and radical and revolutionary sentiments have declined. Strategies of economic development based on tourism, remittances and market-led initiatives have, however, failed to deliver indices of credible 'growth'[2] – the marker for neoliberal success. Corruption has become more prominent in the absence of buoyant economic initiatives.[3] It has proliferated both 'above', through avenues of white collar crime and 'below', where urban gangs, formed in the crucible of the internecine warfare of the seventies, have established profitable political and economic space and autonomy for themselves in the notorious 'garrison' communities of the inner cities (see Figueroa and Sives, 2002). I have elsewhere described this prolonged, fraught moment, where the old hegemonic bloc of the middle class and anti-colonial politicians has lost control over the social direction of the country while retaining some modicum of political control, as one of 'hegemonic dissolution' (Meeks, 1995b). It is both the failure of the old and newer elites to drive the country in the direction they wish, as it is the failure of the popular majorities to wrest it away from them. The result is an era of uncertainty defined by the evacuation of notions of ethical morality from political and social discourse and their replacement by atomism, dog-eat-dog sentiments and the reversion to violence as the first move in conflict resolution. The postcolony in the Caribbean is not to be directly equated with Africa's parallel postcolonial moment, but anyone reading Achille Mbembe will recognise the points of commonality, even as the differences confirm that all social and political theorising must inevitably rest on the deep understanding of a particular situation.[4]

Much of the critical scholarship that has emerged from the Caribbean and its diaspora in this period has sought, while using different lenses and approaches, to understand the rise and fall of the long radical Caribbean seventies, the character of this articulated post-insurrectionary interregnum and possible futures beyond it. There is, for instance, Hilbourne Watson's work in political economy, which locates the Caribbean as a minor link in the worldwide cybernetic, information, robotic revolution, with deeply pessimistic implications for Caribbean sovereignty or any autonomous project of nation-building (see, for example, Watson, 1994). There is Obika Gray's study (2004) which explores in detail the social history of the Jamaican inner-city communities and redefines the role of the state as a predatory enterprise. Deborah Thomas also explores the Jamaican inner-city to understand its denizens' complicated and contradictory culture of 'modern blackness' (Thomas, 2004). And in her more recent work *Exceptional Violence: Embodied citizenship in transnational Jamaica* (2011), she examines the persistence of structural violence against the urban poor, in order to consider what 'repair' might look like and how the incorporation of 'affect' might help in redefining the boundaries of sovereignty. There is Percy Hintzen's attempt to think through the form that a new democracy for the Caribbean based on local empowerment might take (Hintzen, 2018). There is Paget Henry's work on Caribbean philosophy, which seeks to open up a new, foundational archive for both historical exploration and political action, through the elaboration of what he describes as 'Afro-Caribbean philosophy'. There is a buoyant and growing Caribbean feminist scholarship, led by Eudine Barriteau, Rhoda Reddock and Patricia Mohammed (see, for instance, Barriteau, 2003 and Mohammed, 2002) and many others, which, unbowed by the crisis and travails that followed the collapse of the Grenada Revolution in 1983, has sought to introduce gender as a critical avenue through which to understand and confront the neoliberal moment.[5]

The problem space of Scott's tragedy

And, more directly for the purposes of this essay, there is David Scott's work (1999; 2004; 2014), which over the past three decades has attempted to interrogate the meaning of the postcolonial Caribbean directly and elaborate alternative methodologies to understanding it. Scott's *oeuvre* is of the utmost importance, both for its erudition as well as the many unquestionable insights it provides into both the contemporary Caribbean condition and the theorising around it. At its heart is the complex project of thinking through the foundations for both structural and political stasis in the contemporary Caribbean postcolony. Scott's approach travels through three phases. Firstly, he posits the relevance of identifying time and temporality as critical theoretical variables in approaching a given social moment; secondly, in locating a specific temporal context, he seeks to identify and map the 'generational sensibilities' that accompany it. And thirdly, he searches for and presents for scrutiny what he considers as more appropriate and meaningful ways of reading history. Scott proposes the abandonment of what he considers the romantic, progressivist lens that has previously dominated Caribbean history-telling and its replacement with one imbued with what he describes as a 'tragic sensibility'.[6] This approach, he posits, will more accurately reflect the real world that has been far more tragic than triumphant. It will guard, he suggests, against the hubris that inevitably accompanies romantic narratives that assume that the 'arc' of history bends towards justice. While these three elements are closely interrelated, it is the foregrounding of the notion of the tragic sensibility with which I have the greatest concern and which will occupy much of the rest of this chapter.

Scott's *oeuvre* is still very much a work in progress, though its substantial outlines are developed across three central books, which one can consider as a trilogy. In *Refashioning Futures: Criticism after postcoloniality* (1999) he develops, through a series of neo-Foucauldian essays on postcolonial Sri Lankan and Jamaican politics, the suggested outlines and foundations for alternative Caribbean futures. In *Conscripts of Modernity: The tragedy of colonial enlightenment* (2004) he returns to C. L. R. James's classic portrayal of the San Domingo (Haitian) Revolution in order to elaborate in detail his critical perspectives on history and history writing and his theory of the tragic. In the third, *Omens of Adversity: Tragedy, time, memory, justice* (2014), he engages in a specific meditation on the Grenadian Revolution, the third of the self-proclaimed Caribbean Revolutions (Haiti, Cuba and Grenada, if Nicaragua is understood as a Central American phenomenon) and builds on his earlier identification of the importance of tragedy to elaborate questions of temporality and specifically to identify the importance of generational sensibilities. At the heart of this notion is the assertion that the ageing Caribbean generation of the 1970s, those who were on the side of radical change, are living in a time which to them appears 'out of joint'.[7] They exist in a kind of time warp, in which the 'problem-space' in which their politics of radical nationalism and revolution existed has passed. This disorientation leaves them stranded in a no man's land of political meaninglessness, 'lost in space', as it were, and therefore incapable of fully grasping, much less acting upon, the new times that we are living in.

There are some substantial aspects here with which I find easy agreement. The Left of the 1970s, with its crudely Hegelian sense of imminent revolution and willingness to bypass popular opinion in favour of 'historical necessity',[8] may very well have hastened its own destruction. Had the Grenadian 'comrades' for instance been somewhat humbler, more willing to compromise, with a greater appreciation that it could all end, as it did, in tragic destruction, could they have possibly avoided the worst possible outcome? The invocation of 'what ifs' may inevitably be futile, but, nevertheless, if Coard, Bishop and both sides of the 1983 New Jewel Movement crisis, had paused and considered tragedy as the more likely denouement, could history have travelled along a different path? More tellingly for future seemingly irresolvable political impasses, what benefits might a tragic sensibility, driven by fear of the greater likelihood of failure and defeat, yield in the direction of eliciting caution, compromise and possibly, survival? However, and beyond this, there is something in Scott's invocation of the tragic that takes it beyond the role of a mere warning signal and leaves one with an overarching sense of emptiness, of a political void in which radical change and revolution become dangerous chimera, leaving room only for a nihilistic and frozen politics of retreat and closure.

As such, I distinguish between Scott's 'tragic sensibility', in which one's entire world view is informed by and tilted in the direction of 'the tragic' and what I would wish to advance as a necessary 'sensitivity to tragedy', in which we keep the possibility of the tragic outcome as a flashing amber signal on our dashboard, for easy reference when appropriate, but not as the sole or even primary source of information and direction. In order then, to take this distinction beyond the immediate moment of instinctive concern and to develop an alternative approach to thinking about the contemporary Caribbean, I want to focus more attention on the second of these three books – *Conscripts of Modernity* – which is the lynchpin on which the other two gain substantial support.

Conscripts, as intimated previously, is set against the background of the Haitian Revolution, as famously captured in Cyril Lionel Robert (C. L. R.) James's 1938 masterpiece *The Black Jacobins: Toussaint L'Ouverture and the San Domingo revolution* (James, 1989). In order to gain purchase on Scott's argument (but also to invoke James's deep wellspring of optimism), I am going to sketch the barest brushstrokes of James's story, as a pathway to exploring Scott's interventions, and my agreements and disagreements with him. I am determined to invoke again the story of the Haitian Revolution, because as Trouillot so eloquently argued (1995), it was an impossibility in a world of white supremacy and therefore had to be silenced and erased from world history. In closing, I want to reflect on the contemporary global moment and the very notion of revolution to leave with a somewhat more optimistic approach to imagining Caribbean and, more generally, postcolonial futures.

The Haitian revolution

The Black Jacobins is the history of the only successful slave revolt, the only successful black revolution against slavery and the creation of the second independent country (following the United States) in the Americas. To the extent that this history is better known today, with the important work of scholars like Trouillot (1995), Blackburn (1988), Genovese (1979), Dubois, Fick (1990), and many others (e.g., Bender et al., 2011; Getachew, 2016; Buck-Morss, 2009; Forsdick and Høgsberg, 2017; and Bogues, 2017), it is because of James's foundational intervention. *The Black Jacobins* is simultaneously scholarly and passionate. It is reflective of James's maturing Marxist approach to history, yet reads history with a brash agnosticism rooted in his own appreciation of the particularities of the Caribbean, the profound impact of slavery and the plantation and an acute sense of the interconnectedness between the plantation economy and the consolidating mercantilist capitalism of France and Western Europe. Events in the Empire are intimately connected with her colonies and when revolution begins in France in 1789, its repercussions are almost immediately felt in the Caribbean. In the highly racialised structure of St Domingue (San Domingo for James), on the western side of the island of Hispaniola and the richest sugar colony in the world, the whites are immediately divided between royalists and supporters of the revolution. This soon spills over to the mulatto caste, many of whom are wealthy inheritors of their white fathers' wealth but deprived by the *code noir*[9] of full social and political rights. Few imagine that the demonstrations, riots and general turmoil that begins will impact on the mass of black slaves, who constitute the overwhelming majority of the population.

However, as the struggle in France intensifies and becomes more radical, so too does the nascent unrest among the blacks, and in 1791 there is a general rising. At first, it is inchoate and resembles other similar uprisings that have occurred across the plantation arc of the Americas; but things soon change. James underlines the entry among the rebels of an old house slave, Toussaint Breda, who will soon rename himself L'Ouverture (the Opening). It is Toussaint as general, strategist, politician and statesman, who forges a modern, highly trained and effective black army. He is able to brilliantly manoeuvre among the various forces arrayed across the revolutionaries: the Spanish, occupying Santo Domingo to the East; the English, who have entered to capture the now prostrate French colony for themselves; and the French, the principal enemy against whom Toussaint is initially at war. But with the shifting of French politics to the left and the elevation of the Jacobins in Paris, the popular democratic mood in the metropole leads, finally, to the historic abolition of slavery. Toussaint, recognising the opening provided by this epic moment, changes tack, joins forces with the contingents of revolutionary (Jacobin) France, becomes the Black Council of St Domingue and rules effectively on behalf of France over a newly freed population of blacks, mulattos and the remaining whites. Notably, for the events that will soon follow, Toussaint does not at this time contemplate an independent state, but a continuing relationship with France, which in his reading, is now both the guardian of liberty and a requirement for the maintenance of 'civilisation', read here primarily, though in a deeply conflicted way, as access to trade, manufactures, culture and, crucially, weapons for self-defence. Toussaint's approach then, simply stated, believed first in freedom for the blacks, but this required the support of France, its 'civilisation' and its continued economic presence.

Meanwhile in Paris, the course of and prospects for the revolution are changing. The Jacobins – guardians of the emancipation proclamation – are eclipsed and suppressed and soon thereafter, Napoleon ascends to power. Bonaparte – a racist and a state-builder – possesses none of the idealism of the previous regime, but driven by support from the powerful interests of mercantile and slave capital, as well as his own imperialist predilections, begins preparing to re-establish slavery and with it, profitability in St Domingue and the other colonies. In December 1801, the first ships, bearing an army of 12,000 men under the command of Napoleon's brother-in-law, General LeClerc, sail into the harbour of Le Cap, the main port on the colony's northern shore, with precise instructions from Paris. The generals of the black army, most of all Toussaint, must be fooled to believe that the French army is still representative of their liberty, equality and fraternity. Under this guise, they must land safely, entrench themselves and then decapitate the leaders and disarm the rank and file of the black army. This would be the necessary prelude for a re-establishment of slavery.

LeClerc is allowed to land and is at first met with uncertainty and only limited resistance. Toussaint is unwilling to commit his forces against France, but there is grave concern and foreboding as to why, if France is not hostile, such a massive army has been sent. When it becomes obvious that it is an army of enslavers, there begins to emerge a more widespread and determined resistance. LeClerc, who imagined that the powerful and triumphant French army would easily defeat these black rebels, begins to see the extraordinary military capabilities of his foes. Then, surprisingly and unexpectedly, Toussaint yields, parlays with LeClerc for peace, demobilises and retreats to his own small estate. This is all and more that Napoleon could have hoped for and soon Toussaint is arrested, forced on board a French ship and conveyed to a brutal jail in the cold Jura Mountains, where he dies of humiliation and exposure.

The capture of Toussaint, however, is not met with resignation, but alarm and more rapid mobilisation among the leading black generals as well as contingents of autonomous resistance fighters. Even more alarmingly, word reaches St Domingue that Napoleon has restored slavery in the smaller eastern Caribbean colonies of Martinique and Guadeloupe. This leads to a new and final phase of war, in which the black army under Dessalines, Christophe, Maurepas and others, unites with the mulatto army under Petion and fights the final War for Independence, ending with the decisive defeat of the French, the declaration of independence on 1 January 1804 and the inauguration of the first black republic – the state of Haiti.

Scott intervenes

It is on this narrative presented here in miniature (and undoubtedly, in my compression, with significant damage!), that Scott builds his case. James, he proposes, wrote the history of the revolution initially as a romance. It is rooted in Enlightenment imperatives of the inevitability of progress, of right triumphing over wrong and of redemption for the heroes at the end of the day.[10] These unilinear notions fail, he suggests, to account sufficiently for the role of contingency, of uncertainty in history-making and the fact that outcomes are seldom if ever optimal, or even good. Further, James in writing the book, fails to consider and account for the 'problem space' within which he is writing and how it differs with the problem space of St Domingue at the time of the revolution, or with further problem spaces that have cascaded since the original volume was published in 1938. The set of problems that occupied James in 1938, Scott suggests, were related to how to encourage anti-colonial revolutions in the Caribbean, but even more notably, in Africa. These were quite different from Toussaint's conundrum, of trying to find a path beyond racial emancipation to economic prosperity for a poor, isolated, singular black state.

These, Scott suggests, are to be even further differentiated from the problem space of the early 1960s, when in the second edition of *The Black Jacobins*, James inserted seven new paragraphs to the final chapter, 'The War of Independence'. In this new intervention, Scott suggests that James shifts register. Instead of the story of victory against overwhelming odds, which is largely the framework for the rest of the book, James meditates on Toussaint's ultimately tragic dilemma. Torn between his burning goal to consolidate freedom for his people and his competing certainty that without France there could be no survival in a 'civilised' sense, Toussaint was effectively disarmed. This moment of uncertainty, vacillation and paralysis provided the opportunity for his laying down of arms and his capture, leading to his tragic incarceration and death. It was, in James's words, a '*hamartia*', a tragic flaw in Toussaint himself that cost him his freedom, his life and very nearly the entire revolution (Scott, 2004: 153–4).

Scott's assertion is that the insertion of these paragraphs, the rumination on tragedy and the tilt away from a romantic to a tragic lens, is not coincidental, but rather derives from the different problem space of the early 1960s when these were inserted, which was far divorced from the problem space of 1938. In the 1930s, the widespread labour upheaval in the West Indies in the wake of the Great Depression, and the rise of anti-colonial movements in India, Asia and the African continent, all suggested the likelihood of imminent success for anti-colonial struggles. By the 1960s, these hopes had either been tempered or dashed. The specific Caribbean disappointments, with the failure of the attempt at Federation[11] were accompanied by increasingly dismal prospects for new postcolonial advances on the African continent. James, therefore, was seeking to think through some way to temper the optimistic romanticism that permeated the earlier book, with the sobriety that the new situation demanded. Even more profoundly, Scott continues, if *The Black Jacobins* is read today in a twenty-first century post-Bandungan world, its hopeful, romantic, triumphalism gives limited insight either as a model of what is to be done, or prospect of what the future might look like. To quote Scott at length:

> *The Black Jacobins* is an anti-colonial history written out of and in response to a particular colonial present and projected towards a particular postcolonial future ... That future which constituted James's horizon of expectations (the emergence of nation-state sovereignty, the revolutionary transition to socialism) and which the Black Jacobins anticipated, we live today as the bleak ruins of our postcolonial present. Our generation looks back, so to put it, through the remains of a present that James and his generation looked forward to (however contentiously) as the open horizon of a possible future. James's erstwhile future has elapsed in our disappearing present. But if this is so, if the longing for total anti-colonial revolution, the longing for the overcoming of the colonial past that shaped James's horizon of expectations in the Black Jacobins is not one that we can inhabit today, then it may be part of our task to set it aside and begin another work of reimagining the futures for us to long for, for us to emancipate. (Scott, 2004: 45)

Beyond tragedy

Let me start with what is as yet only a partial response to this main conclusion of Scott's study by addressing his central point that 'the political space for a certain kind of anti-colonial revolution no longer exists'. I wish to argue with this assertion. If by this, he means the likelihood, of single-state, Cuban or Grenadian revolution, with intrepid guerrillas battling corrupt dictators, then I would agree, that the peculiar conjuncture of the contemporary world, the power of imperial militaries and the all-encompassing ability of finance capital to make recalcitrant regimes scream, as evident today in the instance of Venezuela, weigh heavily against the likelihood of single-state revolutions surviving. We should qualify this, however, with the recognition that the idea of a single-state revolution of the Haitian, Cuban, Grenadian, and Nicaraguan variety, was always tentative and in small postcolonial instances like these, predicated on close alliances with powerful patrons – Jacobin France, for Toussaint and the Soviet Union for Fidel Castro. This was Toussaint's dilemma as captured by James. Whether one wishes to read Toussaint as wedded to a false notion of the superiority of French civilisation, or simply his recognition that in order to clothe, feed, build shelter and defend themselves, free black people would require close alliances with powerful states, it is evident that he was clear that in a white slaveholder world, St Domingue would find it difficult to survive on its own. When Napoleon took power, this one hope of support from Jacobin France – a reasonably well-intentioned power – was eliminated and the rest of Haitian history, which one cannot even begin to elaborate on here, was largely determined by this hard fact of isolation in a white, imperialist world.

From this perspective, the world of 1804 is not so dramatically different from that of 1938, 1959, or the long seventies of Caribbean Black Power and popular insurrection. In all instances, locally based movements in small states seeking to enact radical social change faced daunting prospects in a world dominated by hostile powers. The problem space, then as now, is – as Venezuela most recently illustrates – that if such movements arise and are fortuitously able to take power, do they have powerful allies, or not?

What is admittedly different is that when Scott wrote *Conscripts* in 2004 and up until very recently, there has been no dominant and self-evident counter-hegemonic philosophy to guide and drive new movements. For the almost four decades since the collapse of the radical, national liberation and revolutionary movements, the decisive defeat of Bandung[12] and the demise of 'really existing socialism', there has been no confidence in a theory of revolution in the way in which anti-slavery thinking drove Toussaint and the masses of St Domingue, or as Fanonion perceptions, Black Power and Marxism drove the anti-colonial radicals of the 1970s. Whether the absence of a clear, guiding philosophical frame is an indication that there can be no clear frame at all, or that there might be one in the making, is the distinction between Scott's absolute partition of historic 'problem spaces' into watertight compartments and the extent to which we might wish to take a different approach, in which historical periods overlap and leak into each other; the extent to which in other words, there is still room to build new movements, albeit movements with new programmes, and different trajectories that move beyond the boundaries of twentieth-century nationalism and the nation-state and the elevation of the 'political kingdom' as the inevitable avenue to human liberation.

This segues into a second of Scott's assertions, in which he argues that we should abandon the 'longing for total revolution', as this world no longer exists. One can agree that the world of the twenty-first century, certainly the Caribbean twenty-first century, a world largely beyond slavery and colonialism, and deeply linked with digital networks and transnational diasporas, is not that of eighteenth-century, transatlantic mercantile capital. However, if we consider the conditions of the crisis of the second decade of the new century, then it might be worthwhile thinking about another critical dimension of revolutions. If the economic conflicts between the interests of the aristocracy and mercantile/financial/slavery capital of the eighteenth century contributed to the collapse of feudalism and the absolute defeat of the slave system in one colony, then what are the portents for a global crisis in the third decade of the twenty-first century? I want to suggest that if we think of Lenin's classic definition of a revolutionary situation[13] and his description of the ruling classes not being able to continue ruling in the old way as one of the critical conditions and portents for a revolutionary situation, then it would be reasonable to suggest that this aspect of his proposal is worth serious consideration in today's world.

Think of, for instance, beyond the market failures of 2008, the global environmental crisis, manifest most alarmingly in global warming, and the consolidating consensus that the earth is verging on ecological catastrophe. Think also of the vast inequalities engendered and exacerbated by financial capital and the 'new economy' that on one level generate deep discontent, but at another, hinder the sort of possibilities that Keynes saw in demand-led capitalist growth. Think thirdly of the potential for massive structural unemployment in an exponential increase in robotisation that will only accelerate in the near future and the emerging evidence that suggests there is no answer to this new imperative (see West, 2015). I mention these three because they are burning and prominent, but they are already having a tremendous impact at the level of politics and policy, with the demise of the Washington Consensus, the rise of Trumpism[14] and the far right across the globe and the likelihood of damaging and debilitating trade wars, particularly but not exclusively between China and the US in the near future.

So, if the dominant classes cannot rule in the old way, what of the possibilities of rebellion from below? When I first delivered these thoughts at the UCL conference 'After the Event' in May 2019, my subsequent comment was that this was a frightening moment, because while structural crises were imminent, the popular response was fragmented and inchoate. At the time I wrote:

> What makes the present moment particularly frightening however, is that while we can imagine a collapse of the environment, linked into a crisis in the 'forces of production' it is happening at a moment of relative weakness of popular movements, both at the national level and in the form of transnational and global alliances. It is not that there is not deep dissatisfaction against all of these imminent signs of crisis, and nascent transnational movements like Extinction

Rebellion (see Taylor, 2020) and the 2017 Women's March (see Hartocollis and Alcindor, 2017), but that this fightback is too sporadic and limited. The forces of progressive resistance are a few steps behind the consolidating wave of a global right-wing insurgency. However, far from there being quiescent belief in the rightness of the present order, I suggest that popular majorities, under the weight of hard imperatives of economic survival and lacking a clear, well-defined understanding of what to fight for, remain relatively disengaged, and on the sidelines. (Meeks, 2019)

Since then, things have moved at warp speed. 'There are decades where nothing happens: and there are weeks where decades happen'.[15] The dramatic 2019 anti-neoliberal and anti-authoritarian uprisings, most notably in Chile, Sudan, Lebanon, India, and Hong Kong (see, for instance, Wright, 2019) among many others, and then in 2020 the unprecedented upwelling of anti-racist and anti-fascist sentiments arising from the George Floyd murder by police in the US that spread across the globe (see Kirby, 2020), despite and in the face of the global COVID-19 pandemic, have upended that earlier portent. The rapidity of mobilisation, the sheer scale of the popular protests, the instantaneous sharing of information surrounding programmes, strategies and tactics, were all present in 2019 and then immeasurably amplified in the summer of 2020. Black Lives Matter demonstrations, emanating from the Floyd murder took place in May and June on a daily basis in cities and small towns across America and were soon described as 'the broadest in US history' (Putnam et al., 2020). Amazingly, the demonstrations jumped national boundaries and Black Lives Matter protests proliferated on all continents, addressing the specific question of police violence against black people in the US, but also incorporating anti-racist and anti-authoritarian themes specific to their localities.

The epoch of quiescence and retreat, the 'problem space' Scott correctly, if somewhat one-sidedly, identifies that occurred at the end of the Bandung era, at the end of the 'national liberation' moment is itself, drawing to a close. A new era of popular upwelling[16] has begun. The popular programme is not yet written in stone but given the centrality and salience of anti-racism to the current moment, it might be useful to peruse some of the thematic demands in the 2020 Policy Platform of the Movement for Black Lives, the driving organisation behind Black Lives Matter:

> End the war on Black communities
> End the war on Black youth
> End the War on Black Women

> End the War on Black trans, queer, gender non-conforming and intersex people
> End the war on Black health and Black disabled people
> End the war on Black migrants
> End to all jails, prisons and immigrant detention
> End the death penalty
> End the war on drugs
> End the surveillance on Black communities
> End to pretrial detention and money bail
>
> (Movement for Black Lives, 2020)

Many of these are, of course, specific to the US context; but there is a central core of demands that question the permanency of national boundaries (ending the war on black migrants), centre the importance of gender and sexuality as inalienable rights, and argue for the erosion of the state as presently constituted (end to jails, prisons and immigration detention). The emerging programme of liberation is therefore distinctly anti-racist, transnational and if not anti-statist, certainly questioning the limits, boundaries and powers of states as presently constituted.

How does this remarkable new turn square with Scott's proposal that the 'longing for total anti-colonial revolution' should be abandoned? I am not sure where invoking this notion as originally mooted by Bernard Yack really leads (see Yack, 1986). If it ends in the recognition of the need to turn things upside down, then there is a lot in the present moment that requires policies and movements that will advocate radical, upending changes, for instance, in carbon-reducing environmental policy, the taxation of financial profits to reverse gaping inequalities, the curtailment of inordinately high budgetary spending on arms and the shift of resources to health, welfare and, again, the environment. These, if grouped together with many of the demands as expressed in the Movement for Black Lives Platform and accompanied by new, more democratic and inclusive modalities of governing, could be considered revolutionary and very much worth both longing and fighting for.

But undoubtedly, too, the idea of revolution is moving away from its singular location in the nation-state. The future is already evident in these transnational alliances as vividly demonstrated above, which have the potential to move beyond demonstrating to build coalitions around common platforms and across differing matters of concern in areas such as saving the environment, fighting against racial, gender and sexual structural discrimination, and fighting for fair housing, against gentrification and for community survival and the preservation of jobs. All of these movements are already out there but lack the common sense of purpose and programme or an underlying platform for the kind of world they are fighting for. I think of Stuart Hall's *Kilburn Manifesto*, written as a collaborative venture shortly before his death in 2015, as one particularly fertile source of thinking through new platforms and programmes (Hall et al., 2015). While one of its weaknesses is that it is a proposal focusing on Great Britain, this also provides it with the strength of local specificity. Its paramount question 'what and who is the economy for?' is one that resonates and could form the basis for thinking about other similar manifestos for specific places as well as transnational ones.

So, my suggestion is that while Scott is right, that a particular definition of single state-bound anti-colonial revolution may have passed its time of conceptual usefulness, the conditions for revolt are in many other respects ripe and the mythos of 'revolution', with its deeply inbuilt connotations and history of breaking decisively with the past, still has a useful purpose and should not be abandoned yet.

Freedom and the sublime

In his epic composition 'Concrete Jungle' on the *Catch a Fire* album, Bob Marley stakes a claim for a yet to be achieved freedom beyond the colonial moment: 'No chains around my feet but I'm not free / I know I am bound here in captivity' (Marley, 1973). If we think of Marley's invocation, which recognises that physical restraint is no longer the primary means of social control, then we can explore his assertion in order to recognise how notions of freedom have expanded exponentially in the postcolonial era to include freedom from male exploitation and abuse; freedom to explore, decide and live one's chosen sexuality; freedom to move without hindrance across boundaries in search of work; freedom from pollution and the right to enjoy a clean environment; freedom from arbitrary violence and war and freedom from want. This partial, but nonetheless revealing list suggests the foundations for a further re-thinking of freedoms beyond negative/positive binaries and even beyond Amartya Sen's more nuanced notions of human capability (1999) to imagine new programmes and policies that, while not driven by pre-determined teleologies, might pioneer new horizons for human thriving.

We might define the present moment then, using Scott's framework, as a new problem space, but it is a problem space still animated by the spectres of the past even as it demands new expansive definitions of freedom and requires new political forms to fight for and achieve its always expanding objectives. In this sense, therefore, the 'longing for total revolution' is not at all a mythopoetic chimera that needs to be exorcised, but rather a necessary narrative that while always under revision, can provide intellectual purchase, motivational purpose and directional compass for ongoing projects of radical change.

At the 2019 Brown University conference 'Unlearning Imperial Rights/Decolonizing Institutions', I asked the African American thinker Hortense Spillers, if Hegelian notions of synthesis and religious notions of redemption no longer provide illumination for our groping in the darkness, what new thinking could potentially animate us and provide direction in the storm? After a short pause, Spillers responded that we could, perhaps, look to the cycle of life and particularly the inspirational moment of birth as a lodestone. Birth is the ever-present new, and while bearing inevitably the options of failure and tragedy, it is also laden with possibilities of transformation and hope. The purpose of living then, always possesses at its very core, hidden as it were, in plain sight, the foundations for optimism and hopefulness.

There is one final feature of James's reflections, which I think Scott misses altogether. It is the typically Jamesian invocation of the power and possibilities that people have when they dare to hope, see freedom within their grasp or fear that, once attained, it might slip away. This I wish to refer to as the phenomenon of the *sublime*[17] in the revolutionary moment and it is at the very heart of James's *Black Jacobins*. Under Toussaint's leadership, black people have been living free in St Domingue for five years. It is a difficult time: the sugar economy is in a state of collapse and there are continuing threats from the British in Jamaica and the Spanish who occupy the eastern two-thirds of the island. Further, in order to keep the economy alive, Toussaint has insisted that people return to the hated estates, though now in a new capacity as paid labourers. It is a fraught, compromised moment, but it is freedom, nonetheless.

But now, Napoleon's army has returned, Toussaint is captured and transported to his eventual death and the truth is out that slavery has been restored in neighbouring colonies, and St Domingue is targeted to be next. This realisation signals the beginning of the Black army's final battle for liberation, which James captures in graphic, unforgettable prose, of which I mention two instances. The first is from a French soldier, Lemmonier-Delafosse, who had served during the war. James notes for emphasis, that he believed in slavery, but found this to say about the character and humanity of his Black adversaries:

> But what men these blacks are! How they fight and how they die! One has to make war against them to know their reckless courage in braving danger when they can no longer have recourse to stratagem. I have seen a solid column torn by grapeshot from four pieces of cannon, advance without making a retrograde step. The more they fell the greater seemed to be the courage of the rest. They advanced singing, for the Negro sings everywhere, makes songs on everything. Their song was a song of brave men and went as follows:
>
>> *To the attack grenadier,*
>> *Who gets killed that's his affair.*
>> *Forget your ma,*
>> *Forget your pa,*
>> *To the attack, grenadier,*
>> *Who gets killed that's his affair.*
>
> (James, 1989: 368)

The second, is among the correspondence written by General LeClerc to Napoleon shortly before his death in late 1802. James notes that the French had arrived in St Domingue the year before, covered with glory from the European campaigns, and with the hubristic belief that they would quickly dismantle this black army of their racial inferiors. I quote only the immediately relevant section:

> ... I have decided to send you General Boudet ... Believe what he will tell you. We have in Europe a false idea of the country in which we fight and the men whom we fight against ...
>
> (James, 1989: 353)

What Lemmonier-Delafosse saw clearly and Leclerc realised too late at the end of his life, was not the bravery of black people *per se*, but the heroic stance of armed and capable black women and men in the throes of social revolution, who were unwilling under any circumstances to yield and return to a life of slavery and degradation.[18] This romantic, mythopoetic, but also, ultimately, true and compelling portrait of a moment in Haiti's revolution, provides a powerful coda and reminder that whether the struggle is to secure a free foothold on the western side of Hispaniola, to secure the civil rights of black people in the United States, or to oust a ruthless kleptocratic dictator in the Sudan, the majesty of mobilised people transcends historical eras. James sought to invoke that intangible spirit of revolution as a motivation and source of optimism for twentieth-century anti-colonial struggles. Twenty-first-century revolutionary transnational movements in an entirely different problem space, might wish nonetheless to learn from the archive of revolution, drawing inspiration from its history without being transfixed by its tragedies, even as they fight for significantly new objectives, though in necessarily modified forms, against both old and new opponents.

Notes

1. See Lewis, 1998, especially pp. 85–123.
2. See Polanyi-Levitt, 2005: 109–212.
3. Of 180 countries measured on the 2019 Corruption Perception Index, three Caribbean countries were among the most corrupt, with Jamaica at 74 and Guyana and Trinidad and Tobago tied at 85 at the bottom. (Numerous tied ratings accounted for the only 85 levels.) See Corruption Perception Index, 2019.
4. See Mbembe, 2001. Mbembe's powerful, poetic and subtle text does not present itself for easy summary. Beyond his deep cynicism surrounding the corruption, brutality and sheer absurdity of the regimes that inhabited postcolonial Africa, particularly those of the francophone sphere, he nonetheless leaves the door open for hope. Even as he describes the postcolonial era as 'a time of unhappiness' (238) in which 'force cohabits with buffoonery, caprice with brutality' (238), he imagines this as a temporary phase: 'On the other hand, the time of unhappiness is like a tidal wave, and we know that a tidal wave comes and goes, flows in and out' (238). While postcolonial time is therefore one of unhappiness, it is also a time of possibilities (241). One wonders whether Scott's tragic sensibility (see following section) leaves any door open for transformative possibilities in the way Mbembe so clearly does.
5. See for my earlier attempt to engage critically with some of these approaches, Meeks, 2007.
6. Read especially Scott, 2004, Chapter 5: 'The tragedy of colonial enlightenment', pp. 170–208.
7. For his use of this phrase from *Hamlet* see Scott, 2004: 162.
8. See this argument in Meeks, 2017.
9. The infamous Royal Code of 1685 that defined conditions of slavery in the French colonies.
10. In Scott's words, James writes in a tradition of 'romantic vindicationalism'. See for instance, Scott, 2004: 79.
11. For a contemporary revisiting of the importance of federations in the failed anti-colonial attempt at 'worldmaking', see Getachew, 2019.
12. For Scott on Bandung, see Scott, 2004: 30.
13. Lenin's precise words were 'When it is impossible for the ruling classes to maintain their rule without any change …'. See Lenin, 1964.
14. This draft was first written in December 2020, in the moment between Joe Biden's victory at the polls and his January 2021 inauguration, with no certainty that Donald Trump would actually concede and leave office voluntarily. The unprecedented attempt to deny the electoral results, leading ultimately to the storming of the Capitol by a Trumpian mob on 6 January, is now of course, history. Trump eventually stepped down and Biden was inaugurated, but his denial of the election result continues, even as more than 500 would-be insurrectionists face trial in the coming months. What is certain, however, is that based on his continuing popularity in the Republican Party, the legacy of Trumpism – neo-fascist, racist nationalism – will endure. Trump's remarkable support by some 73 million voters (Biden received more than 80 million) suggests the deep resentment felt by sections of the white working and middle classes on their perceived loss of not only the election, but their social, racial and economic status and the inherent dangers for the US and the world that lie ahead.
15. Purportedly written by V. I. Lenin, though with much controversy surrounding it, the saying is nonetheless aptly reflective of moments when life accelerates, as in the summer of 2020.
16. I am searching for a description of the present moment that falls short of proclaiming global insurrection, yet recognises that the present moment of popular unrest goes far beyond the normal decades-long, sporadic resistance to neoliberalism.

17. I use sublime here in the sense in which it is understood in chemistry, as a compound that changes directly from a solid to a gas. This is to suggest the extent to which 'revolution' is both ephemeral yet has been in the past and may be utilised in the future as a framework to mobilise and fight for radical change.
18. And from a different perspective, the moment after the taking of power in Grenada in 1979, think about this sentiment expressed by Theresa Simeon, suggesting possibility untethered, that anything, against any odds, might be achieved: 'Then when the revolution happened, I was in the States. So I came back here, I really wanted to make up for not being here. I started going to the rallies … I was so impressed I'd never seen people so together and united like that before in Grenada. I was thinking, how can I help? I knew we needed a lot of money and I wondered, how can I raise some? Then in November 1979 we heard about the international airport idea. So I called my friends together, and twenty-two of us decided to form the St. George's development committee … All this involvement has changed my life so much … We are much more involved in the revolution and always being called upon to help'. Interview with Theresa Simeon in Searle and Hodge, 1982: 73.

References

Barriteau, Eudine (ed.). 2003. *Confronting Power, Theorizing Gender: Interdisciplinary perspectives from the Caribbean*. Kingston: University of the West Indies Press.
Bender, Thomas, Dubois, Laurent and Rabinowitz, Richard. 2011. *Revolution! The Atlantic World Reborn*. London: D. Giles; and New York: New York Historical Society.
Blackburn, Robin. 1988. *The Overthrow of Colonial Slavery*. London and New York: Verso.
Bogues, Anthony. 2014. 'The Abeng newspaper and the radical politics of postcolonial blackness', in Quinn, Kate (ed.), *Black Power in the Caribbean*. Gainesville: University Press of Florida, 76–96.
Bogues, Anthony. 2017. 'The black Jacobins and the long Haitian revolution: Archives, history and the writing of revolution', in Forsdick, Charles and Høgsberg, Christian (eds), *The Black Jacobins Reader*. Durham, NC and London: Duke University Press, 197–214.
Buck-Morss, Susan. 2009. *Hegel, Haiti and Universal History*. Pittsburgh: University of Pittsburgh Press.
Carrington, Edwin. 1971. 'Industrialization by invitation in Trinidad since 1950', in Girvan, Norman and Jefferson, Owen (eds), *Readings in the Political Economy of the Caribbean*. Kingston: New World, 143–50.
Corruption Perception Index. 2019. www.transparency.org.
Fick, Carolyn E. 1990. *The Making of Haiti: The St Domingue revolution from below*. Knoxville: University of Tennessee Press.
Figueroa, Mark and Sives, Amanda. 2002. 'Homogenous voting, electoral manipulation and the "garrison" process in post-independence Jamaica'. *Journal of Commonwealth and Comparative Politics*, 40(1): 81–108.
Forsdick, Charles and Høgsberg, Christian (eds). 2017. *The Black Jacobins Reader*. Durham, NC and London: Duke University Press.
Genovese, Eugene D. 1979. *From Rebellion to Revolution: Afro-American slave revolts in the making of the modern world*. Baton Rouge: Louisiana State University Press.
Getachew, Adom. 2016. 'Universalism after the post-colonial turn: Interpreting the Haitian revolution'. *Political Theory*, 446: 821–45.
Getachew, Adom. 2019. *Worldmaking after Empire: The rise and fall of self-determination*. Princeton: Princeton University Press.
Gray, Obika. 2004. *Demeaned but Empowered: The social power of the urban poor in Jamaica*. Kingston: University of the West Indies Press.
Grenade, Wendy (ed.). 2015. *The Grenada Revolution: Reflections and lessons*. Jackson: University Press of Mississippi.
Hall, Stuart, Rustin, Michael and Massey, Doreen (eds). 2015. *After Neoliberalism? The Kilburn Manifesto*. London: Lawrence and Wishart.
Hartocollis, Anemona and Alcindor, Yamiche. 2017. 'Women's march highlights as huge crowds protest Trump: "We're not going away"'. *New York Times*, 21 January. https://nyti.ms/3WHBnK9.

Hintzen, Percy. 2018. 'Towards a new democracy in the Caribbean: Local empowerment and the new global order', in Meeks, Brian and Quinn, Kate (eds), *Beyond Westminster in the Caribbean*. Kingston and Miami: Ian Randle Publishers, 173–98.

Huber-Stephens, Evelyn and Stephens, John D. 1986. *Democratic Socialism in Jamaica*. London and Basingstoke: Macmillan.

James, C. L. R. 1989 [1938]. *The Black Jacobins: Toussaint L'Ouverture and the San Domingo revolution*. New York: Vintage.

Jefferson, Owen. 1971. 'Jamaica's post-war economic development', in Girvan, Norman and Jefferson, Owen (eds), *Readings in the Political Economy of the Caribbean*. Kingston: New World, 109–20.

Kaufman, Michael. 1985. *Jamaica under Manley: Dilemmas of socialism and democracy*. London: Zed.

Kirby, Jen. 2020. '"Black Lives Matter" has become a global rallying cry against racism and police brutality'. *Vox*, 12 June. https://www.vox.com/2020/6/12/21285244/black-lives-matter-global-protests-george-floyd-uk-belgium.

Lenin, V. I. 1964. 'The collapse of the Second International', in *Collected Works*, Vol. 21, August 1914–December 1915. Moscow: Progress Publishers, 213–14.

Lewis, Patsy, Clegg, Peter and Williams, Gary (eds). 2015. *Grenada: Revolution and invasion*. Kingston: University of the West Indies Press.

Lewis, Rupert. 1998. *Walter Rodney's Intellectual and Political Thought*. Kingston: University of the West Indies Press.

Marley, Bob. 1973. 'Concrete Jungle', *Catch a Fire,* Island Records.

Mbembe, Achille. 2001. *On the Postcolony*. Berkeley: University of California Press.

Meeks, Brian. 1993. *Caribbean Revolutions and Revolutionary Theory: An assessment of Cuba, Nicaragua and Grenada*. London and Basingstoke: Macmillan.

Meeks, Brian. 1996a. 'The 1970 revolution: Chronology and documentation', in Meeks, Brian, *Radical Caribbean: From black power to Abu Bakr*. Kingston: University of the West Indies Press, 9–36.

Meeks, Brian. 1996b. 'The political moment in Jamaica: The dimensions of hegemonic dissolution', in Meeks, Brian, *Radical Caribbean: From black power to Abu Bakr*. Kingston: University of the West Indies Press, 124–43.

Meeks, Brian. 2007. *Envisioning Caribbean Futures: Jamaican perspectives*. Kingston: University of the West Indies Press.

Meeks, Brian. 2017. 'Jamaican roads not taken: Or a big "what if" in Stuart Hall's life', *Boundary2*, December. https://bit.ly/3zXsX7F.

Meeks, Brian. 2019. 'On the question of optimism in troubled times'. Paper presented at the conference 'After the Event: Prospects and Retrospects of Revolution', University College London, 15–17 May.

Mohammed, Patricia (ed.). 2002. *Gendered Realities: Essays in Caribbean feminist thought*. Kingston: University of the West Indies Press.

Movement for Black Lives. 2020. *Vision for Black Lives – 2020 Policy Platform*. www.m4bl.org.

Polanyi-Levitt, Kari. 1984. *Jamaica: Lessons from the Manley years*. Kingston: Maroon Pamphlets.

Polanyi-Levitt, Kari. 2005. *Reclaiming Development: Independent thought and Caribbean community*. Kingston and Miami: Ian Randle Publishers.

Puri, Shalini. 2014. *The Grenada Revolution in the Caribbean Present: Operation urgent memory*. London and Basingstoke: Palgrave Macmillan.

Putnam, Lara, Chenoweth, Erica and Pressman, Jeremy. 2020. 'The Floyd protests are the broadest in U.S. history – and are spreading to white, small-town America'. *Washington Post*, 6 June. https://wapo.st/3G4S9gi.

Ryan, Selwyn, Stewart, Taimoon and McCree, Roy (eds). 1995. *The Black Power Revolution 1970: A retrospective*. St Augustine: ISER, University of the West Indies.

Samaroo, Brinsley. 2014. 'The February revolution (1970) as a catalyst for change in Trinidad and Tobago', in Quinn, Kate (ed.), *Black Power in the Caribbean*. Gainesville: University Press of Florida, 97–116.

Scott, David. 1999. *Refashioning Futures: Criticism after postcoloniality*. Princeton: Princeton University Press.

Scott, David. 2004. *Conscripts of Modernity: The tragedy of colonial enlightenment*. Durham, NC and London: Duke University Press.

Scott, David. 2014. *Omens of Adversity: Tragedy, time, memory, justice*. Durham, NC and London: Duke University Press.

Searle, Chris and Hodge, Merle. 1982. *Is Freedom We Making: The new democracy in Grenada*. St George's, Grenada: Fedon Publishers.

Sen, Amartya. 1999. *Development as Freedom*. New York: Alfred A. Knopf.

Taylor, Matthew. 2020. 'The evolution of Extinction Rebellion'. *The Guardian*, 4 August. https://bit.ly/3hiUgmf.

Thomas, Deborah. 2004. *Modern Blackness: Nationalism, globalization and the politics of culture in Jamaica*. Durham, NC and London: Duke University Press.

Thomas, Deborah. 2011. *Exceptional Violence: Embodied citizenship in transnational Jamaica*. Durham, NC and London: Duke University Press.

Trouillot, Michel-Rolph. 1995. *Silencing the Past: Power and the production of history*. Boston: Beacon.

Watson, Hilbourne (ed.). 1994. *The Caribbean in the Global Political Economy*. Boulder, CO: Lynne Rienner Publishers.

West, Darrel M. 2015. 'What happens if robots take jobs? The impact of emerging technologies on employment and public policy'. Center for Technology innovation at Brookings, 26 October. https://brook.gs/3A4Jc2J.

Wright, Robin. 2019. 'The story of 2019: Protests in every corner of the globe'. *New Yorker*, 30 December. https://bit.ly/3WRRzsn.

Yack, Bernard. 1986. *The Longing for Total Revolution: Philosophic sources of social discontent from Rousseau to Marx and Nietzsche*. Princeton: Princeton University Press.

Afterword

Behrooz Ghamari-Tabrizi

This volume began with Rosa Luxemburg's famous assertion that before a revolution happens, it is perceived as impossible, but that after it has happened, it is seen as having been inevitable. After reading the chapters in this book on revolutionary experiences from Peru to Yemen, and from the Caribbean to Iran, we might think differently about the condition and contingencies that simultaneously inform the impossibility and the inevitability of revolutions. Luxemburg, like many of her contemporaries and later generations of revolutionaries and those who theorise about revolutions, looked at revolution *sui generis* and independently from the lives of those who make it possible. Revolutions were seen more in terms of a temporal rupture, or as Massimiliano Tomba (2019) has recently called it 'insurgent universalities', rather than how they were experienced and lived. As we have seen in this volume, these two ways of understanding revolutions do not exist in binary opposition. Observing one without the other, however, forces us to understand revolutions only in terms of their success or failure. This book has taken us beyond the question of success and failure in order to situate the unfolding of the revolutionary impulse and events in relation to the lives of those who have lived it.

The idea here is not to be stoic or to view revolutions and their outcomes in ambivalent terms, but to see the revolution in its own context without locating it in relation to a universal referent by which its success or failure is measured. All of the preceding chapters have in one way or another sought to locate the revolution in unlikely places: the entire ambit of the lifeworld from the thunderous moments of revolutionary uprising to the mundane concerns of everyday life, or before and after the 'event'. Each has provided a subtle but significant anthropological shift in the study of revolutions.

'Revolution' carries a paradoxical meaning in itself – its original meaning of a natural 'circular motion' and a progressive march towards the future. It is only after 1789, or more precisely 1793, that Revolution became a temporal abbreviation, a radical disruption in cyclical order of political formations, a rupture or alteration in the course of time (Koselleck, 2004: 43–57). By the beginning of the nineteenth century, revolution had already turned into a historical event with its own independent authority in shaping and giving legitimacy to political violence. For the first time, as Hannah Arendt (1990: 41) observes, '1789 generated a historical precedence for the transformation of revolution from a collective event for the restoration of an old order into its very opposite, a change so radical that [it] turned subjects into rulers.' It spread its shadow over future revolutions and turned them into scripted social and political affairs with fixed causes and known outcomes that were steeped in the universal principles of eighteenth-century bourgeois Enlightenment thought. What was lost in this transformation was the singularity and ambiguity with which this temporal rupture was associated. Not only was the French Revolution singular, but it also operated with a great degree of ambiguity, to the extent that Diderot famously pondered, 'What will succeed this revolution? Nobody knows' (cited in Koselleck, 2004: 24).

Revolutionary moments, *like a thunderbolt from the blue*, tear open the world of possibilities – possibilities that are articulated, albeit in ambiguous terms, in public imaginations of the good life. Revolutionary moments, from the time of the French Revolution to the Arab uprisings of a decade ago, have also been stifled by institutional restrictions, discursive confinements, and the demands of post-revolutionary realpolitik. Such demands often compel revolutionary subjects to abandon their essential desire for *possible* realities and instead become content, as Robert Musil ponders in *The Man without Qualities* (1995), with a pragmatic sense of *real* possibilities.

Where do we stand today in relation to what political theorists began to explore in the 1970s about the end of revolutions? Are all of the revolutions after 1789 staged to repeat the same drama, borrowing lines and symbols from the same cast and production? Are we losing the ability to imagine that *another world is possible* with expressions and desires that do not map onto a temporal geography invented during *The Age of Revolutions*? 1789 became the ground zero of history, an absolute beginning with universal claims on culture and morality – the way Voltaire envisioned: *one geometry, one morality*. A revolution, that in reality was both singular and ambiguous, in the Benjaminian sense *a leap into the open sky of possibilities,* gained historical certainty and universal transformative authority from Haiti to Hanoi, from Moscow to Mozambique. Revolution increasingly turned into a discourse that no longer reflected its formative impulse to alter the temporal map of history. The discursive containment of revolution has led to the realisation of what Rousseau feared in the mid-eighteenth century about the emergence of a particular form of authority that penetrates mankind's innermost thoughts and desires.

Much has been written about the paradoxical core of the Enlightenment: its substantive emancipatory outlook and its instrumental oppressive practice. Enlightenment thought advocated a secular eschatology that promoted the pursuit of worldly happiness against the Christian submission to divine providence. It fostered the desire for earthly gratification against the hope for heavenly salvation. Yet revolutions around the globe, most significantly the Haitian Revolution that inaugurated the nineteenth century, most profoundly expressed a public imagination that rested upon a commitment to the world of possibilities with competing visions of good society. By the mid-twentieth century those utopian visions that had primarily emerged through the spirit, or what Derrida called the 'metaphysics' of the project of Enlightenment, gradually became associated with totalitarianism. The inescapable association between utopia and terror, between the imagined good society and totalitarianism, formed the foundational block of all that was revolutionary.

Revolutionaries often justified the atrocities committed in the name of revolution by references to that 'ultimate end' – those who stood in its way acted against the demands of progress and historical inevitabilities. Revolutionary anticipation, and the uncertainty that defines it, yielded to a predestined goal the terms of which were set from a universal position of exteriority with ambivalence towards the contingencies that inform the particularities of any historical moment. Such a disconnect inhibited societies from recognising their own narrative abilities in envisioning and articulating alternative political, economic, and cultural relations outside universal claims that have conditioned the existing orders. Ernst Bloch went even further to suggest that a society dispossessed of the narrative skill to envision alternative political, economic, and cultural relations is dead. In his vision of utopia and the revolutionary act, Bloch linked the conception of utopia to the principle of hope. In order to delink revolution from terror, Bloch (1986) located the revolutionary core of utopian thinking in the 'not-yet-become' of folklore, in the popular desire to hope and strive for a better life expressed in myth, fairy tales and daydreams.

In different chapters in this book, we have seen moments closer to earlier conceptions of revolution as moments not yet ossified in a new historical epoch, the blueprint of which had already been drawn. Here we see more care and credibility given to a playful and imaginative understanding of history that connected the experiences of life in the past to the possibilities of the yet-to-be-realised future, the creativity through the exercise of which revolutions unfold in a perpetual tension with a temporality that restrains any deviation from the imposed logic of historical necessities. Revolutions do not occur as a fulfilment of progressive inevitabilities. As Walter Benjamin (1996: 402) notes: 'Marx said that revolutions are the locomotive of world history. But perhaps things are very different. It may be that revolutions are the act by which the human race travelling in the train applies the emergency brake.' That image suggests that if humanity allows the train of history to follow its course, already laid down by the steel structure of the tracks, 'we shall [be] hurled into catastrophe, the crash or the abyss' (Löwy, 2013: 186).

This volume has demonstrated with careful analysis what I have argued elsewhere (Ghamari-Tabrizi, 2016): that revolutions have always spread at the threshold of a novelty with an inherent contradiction between the realisation and the rejection of possibilities; between a pause and acceleration in historical temporality; between exits from and inclusion in history; and between the *particular* transformative experiences of life and the discursive demands of universal history. In the second half of the twentieth century, revolution increasingly became associated with terror and totalitarianism rather than with hope and emancipation. From a highbrow philosophical assertion, the end of history turned into an everyday reality that colonised the very essence of imagination and revolutionary thinking and acting. The ability to transcend the present and to think of the world anew appeared to be a story the end of which we already knew, so we told ourselves as the first act was unfolding. Despite restoring faith in the possibility of change, the transformative power of revolutionary imaginations and desires materialised through the imposition of existing possibilities.

Instances abound when historians, political actors, intellectuals, and all those who give voice to revolutionary desires render them as demands that are legible only with reference to the inherent logic of linear historical progress. Revolution is the space of engagement with politics in its imaginative and uncertain terms, a space that allows thinking about possible realities without the inhibiting constraints of real possibilities. Rather than a temporal abbreviation and a violent realisation of a predetermined future, this book has proposed that revolution ought to be understood as a moment of creative pause and a transformative politics, the outcome of which needs to be negotiated in practice. In all these case studies, we have witnessed how every single case generated in fleeting moments the possibility of a different kind of life that did not simply reflect the unfolding of a universal temporality. Revolutions might fail, but the experience of *becoming* in a revolutionary moment gives rise to a transformed subject whose relation with their lifeworld will permanently change. This book has been the story of those subjects.

References

Arendt, Hannah. 1990 [1963]. *On Revolution*. New York: Penguin.
Benjamin, Walter. 1996. *Selected Writings, Vol. 4: 1938–1940*. Cambridge, MA: Belknap Press of Harvard University Press.
Bloch, Ernst. 1986. *The Principle of Hope*, Vol. 1. Translated by Neville Plaice, Stephen Plaice and Paul Knight. Cambridge, MA: MIT Press.
Ghamari-Tabrizi, Behrooz. 2016. *Foucault in Iran: Islamic revolution after the enlightenment*. Minneapolis: University of Minnesota Press.
Koselleck, Reinhart. 2004. *Critique and Crisis: Enlightenment and the pathogenesis of modern society*. Cambridge, MA: MIT Press.
Löwy, Michael. 2013. *On Changing the World: Essays in political philosophy from Karl Marx to Walter Benjamin*. Chicago: Haymarket Books.
Musil, Robert. 1995 [1930–1943]. *The Man without Qualities*. Translated by Sophie Wilkins. London: Picador.
Tomba, Massimiliano. 2019. *Insurgent Universalities: An alternative legacy of modernity*. Oxford: Oxford University Press.

Index

References to images are in *italics*; references to notes are indicated by n.

'Abdul Jalil, Mustafa 87
absence 44, 57, 65–6
al-Absi, Ahmad 'Umar 60
action 94
Adorno, Theodore 76
Africa 178, 184
agency 45, 54
agrarian communities 163
    and Iran 104, 105–6, 110, 118
    and Nicaragua 28–40
    and Peru 133, 149
agriculture *see* agrarian communities
Ahmad, Iman 55, 60, 62
Albania 150
alcohol 81, 95n13, 119
'Ali b. Muhammad 47, *48*, 49–51, 62
Aliabad *see* Iran
American Revolution 3, 4
Amin, Qasim 49
ancien régimes 58, 67n1, 154, 164, 170
Anderson, Benedict 25–8, 38, 39
anti-authoritarianism 188
anti-colonialism 184–5, 186, 189
anti-fascism 188
anti-neoliberalism 188
anti-racism 188–9
APRA (Popular American Revolutionary Alliance) 132–43, 152
    and disaffection 149–51
    and embodiment 145–9
    and missions 143–5
Arab Spring 1–2, 11, 154, 198
Arendt, Hannah 198
Argentina 66
aristocracy *see* elites
arts of deception 137–43
Australia 45, 63, 70n51, 74
authoritarianism 22

Bandera Roja (Red Flag) 150
Bandung 186, 188
Barakat, 'Abdullah 49, 59, 62
Barriteau, Eudine 178
Barthes, Roland 44
Bateson, Gregory 74
Ben Ali, Zine El Abidine 1
Benjamin, Walter 2, 200
Berlin wall 44

Berman, Marshall: *All that is Solid Melts into Air* 161
Biden, Joe 193n14
Bishop, Maurice 176–7
Black Lives Matter movement 14–15, 188–9
Black Power movement 175–6, 186
Bloch, Ernst 199
boredom 13, 73, 74–7
    and Libya 80–4, 85–7, 90–2, 94
Bouazizi, Mohamed 1
Braudel, Fernand 7
Britain *see* Great Britain
Buck-Morss, Susan 155, 161–2
bureaucracy 165–6
Burkina Faso 2

capitalism 75, 132, 133
Caribbean 3, 14–15, 175–81, 186–7; *see also* Cuba; Haitian revolution
Castro, Fidel 14, 158, 164–6, 173n1, 185
    and 'words to the intellectuals' 162–3, 166–7, 171
Castro, Raúl 166
caudillismo (strongman politics) 22
censorship 165
Certeau, Michel de 64
Chachapoyas (Peru) 133, 136, 137–45, 147, 150
change 5, 10, 74, 169–70
    and Cuba 14, 164–5, 166, 167
    and Iran 103–4, 109–10, 113–14
    and Peru 134, 150–1, 152
    and Yemen 49, 60
charisma 156, 167
Chávez Várgas, Manuel 133, 134, 135–43
    and forms of embodiment 145–9
    and missions 143–5
Chile 188
China 150, 161, 166, 187
Christianity 121
class 105, 107, 113, 117, 118; *see also* elites
clientelism 22, 24, 33
coastal plantations 132, 149
coffee 28–9, 30
Cold War 165
collectivisation 29, 30–2, 133
colonialism *see* anti-colonialism; postcolonialism

communism 133, 150, 162
connections (*wasta*) 79–80
continuity 23–5
'Contra' war 29
conversion 10
convivencia (mutual coexistence) 149–50
cooperatives 28, 29–32
coronavirus pandemic 108, 119, 188
corruption 105, 110, 118, 120, 121
    and Caribbean 177, 193n3
cosmogony 156–7, 161–8, 170–1
Costa Rica 30
crime 89, 90, 177
Cuba 3, 14, 155, 157–61, 173n1
    and cosmogony 161–8, 170–1
    and Grenada 176
    and Peru 150
    and Soviet Union 185
culture 157, 168–71
Cyrus the Great 121

deception 137–43
democracy 77–8, 178
    and Peru 132–3, 134, 135, 148–9
Derrida, Jacques 199
development 32–4, 39, 109–10, 162–3
Dhufar 7
Díaz-Canel, Miguel 166
dictatorship 22
disappeared 51–5, 57, 62, 66
disinformation 22
divinity 25–6
Domanska, Ewa 66
double bind 74, 95n2
drugs 81, 95n13
durability 23–5

ecological disaster 10
economics 189
    and Caribbean 175, 177, 186–7
    and Cuba 166
    and Iran 119
    and Peru 132, 133
education 37, 38, 58
    and Cuba 164
    and Iran 104, 118, 121
    and Libya 87
Edwards, Elizabeth 45–6, 63–4
Egypt 43, 47, 49, 68n14
    and 2011 revolution 75, 95n3
elites 132, 133, 134, 135, 149
embodiment 146–8
employment 79–80, 84–5, 104–5; *see also* unemployment
Enlightenment 11–12, 172, 183, 198–9
ennui *see* boredom
environmental crisis 187, 189
equality 134–5, 148–9
ethnicity *see* race
executions:
    and Iran 118, 121
    and Yemen 50, 51, 60, 61–2, 66
Extinction Rebellion 187

failure 6–7, 23, 25, 173n1
Fatemeh 107

femininity 84–5
firearms 89–90
Floyd, George 188
Foucault, Michel 11
France 88
    and Haitian revolution 181–3, 184, 185–6, 191–2
    see also French Revolution
freedom 190–1
French Revolution 3, 4, 154, 161, 198–9
FSLN *see* Sandinistas

al-Gaddafi, 'Aysha 85
al Gaddafi, Col Mu'ammar 73, 76, 77–8, 79, 80, 83, 86, 89
    and railways 96n22
    and revolt 87, 88
    and Sufism 92
    and women 84, 85, 96n19
Gairy, Eric 176
gangs 90, 177
gas 88
Gell, Alfred 45, 56
Germany 156
Gould, Jeffrey 34
governance:
    and Iran 110, 112–13, 119–20
    and Libya 77–9, 82–3, 84–5, 88–90
    and Peru 137, 143, 149
Gray, Obika 178
Great Britain 77, 105, 175, 182, 190, 191
Greece 160, 167
Grenada 5, 14, 176–7, 178, 194n18
    and Scott 179, 180
Guadeloupe 183
Gualiqueme (Nicaragua) 28–40
Guardia Civil 137–45
Guevara, Che 150, 158, 163, 173n1

Hadi 'Isa 49, 50
Haitian revolution 11, 179, 180–6, 191–3, 199
Hall, Stuart: *Kilburn Manifesto* 190
al-Hamdi, Ibrahim 58, 69n30
Hassan 106
healthcare 164
Henry, Paget 178
Hintzen, Percy 178
history 5, 8–9, 45–6
Holbraad, Martin 3
Honduras 30
Hong Kong 188
Husein, Imam 102–4, 106–7, 108, 110, 111, 115–17
    and Karbala shrine 121
    and Moharram 118–19, 123

Idris as-Sanusi of Libya, King 77
imagined community 27, 28
immobility 80, 85–6, 88, 89, 90, 93, 96n22
imprisonment 21
inaction 94
Inca Empire 133, 134–5
independence movements 175
India 183
indigenous people:
    and Australia 45, 63, 70n51, 74

and Nicaragua 34–7, 38
and Peru 134–5, 143
industry 132, 134, 163
infrastructure 32, 33, 96n22, 163
intelligence 136
Iran 3, 104–6, 122–3
    and Hussein 115–17
    and Islamic decline 117–22
    see also Iranian Revolution
Iranian Revolution 2, 11, 13, 102–4, 106–9
    and aftermath 109–22
Iran–Iraq War 108, 111, 118
ISIS (Islamic State of Iraq and Syria) 88
Islam 2, 11, 75
    and Libya 33, 88, 91–4, 97n31
    see also Shi'a Islam
Israel 108
Italy 88

Jalila Agha 51–5, 64–6
Jamaica 175, 176, 177, 178, 179, 191
James, C. L. R. 179
    The Black Jacobins: Toussaint L'Ouverture and the San Domingo revolution 180–5, 191–3
Jameson, Fredric 5
Jamil, Jamal 47, 49, 68n15
Jasmine Revolution 1
jihadism 10, 88

Karbala 102, 107, 110, 114, 115
Khomeini, Ayatollah 106, 117, 121
Koselleck, Reinhart 154

land:
    and Cuba 163
    and Iran 104, 105–6, 120
    and Nicaragua 28–32, 38–9
    and Peru 132, 133, 134, 149
Latin America see Caribbean; Nicaragua; Peru
Latour, Bruno 168
leadership 156, 167
Lebanon 188
Leclerc, Charles 182, 183, 192
Left politics 22
Lenin, Vladimir 155, 187
lethargy 13, 73, 81
Libya 3, 13, 73–4, 76–7, 87–90
    and boredom 80–4, 85–7, 90–2
    and al-Fatah revolution 77–80
    and Sufism 92–4
    and women 84–5
literacy 36–7, 163
longue durée 7, 14, 131–2; see also APRA
L'Ouverture, Toussaint 182, 183, 184, 185–6, 191
Luxemburg, Rosa 2, 197

Malia, Martin 161
Manley, Michael 176
Marley, Bob 190
marriage 85–6, 87, 92, 110
Martinique 183
martyrdom see Hussein, Imam
Marx, Karl 200
Marxism 155, 165, 181, 186

Mbembe, Achille 178, 193n4
media 27, 41n3
Melanesia 169
memorial sites see photography
mestizaje (mixed races) 34–7, 38
meta-change 165
metonymy 44, 65
Mexico 2
Middle East see Iran; Syria; Yemen
migration 30, 80, 175
    and Iran 109, 113, 118
military 132, 177
militias 88–90, 96n30
Mohammad, Prophet 106
Mohammad Reza Shah 105, 107–9
Mohammed, Patricia 178
Moharram rituals 111, 113, 115, 117, 118–19
monarchy 25–6, 77, 78
mosques 111–12, 113, 114
Mossadeq, Mohammed 105, 108
Movimento de la Izquierda Revolucionaria (MIR) 150
Murillo, Rosario 22
Musharbash, Yasmine 74
Musil, Robert: *The Man Without Qualities* 198
Muslims see Islam

Napoleon Bonaparte 182, 183, 185–6, 191, 192
al-Nasser, Jamal 'Abd 17, 68n14
nation states 26–7
nationhood 25–8
nature 168–71
Navaro, Yael 7–8
neoliberalism 177, 178
nepotism 76, 79
New Jewel Movement 176, 180
newspapers 27
Nicaragua 3, 12, 21–5
    and agrarian community 28–40
    and development 32–4
    and *mestizaje* 34–7
North Africa see Egypt; Libya; Tunisia
novels 27
nuclear weapons 108, 110, 114

Obama, Barack 166
oil 88
oligarchy see elites
oppression 160, 164
Ortega, Daniel 22–3, 31, 33, 40

Pahlavi regime 103, 106, 108, 118
Palestine 121
paramilitaries 21; see also militias
Patria Roja (Red Nation) 150
patronage 79–80
PCP-SL see Shining Path
peasantry see rural communities
peopledom (*jamahiriya*) 77–9, 82–3, 86, 87, 90
perdurance 154–6
permanence 154–6, 157
    and Cuba 158, 159–61, 167–8, 170–1
Perry, John 40n1
Peru 3, 13–14, 131–2, 151–2; see also APRA

204   INDEX

Peruvian Communist Party (PCP) 150, 151
photography 13, 43–6, 63–4
    and Yemenis 47, *48*, 49–51, 56–63, 64–6
Plan Techno 32
police:
    and Jamaica 176
    and Libya 89
    and Nicaragua 21
    and Peru 137–45
    and Yemen 59, 62–3
politics 26–7, 168
    and Caribbean 176–8
    and Cuba 159–61, 162–3, 166–7
    and Iran 105–6
    and Nicaragua 21–4
    see also APRA; democracy; governance
population growth 112
populism 22
postcolonialism 177–8
poverty 114, 118
    and Caribbean 175, 178
    and Nicaragua 23, 30, 32, 35, 37
    and Peru 133, 134, 143, 145–6
Prado, Manuel 149
presence 44, 65–6
propaganda 136, 143–5
prophetic invention 10
protests 21, 117, 188; *see also* Arab Spring
public speaking 146–8

Al Qaeda 88
Qa'id, Ahmad 52–3, 54
Qatar 88
Qavams 105–6

race 181–3, 185–6
    and Caribbean 175–6
    and Nicaragua 34–7, 38
    see also Black Lives Matter movement; Haitian revolution; indigenous people; *mestizaje*
radical politics *see* revolution
Ramazan 111, 113, 114, 116, 117
Rastafari 175
rebellion 11
Reddock, Rhoda 178
refugees 29
religion *see* Christianity; Islam
repression 22–3, 119–20
revolution 3–4, 154–7, 197–201
    and boredom 74–5
    and change 169–70
    and definition 2–3
    and development 32–4
    and event 9–12, 37–8
    and freedom 190–1
    and land 30–2
    and Libya 73–4, 76–80, 87–90
    and *longue durée* 131–2
    and *mestizaje* 34–7
    and Nicaragua 23–5
    and temporality 4–9
    and transnational movements 188–90, 193
    and Yemen 49–63, 64–6
    see also American Revolution; Cuba; French Revolution; Grenada; Haitian revolution; Iranian Revolution; Russian Revolution; Sandinistas; Shining Path
Revolutionary Guards 109
Right politics 22, 188
Rigoberto Cruz Cooperative 28, 29–32
rituals 111–17
Rodney, Walter 176
Runia, Eelco 44, 65
rupture 9–10, 50, 156, 159–61
rural communities 118
    and Nicaragua 24, 25, 28–40
    and Peru 136, 145–9
Russian Revolution 3, 4, 154, 155, 156, 161; *see also* Soviet Union

St Domingue *see* Haitian revolution
Salih, 'Ali 'Abdullah 50, 68n22, 70n47
al-Sallal, Col 'Abdullah 61, 70n45
San Domingo *see* Haitian revolution
Sana'a (Yemen) 47, 49–51
sanctions 110, 114
Sandinistas 12, 21–5, 32–3
    and rural communities 29, 30, 31, 38–40
Sartre, Jean-Paul 75–6, 95n5
Saudi Arabia 88
Schielke, Samuli 7, 75–6, 77
Scott, David 6, 14, 178–81, 183–5, 186–7, 188–91
Sebald, W. G. 44
Sen, Amartya 190
Sendero Luminoso see Shining Path
Shah *see* Mohammad Reza Shah
shari'a law 89
Shariati, Ali 106–7, 117
al-Shaybani, 'Abd al-Karim 59, 62–3, 64
al-Shaybani, Umhani 55–63, 64–5
Shi'a Islam 102–4, 106–9, 110, 122–3
    and decline 117–22, 124n12
    and Hussein 115–17
    and rituals 111–14
Shining Path 14, 131, 150, 151–2
Shiraz *see* Iran
shrines 111–12, 114, 116
slavery *see* Haitian revolution
Smith, Benjamin 45
smoking 80–1, 82, 83
socialism 22, 77, 83, 133, 166, 171
Somoza Debayle, Anastasio 23, 29
Sontag, Susan 43
sovereignty 25–7, 28
Soviet Union 14, 150, 162, 176
    and Cuba 165, 166, 185
Spain 182, 191
Spillers, Hortense 191
sport 83
Sri Lanka 179
stagnancy 73, 74, 76–7, 82–4, 85–7, 91–2
    and Cuba 165, 166–7
Stalin, Joseph 155
state, the 165–6
student protests 21
Sudan 188, 192
Sufism 92–4, 97n33, 121
surveillance 136, 138–9, 163
Syria 2, 11

temporality 4–12, 24, 28, 63
territory 25–7; *see also* land
terrorism 21
Thomas, Deborah 178
time 162, 179
Tomba, Massimiliano 197
totalitarianism 200
Trinidad and Tobago 175, 176
Tripoli *see* Libya
Trump, Donald 108, 110, 114, 166, 193n14
Tsipras, Alexis 160, 167
Tunisia 1
tyranny 102

unemployment 80, 87, 90, 110
   and Caribbean 175, 187
United States of America (USA) 188, 192
   and Caribbean 187
   and Grenada 177
   and Iran 105, 108, 110, 114
   and Nicaragua 21–2, 30
urbanisation 109–10
USSR *see* Soviet Union
utopianism 199

Venezuela 185, 186
Vietnam 166
violence 11, 62, 178
Voltaire 198

Wagner, Roy 157, 169–70
Watson, Hilbourne 178
Weber, Max 156
Williams, Eric 176
Wilson, Alice 3, 7
women 187–8
   and Iran 104, 107, 111, 112–16, 117, 118
   and Libya 80, 84–5
   and Nicaragua 29
   and Peru 133
   and Yemen 51–62, 65–6, 67n9
al-Wushali, Hamud 51–5, 60, 62, 66

Yack, Bernard 189
Yahya, Imam 47, 55
Yemen 3, 13, 43–4, 46, 51–6
   and photography 47, *48*, 49–51, 56–63, 64–6
young people 13
   and Iran 118–19, 120–1
   and Libya 76–7, 80–4, 90
   see also APRA
Yurchak, Alexei 171

Zeinab 106, 107
Zoroastrianism 121
al-Zubayri, Muhammad 60, 70n44

www.ingramcontent.com/pod-product-compliance
Lightning Source LLC
LaVergne TN
LVHW050008140426
836100LV00010B/60